AGAINST LIBERATION

Putting animals in perspective

Michael P. T. Leahy

London and New York

First published 1991
by Routledge
11 New Fetter Lane, London EC4P 4EE

Simultaneously published in the USA and Canada
by Routledge
a division of Routledge, Chapman and Hall, Inc.
29 West 35th Street, New York, NY 10001

British Library Cataloguing in Publication Data
Leahy, Michael
Against liberation: putting animals in perspective.
1. Animals. Treatment of animals by man. Ethical aspects
I. Title
179.3

Library of Congress Cataloging in Publication Data
Leahy, Michael P. T., 1934–
Against liberation : putting animals in perspective / Michael P.T.
Leahy.
p.   cm.
Includes bibliographical references and index.
1. Animal rights–Philosophy.   I. Title.
HV4708.L43   1991
179'.3–dc20   90-23775

ISBN 0-415-03584-8

TO ROSEY, ISABEL AND MILES

CONTENTS

ACKNOWLEDGEMENTS

I am grateful to Messrs Faber & Faber, and to the author, for permission to use Ted Hughes' poem 'Hawk Roosting' as my frontispiece; and also to Basil Blackwell in allowing me to quote extensively from the posthumously published works of Ludwig Wittgenstein, most notably *Zettel* and *Philosophical Investigations*. Although I have been assembling the material for this book for some time, I would have been unable actually to write it without the generosity of my university in granting me two terms of sabbatical leave during 1989–90, and the expert secretarial assistance of Nicola Kerry who typed (and retyped) the manuscript.

My thanks are also due to the research laboratories and other institutions connected with the use of animals that permitted me to visit them and to friends and academic colleagues, in various places who, over the years, have discussed the often complicated issues with me. My greatest debt, it hardly needs saying, is to my wife and children to whom the book is dedicated. They have twice had to endure the less acceptable face of sabbatical leave – that of a restless writer perpetually in the way and needing to be fed. I hope the cups of tea have not fuelled a lost cause; if they have, it is nobody's fault but mine.

LIST OF ABBREVIATIONS

AR   Aristotle (1959) *The 'Art' of Rhetoric*, J. H. Freese (tr.),
London: William Heinemann.

BB   Wittgenstein (1958) *The Blue and Brown Books*, Oxford:
Basil Blackwell.

DA   Aristotle (1986) *De Anima (On the Soul)*, H. Lawson-
Tancred (tr.), Harmondsworth: Penguin Books.

H&R   Haldane, E. S. and Ross, G. R. T. (trs) (1970) *The Philosophical Works of Descartes*, 2 vols, Cambridge: Cambridge
University Press.

NE   Aristotle (1976) *The Nicomachean Ethics*, J. A. K. Thomson
(tr.), Harmondsworth: Penguin Books.

P   Aristotle (1948) *The Politics of Aristotle*, E. Barker (tr.),
Oxford: Clarendon Press.

PI   Wittgenstein (1958) *Philosophical Investigations*, 3rd edn,
New York, Macmillan. (First pub. 1953.)

ST   St Thomas Aquinas, *Summa Theologica*, in A. C. Pegis (ed.
and tr.) (1948) *Introduction to Saint Thomas Aquinas*, New
York: Random House.

Z   Wittgenstein (1967) *Zettel*, G. E. M. Anscombe and G. H.
von Wright (eds), Oxford: Basil Blackwell.

HAWK ROOSTING

I sit in the top of the wood, my eyes closed.
Inaction, no falsifying dream
Between my hooked head and hooked feet:
Or in sleep rehearse perfect kills and eat.

The convenience of the high trees!
The air's buoyancy and the sun's ray
Are of advantage to me;
And the earth's face upward for my inspection.

My feet are locked upon the rough bark.
It took the whole of Creation
To produce my foot, my each feather:
Now I hold Creation in my foot

Or fly up, and revolve it all slowly –
I kill where I please because it is all mine.
There is no sophistry in my body:
My manners are tearing off heads –

The allotment of death.
For the one path of my flight is direct
Through the bones of the living.
No arguments assert my right:

The sun is behind me.
Nothing has changed since I began.
My eye has permitted no change.
I am going to keep things like this.

Ted Hughes
Lupercal (1960)

INTRODUCTION

> Language sets everyone the same traps; it is an immense
> network of easily accessible wrong turnings. . . . What I have to
> do then is erect signposts at all the junctions where there are
> wrong turnings so as to help people past the danger points.
>
> (Ludwig Wittgenstein 1980a: 18e)

Books are often bought on the strength of an introduction requiring,
as often as not, a cramped and hurried read in a crowded bookshop.
On the same strength they are sometimes reviewed; but that is a less
reputable story. Most readers with any sort of exposure to the issues
surrounding the increasingly well trampled field of animal liberation
and alleged animal rights, and that is every sane and literate person
over the age of 12, will find this a somewhat unusual book. Some
might think it insidious. For this reason I think it both worthwhile
and only fair to provide the unsuspecting with a foretaste of what I
will be attempting to establish in the coming pages. The oddity of the
book is not the only reason. I see its message as appealing particularly,
but not exclusively, to nonprofessionals who feel that the often
fraught issues of vegetarianism, field sports, the fur trade, animal
experimentation and so on, are best approached with generous
helpings of common sense. Unfortunately the intervening arguments,
in support of common sense and against the varieties of intellectual
extremism, will rarely themselves *be* commonsensical; although, I
hope, not to the point of being incomprehensible to readers prepared
to treat the text patiently.

The contemporary background

So what is unusual or odd about my contribution to the moral and
philosophical issues which bedevil discussion of our treatment of

1

animals? Several significant books have appeared in recent years, most notably by Andrew Linzey (1976), Stephen Clark (1977), Bernard Rollin (1981), Mary Midgley (1983), Tom Regan (1983), Vicki Hearne (1987), and, best known of all, Peter Singer (1983) whose *Animal Liberation*, first published in 1975, is generally credited with having galvanised contemporary enthusiasm in topics with a considerable history but, until then, a low profile. These have generated numerous satellite articles in the so-called scholarly press and even the publication of new journals, such as *Ethics and Animals* and *Between the Species*, exclusive to the area. Neither has the press, nor television, of the western world been idle. The quality newspapers bristle with items about intensive farming, hunt saboteurs or endangered species and magazines such as *Newsweek* and the UK Sunday Supplements highlight lengthy reports on topics such as recent research on animal learning, the less than peaceable activities of the Animal Liberation Front, and the use of animals in science. As if all this were not enough it is dwarfed by a wealth of scientific and technical literature from relevant disciplines as diverse as ethology, bio-medicine, economics and jurisprudence.

If there is no merit in merely treading paths adequately laid by others, then why yet another book? Now the paths laid by Regan, Clark, Rollin, Midgley, Linzey and Singer are substantial enough in radiating a deep commitment to matters animal, which is no bad thing, and have eased the way for considerable numbers of devotees to follow them. Furthermore they all lead in roughly the same direction. Unfortunately, despite its warm-hearted and often intuitive appeal, I am firmly convinced that it is the *wrong* direction. To drop the metaphor: these authors, although they differ from each other considerably in the nature and emphasis of their arguments, for example, Rollin (1981) is authoritative on animal experimentation and Linzey (1976) on the religious dimension, tend to agree substantially in their conclusions. They share the conviction that the treatment of animals by western society in the well publicised and contentious areas to which I have referred is little short, and sometimes nothing short, of criminal. These writers are therefore, and understandably, very sympathetic towards, and in most cases influential advocates for, all sorts of claims made on behalf of animals and the consequent reforms that these imply. These claims, in most cases, go far beyond the prevailing legal requirements (some advocate, for instance, that vegetarianism is a moral duty or that 'intensive' farming should cease forthwith) and are extreme enough to strike ordinary mortals as idealism born out of crankiness. Nonetheless their appeals leave in their wake a residue of guilt, the product of smooth and apparently compelling argument, the substance of which is that we ordinary mortals who eat meat, go fishing, or visit zoos, are pretty frightful in our complacency.

I do not pretend to be the first to have entered the lists against the received views of the liberationists. Anthony Kenny's *Will, Freedom and Power* (1975) and R.G. Frey's *Interests and Rights* (1980) in very different ways anticipate attacks that I shall employ. Both are important, mainly because they are practically the only writers to acknowledge the importance of the writings of Ludwig Wittgenstein for our understanding of the ontological and psychological issues involved; what exactly we are talking about in discussing, say, whether dogs *think*. Wittgenstein (1889–1951) is a towering figure in contemporary philosophy, competing with Einstein and Freud as the greatest theorist of the present century, and it is incredible that his many references to the nature of animals are almost totally ignored by the liberationists.[1] Frey is sent packing almost as abruptly and it is only Regan and to a lesser extent Midgley, of the writers so far cited, who subject Frey's views to any sort of extended scrutiny. But my pre-eminent task will be to tease out in considerable detail the implications of what Wittgenstein has to offer to a particular picture of human, then by subtle contrast animal, nature and then to follow up, on my own account, the implications for the practical issues involved.

Konrad Lorenz and choosing a dog

At the outset I offered a foretaste of my method. This I have so far failed to deliver. So, by way of example, I turn to a passage in one of Konrad Lorenz's deservedly celebrated books, *Man Meets Dog* (1959), although most readers will be more familiar with his earlier *King Solomon's Ring* (1964), first published in 1952. Lorenz is discussing the factors governing the choice of a dog both individually and in terms of breed. Red Setters show devotion but are 'too sentimental' whereas Sealyhams show fidelity and a genuine love of fun. He is patronising towards the 'good honest Boxer' or Airedale that lacks sensibility and 'independence of character'. Whilst allowing that they will not appeal to everyone his preference is for 'dogs not too far removed from the wild form' and of lesser pedigree; hence his favourite Chow-Alsatian crossbreds (1959: 82). He continues with this observation:

3

A mistake often made by animal lovers without much knowledge of dogs is to choose one which makes the friendliest overtures on first acquaintance. But one must not forget that one is thereby inevitably choosing the greatest *fawner* and that one will be less pleased later on when the dog greets every stranger in the same way . . .

Sycophancy is one of the worst faults a dog can have and, as I have already mentioned, it comes from a persistence of the indiscriminate friendliness and *servility* which very young dogs show towards all people and adult dogs. It is a *defect* only in adult dogs; in young ones it is perfectly normal and in no way reprehensible.

(Lorenz 1959: 84–5, my italics)

It is instructive to remember that Lorenz's views, which might have emanated merely from an intelligent and experienced breeder of dogs, are in fact those of a scientist of international repute and a pioneer of that branch of zoology known as ethology. His preoccupation with pets, birds, fish in tanks, and farm animals was not just an excess of 'Noah's Ark Syndrome' but born of the early ethologists' concern with instinct and the need to describe the behavioural repertoire of his subjects.[2] Those species capable of being kept in captivity and yet under conditions as near natural as possible, like dogs, cats, fish and small rodents, make the ideal subjects for prolonged scientific observation and experiment. So we have an expert speaking. Despite the homely and approachable nature of his remarks, which immediately engage the most casual reader, Lorenz knows what he is talking about. Yet nonetheless controversy is close to the surface. I am not thinking of the debate that might ensue upon, say, an enthusiast for Airedales or Red Setters defending the breed; Lorenz is generous in allowing for personal idiosyncrasies when it comes to a choice of pet. What is at issue is the *language* that he employs. Many will uncritically agree with him; fawning dogs seeming to be as contemptible as fawning people, grovelling towards those they regard as their betters. Angela Lambert (1989), in her recent account of the pre-war English debutantes, found that many of them were still waited upon by women considerably older than themselves, part servants and part companions, whose loyalty, devotion, and lack of remuneration, seemed almost slavelike. As she describes it, they seemed to regard themselves as a lower form of life destined only to serve the whims of

4

the aristocracy. People who find such states of affairs contemptible rather than touching might well compare the 'servility' of these women with the shortcomings of Lorenz's 'fawner'. Note the depths of his disapproval which seems to amount to moral condemnation by contrast with the virtues of 'aloofness' and 'exclusiveness':

> Unfortunately, it is impossible to foretell whether the playful young pup will grow into a sycophant or whether, with maturity, he will acquire the necessary aloofness towards strangers. . . . Chows develop this exclusiveness early and even at eight or nine weeks of age they show marked individuality of character.

> (Lorenz 1959: 85)

With all of this, as I have allowed, many will agree. But many will not and one does not have to be particularly knowledgeable about dogs to register a mild protest. Lorenz, perhaps in his eagerness to commend the chow and alsatian, might be thought improperly to elevate these breeds and, just as improperly, to demean those he objects to. The procedure is improper because he trades on the language of what are *human* virtues and vices rather than canine ones. This is my view. The evidence offered by Lorenz for the labels of fawner or sycophant, both offensive rebukes if directed at people, is that the offending dogs are indiscriminate in their friendliness and quick to give it.

Now this behaviour, other things being equal, is a vice neither in animals nor humans; indeed it might well be accounted a commendable trait akin to gregariousness. But the qualification is important since if things are *not* equal (if we have, let us say, only the *appearance* of friendliness) then the proper diagnosis might be more insidious since fawners, flatterers, sycophants and toadies are notoriously pleasant when it suits them. So is the groveller. So what is necessary to be one; with all of the implicit moral censure? (And it *is* implicit. The phrase 'a well-intentioned toady' or 'an honest sycophant' carries a distinct whiff of self-contradiction.) What is necessary in order to qualify as one of these dubious characters must involve some combination of self-abasement and insincerity; dishonesty in the service of self-advancement. To be merely servile, like the ancient companions, is not to be a sycophant; but if they *despise* the mistress they obey then it is. Furthermore all of these character ascriptions carry with them some sort of self-awareness; awareness, albeit not always clearly focused, that one is *being* insincere or whatever. What could be meant by describing someone as an unwitting sycophant?

At best the person in question might give the *appearance*, to a casual observer, of behaving in this unacceptable fashion. Perhaps he gushes or his manners are artless, but if the required insincerity is not present, then it is *wrong* to label him as if it were. A person with this undeserved stigma of moral fault, which cloaks something far less odious (indeed artlessness of manner can be a very attractive trait), is very close to those dogs of which Lorenz has such a low opinion. There is a difference also. A person, being *compos mentis*, is *capable* of the type of insincerity required to be correctly labelled a sycophant. Its presence was simply ruled out for the purposes of the example; most people, most of the time, are not insincere. But with dogs, momentous difficulties arise when we try to make sense even of their *capability* for the sophistication necessary to exhibit anything like insincerity, let alone its actual presence. Indeed any form of pretence, of which insincerity is a less reputable species, if attributed to dogs in an other than technical or metaphorical sense raises similar problems.

> Why can't a dog simulate pain? Is he too honest? Could one teach a dog to simulate pain? Perhaps it is possible to teach him to howl on particular occasions as if he were in pain, even when he is not. But the surroundings which are necessary for this behaviour to be real simulation are missing.
>
> (Wittgenstein 1958b: sect. 250)

Lest an exasperated reader, familiar with certain examples of apparent simulation in all sorts of animal behaviour, is tempted to close the book at this point I shall, once again, anticipate what is to come. Several small mammals, such as the American opossum, 'sham dead' when confronted by a predator who, if they are lucky, loses interest in a stationary victim and moves on to more exciting matters. The opossum lives to die another day. But it has not been cleverly shamming. The explanation is a state called thanatosis; a temporary paralysis, akin to hypnosis, brought about by the shock of confrontation. Thanatosis can also occur as a result of a sudden change of position. A frog suddenly turned over upon its back will be similarly paralysed but soon recover. Lorenz himself provided the explanation of another type of extraordinary behaviour. A squirrel in captivity will eat only a certain amount of food. If there is more than it can consume it may well be observed to go through all the motions of burying the surplus on the hard floor of its cage. This act of shadow burying leaves the squirrel content despite the fact that the food is still obviously there to see. But it is a mistake to see this, and many other bizarre 'shadow' performances, as a simulated burial or whatever. Lorenz showed that these were so-called fixed action patterns, a form of complex automatism which lies at the heart of the animal's repertoire of instincts.

These two examples are revealing but not conclusive. Much of this book will be concerned to show, in a sustained way, precisely *why* it is incorrect to attribute to all animals, with the odd rare possible exception, even the *capability* of pretence, insincerity, and a whole range of other 'mental' attributes. What follows from this for the practical and moral issues involved will be intriguing. But the issue facing us here is the value of Lorenz's talk of dogs as fawners and sycophants, and it would seem to ring distinctly hollow if based solely on the evidence of gregariousness on the part of creatures whose capacity for lack of sincerity or related varieties of subterfuge is, to say the very least of my counter-examples, a moot point. With dogs we seem to be on even stronger ground to counter the charges than in the case of the artless and gushing person. In desperation their critic might argue that the lack of social graces masks a schemer whose deceit knows no bounds but for which he has no hard evidence; at least we cannot prove otherwise. This popular device of quibblers is desperate because, lacking evidential support, it would be based purely upon the object of attention being a human being capable of dissembling. But with dogs, if my doubts are justified, even this dubious manoeuvre is not available. But dubious manoeuvres make good rhetoric and there must be many readers influenced by Lorenz's marvellous books who speak slightingly of spaniels or setters because his argument has faltered by too closely identifying dogs with human beings.

In defence of Lorenz

But *does* it falter? Since I am using the Lorenz quotations to provide a foretaste of what will be a lengthy discussion it will be worthwhile to pick at a few more threads. He is an expert naturalist, a fact too well known to benefit from my acknowledgement, so how might he be defended? Firstly, it might be claimed after all that some animals, higher mammals perhaps, are capable of the insincerity and deceit necessary to qualify as sycophants and fawners properly so called. Now I have already given several reasons for doubting that this is possible since it involves our regarding animals as what are called *moral agents*, capable of vice and virtue. Furthermore, none of the liberationist authors that I have so far referred to are prepared to argue that even the highest mammals can be so categorised. Tom Regan (1983: 151–6) allying them with human imbeciles and infants, talks of them as moral *patients*, and these comparisons are typical. However, it is fair to warn the reader that I shall be employing the *type* of argument that disqualifies dogs as authentic sycophants or fawners to undermine the attribution to animals of a whole range of what are often called mental abilities, such as desires, emotions, intentions, preferences, self-awareness, *in the sense in which these terms are used of human beings*. To this escalation of the attack Regan and the others will be seen to be united in implacable opposition.[3]

Secondly, it might be claimed for Lorenz that in training my guns upon the understanding of, say, 'sycophancy' as we might use it or withhold it of aged retainers or artless youths, I am missing the point. He is talking of an exclusively *animal* characteristic. Now there are, of course, such characteristics. Autotomy is the facility possessed by reptiles such as shore crabs by which the reflex action of a special muscle can cast off certain parts of their bodies if they are seized by a determined predator. The rejected claw or whatever grows back. Human beings are not autotomous nor, I think, would it enrich the human condition if we were. Typically the term 'autotomy', apart from a superficial resemblance to 'autonomy', suggests nothing that might be human. Where there *is* such a suggestion the term almost invariably implies a similarity. Thanatosis, discussed above, is not exclusive to animals nor is the term. It has its human analogue in most people's experience of being unable to move or cry out in extreme fear. One is as if momentarily hypnotised, as the explorer David Livingstone discovered in a singularly unenviable way:

> The lion growled horribly in my ear and shook me like a terrier does a rat. The shock produced a stupefaction in me, like that which a mouse must feel when caught by a cat. It induced a sort of state of anaesthesia, in which I felt neither the pain nor the shock, although I was fully conscious at the time. I was like a patient slightly under the influence of chloroform, who sees all the motions of the operation he is undergoing yet can feel no trace of the knife. This extraordinary state was not the outcome of any mental process, but the shock removed all trace of fear, and eliminated all horror – even in the very face of the lion.
>
> (Burton and Burton 1977: 272–3)

Lorenz cannot claim that sycophancy is a trait exclusive to animals, like autotomy, since the term has primary application in the human sphere. It would be unbelievably misleading to use 'sycophant' of animals yet deny any human analogues and this is clearly not Lorenz's intention since, as we have already seen, he is trading on the pejorative implications of the accepted usage. So if there cannot be an identity with this accepted usage then there must at least be a substantial similarity with it; as in the case of thanatosis.

This brings us to a third possible defence of Lorenz and one that will be influential in this book. It develops the idea of there being a 'substantial similarity' between the two uses. Stephen Clark, for example, argues for the presence in many animals, including vervet monkeys and dogs, of 'the roots of conscience' which, like sycophancy, hints at implications of morality (1985: 50). To lack conscience speaks for a degree of insincerity. He continues:

> To be a 'good dog' is to have those virtues of character that must be fairly widespread in a natural population if creatures of that kind are to survive and reproduce. A good dog is discriminating in her choice of mate [and] may show some signs of having preferred the paths of virtue to those of easy gratification. Human animals alone . . . have taken the next step, that of trying to assess their own sentiments in the light of reason.
>
> (Clark 1985: 50–1)

This passage might well fill an astute reader with disquiet. It is a thicket of problems into which I will be venturing later. Let me just hint at the cause for suspicion. The 'virtues of character' picked upon by Clark relate explicitly to reproductive and survival strategies which have enabled some species to flourish at the expense of others which either struggle or become extinct. Now such 'virtues' do not necessarily carry with them either moral agency or moral approbation. The snake that lies in the sun, warms up its ovaries and proliferates is *doing simply that*. If we approve of it and prefer it to its sun-shunning fellows with smaller broods it is simply on the grounds of an efficient survival strategy. But this is not *moral* approval. The successful quarterback or financier is not *thereby* a 'better person' (the phrase which, in a rough-and-ready way, encapsulates the essence of moral approval). Clark, not unlike Lorenz, seems to be equivocating. He establishes a sense of 'virtue' which is undeniably true of animals, namely that they perform certain functions, in this case of survival, efficiently. Such a use is common in English; it is perfectly proper to talk of the virtues of the Volkswagen, or those of bottled water in the

9

tropics. But this sense of 'virtue' is morally neutral. Clark then glides effortlessly on to talk of the dog's discrimination and its preferring 'the paths of virtue'. Here the implication of *moral* approval, the arena in which 'virtue' has its more emphatic location, is clearly intended. It might well be claimed, in Clark's defence, that he is simply pointing to the roots of conscience and that these roots are morally neutral. If this be so, then how do these roots suddenly become invested with moral significance? Indeed the suspicion remains, and I shall attempt to justify it, that the *moral* significance is inextricably involved with Clark's next step, the human one, that of assessing sentiments 'in the light of reason'.

Anthropomorphism and the expert

If the criticisms that I have levelled at Lorenz are plausible then he has done more than unjustifiably demean the dogs he dislikes by harking to the language of moral vice appropriate for humans. He has, in the process, presented a distorted picture of the very nature of these creatures by the implication that they have the *capacity* for the sophistication necessary to deserve such labels as 'fawner'. It might be added, to redress the balance, that he is extravagant and misleading in attributing to his favoured Lupus cross-breds the capacity for the virtues of 'aloofness' and 'exclusiveness'; if, indeed, they *are* virtues. Whether or not, in either case, the element of sophistication, absent in dogs, is again necessary for their proper, morally praiseworthy, attribution. The same might be said of Clark's praise of 'good' dogs as 'discriminating' ones. What Lorenz has done, and it is something that he does frequently, is to indulge in *anthropomorphism*. Yet it is a habit that he also warns against: animals are *animals*, not to be viewed as if they were human beings in similar circumstances and treated accordingly. In *King Solomon's Ring* he casts scorn upon visitors to zoos who,

> are in the habit of wasting sentimental pity on animals that are absolutely contented with their lot. . . . People are specially apt to pity those animals which, owing to their particular emotional associations, play a prominent role in literature, like the nightingale, the lion and the eagle.
>
> (Lorenz 1964: 49)

The eagle is too stupid to suffer from any loss of freedom and the lion too 'enviably indolent'. He also ridicules the idea, popular with almost all shades of liberationist, that the higher mammals have an inborn love of freedom and suffer a perpetual call of the wild:

> The notion . . . that a really tame mongoose, fox or monkey, once let loose, must certainly attempt to regain its 'precious freedom' for good and all, implies a false anthropomorphization of the animal's motive. It does not want to get away, it only wants to be let out of the cage.
>
> (Lorenz 1964: 72–3)

That a scientist like Lorenz, anxious to avoid the expense of false sentimentality upon animals, nonetheless fails to avoid some of its less obvious pitfalls is particularly enlightening. For a start it demonstrates that anthropomorphism is both more elusive and pervasive than is often supposed. It can be crass, of course, and many think this best exemplified in children's books like *The Wind in the Willows*, *Winnie the Pooh* or the Brer Rabbit stories. It might be thought that liberationists would applaud the depictions of animals in these and other wonderful books since the children who read them seem to overflow with fellow feeling for the real things, be they toads, donkeys, mice or the tiniest bug. In fact such works tend to be dismissed for perpetuating objectionable stereotypes: the silly goose, bloodthirsty wolf, sly fox, overweening toad, and the rest. Rollin discusses this very sensibly (1981: 45). But many anthropomorphic flights of wishful thinking are *not* transparently so and it is to the exposure of certain of these, and the consequent implications, that this book is devoted.

The second reason why Lorenz's flirtation with anthropomorphism is enlightening is that it encourages a justifiable scepticism over accepting *every* claim made by experimental scientists in this, as in any other, field. Forensic experts in a court of law can establish incontrovertibly that the fatal bullet was fired from exhibit *A*, and that the clothes of the accused betray minute stains of a blood-type identical with that of the victim. These are the acknowledged fields in which the honest testimony of the expert witnesses is properly accepted by judge and jurors as the truth. But if the ballistician stated his conviction that the defendant murdered the deceased or, even more hazardously, that he murdered out of greed or envy, then these views would be struck from the record and he would probably lose his job. Unfortunately it is rare that an alleged expert will tip his hand as blatantly as this. Life would be simplified were it so. Indeed there are often bitter disputes over precisely where the boundaries of expertise are to be drawn particularly in fields, unlike the law, where no attempts have been made to clarify, let alone codify, an equivalent to the jurist's rules of evidence.

Our own field, that of understanding animals, is notorious for such boundary disputes, in part because there are so many purveyors of alleged expertise jostling for recognition. Here is a revealing, if controversial, example. It will be discussed at length later. Comparative psychologists are much interested in the ability of animals and birds to communicate with each other. Gulls, for example, make a particular call if corn is thrown to them which attracts others but issue a variant of greater range if the offering is fish. Vervet monkeys' alarm calls similarly differentiate predators, whether big cats, eagles or snakes and elicit different responses from their fellows that hear. These are snippets of what are called natural communication systems and their variety is fascinating. That the calls and responses occur in the appropriate contexts tends not to be disputed. But the fur begins to fly when discussion moves to the value of these mutual behaviour patterns as indicators of the *intelligence* of the creatures in question or the nature of the communication with which we are here involved. Ethologists tend to agree that the behaviour involving gulls and monkeys is *instinctive* although in many cases capable of adaptation; it is present in the lowest of creatures, tends to be inflexible (which is why specific birdsong is so easily recognised) and is triggered by precise causes. Now on this view it would be misleading to talk of the gulls *telling* the others that fish is on the menu or of the listening monkeys *being warned*. Careful writers would talk of 'telling' or 'being warned' to indicate an attenuated use; and likewise they might refer to it as 'communication'. It resembles in some ways the 'communication' that takes place within a complicated machine or organic system like the body. But some comparative psychologists and certainly many animal enthusiasts would scorn the inverted commas and talk of the information imparted by one creature to others who *understand* what the first one *says*. Yet there does seem to be an important difference between understanding a sound, which has to do with the *meaning* that it might have, and merely responding to it in an instinctive way.

My own sympathies, in considering the above issue, tend firmly towards the 'instinctive' solution which emphasises the gulf between simply reacting to sounds rather than understanding them. Thus gulls and monkeys are misleadingly described as giving each other information, being warned, and understanding. However, I would not wish my Introduction to leave a reader under the impression that I am in favour of excising such phrases from our talk about animals. This would be a silly crusade. Such talk has a purpose. Sarah Helm (1989: 24) reports a UK rabies expert as describing the virus as 'extraordinarily clever' but there is no implication of a premeditated masterplan to conquer the world. He is remarking upon its extraordinary adaptability:

> Its masterstroke is the way it replicates in nervous tissue – where the immune system is ineffective. Growing in the brain [it] causes madness – and then, with perfect timing, as the host starts to attack other animals, the virus leaves the nervous tissue and enters the saliva.
>
> (Helm 1989: 24)

If this, admittedly somewhat sensationalistic, way of speaking is possible without misconstruction we ought with care and insight similarly to accept that much of our talk about more complex creatures is, as it were, hedged in by emphatic but inexplicit contextual implication. I hope that this book will go some way to providing grounds for such care and insight. Wittgenstein's seminal notion of *language-games* will be an essential methodological aid in showing that what is at issue here is not something exclusive to our talk about animals but a general feature of our understanding of the way that language works.

1

THE UTILITARIAN
BEGINNINGS

Singer and utilitarianism

My Introduction plunged the reader, with few preliminaries, into some heady issues. It is now time to return to those preliminaries and examine the background to the contemporary flurry of concern for animals. It has a varied and enlightening history stretching back as far as one likes to think; primitive man farmed animals as well as hunting them and implicit in both activities is some concern for their welfare and interest in their habits. The earliest written sources usually cited are biblical ones with their obvious importance for the religious attitudes towards animals exemplified in Judaism and Christianity. But the history is not essential for an understanding of the crop of recent theories and will be found more apropos against a contemporary background. So it is to these theories that we turn.

The debate was originally fuelled by moral concerns about *equality* and, for some theorists, *rights* rather than specific discoveries about the nature of animals. The 1970s were relatively successful, some would say enormously so, in boosting reform movements geared to ameliorating the lot of certain allegedly oppressed people, notably women, blacks, and homosexuals. The reasons for the timing are the province of social historians. But what is clear is that the nature of the noisy, prolonged, and often violent debate revolved around claims for *equality* for which the goal for these groups was *liberation*. The claims on behalf of animals, pioneered by Peter Singer, followed in the wake of these advances. They are also explicitly allied. The fact that the phrase 'animal liberation' raises for many people the spectre of balaclava helmets and violence to property is unfortunate since the phrase was coined to recall the charisma and inspiration of the movements for human liberation.

Singer begins from basic considerations about the nature of ethical thinking. As he puts it, 'Ethics takes a universal point of view' (1979: 11). He derives from this a twofold theory of what an ethical judgement should take account of. Firstly, in considering the problem from everyone's viewpoint, my own likes and dislikes are to be taken account of, but they must count for no more than any other person's. These desires and aversions reflect people's *interests*. The remaining task is to select as the right course of action that which has the best consequences for all concerned. This will, of course, involve balancing interests against each other since only in the rarest cases will everyone be satisfied to the full. This second requirement clearly identifies Singer as a *utilitarian* in the late eighteenth- and nineteenth-century tradition of Jeremy Bentham and John Stuart Mill. Their guiding principle of moral action, the 'best consequences', was encapsulated in the well-known phrase 'the greatest possible happiness to the greatest possible number' (Sidgwick 1874: 381).

The principle of equal consideration of interests

If the second feature of Singer's theory points to his being a utilitarian, a label he willingly admits to, the first emphasises his commitment to an uncompromising *equality*. To say that all humans are equal is to say that no one person's interests, or no group's, must take precedence over those of other persons or groups simply because they are that person or a member of that group. It seems to be a corollary of this that when we are deliberating about an outcome with moral implications we must give equal weight to similar interests notwithstanding the sex, race, class, education or abilities of the individuals or groups that have them. This sense of equality is summed up in Singer's principle of equal consideration of interests:

> The principle of equal consideration of interests acts like a pair of scales, weighing interests impartially. True scales favour the side where the interest is stronger or where several interests combine to outweigh a smaller number of similar interests; but they take no account of whose interests they are weighing.
>
> (Singer 1979: 19)

It must be stressed that fairly modest claims are made for this principle. It does not tell us how the 'scales' work. How do we weigh an idler's desire to live a quiet life against that of the professional brass player in the adjoining apartment who needs to practise for several hours each day? A court might eventually make a decision but legitimate disagreement can persist. Nor, more perplexingly, does Singer clarify whether and why all such disputes must necessarily be seen to be *moral* ones. He seems, however, to be attempting to capture what for most of us is an important yet elusive prey; how to give substance to the claim frequently made that in some sense a highly sophisticated representative of the civilised world like Albert Einstein and the most illiterate and impoverished of Ethiopian tribeswomen are nonetheless equal. Yet since Einstein and the peasant could hardly be more different from each other it would be foolish to treat them in exactly the same way. The woman would make nothing of men's clothing, or mathematical papers, and Einstein would not thrive on primitive cuisine and a few goats. But what would be preserved, despite the wildly different provisions made, is an equal respect for the different interests of both of them and it is precisely with this in mind that, it is argued, it would be foolish and uncaring to give them the same things.

Singer's principle is minimal; it enjoins equal concern for others' interests without specifying the forms that it should take nor when it should properly be taken. But it is also an *ethical* principle and by this Singer means that equality is not something for which we qualify or from which we are disqualified in virtue of any particular qualities or abilities we might have as individuals nor as members of ethnic or social groupings. That a child shows an aptitude for playing the violin or acting might well justify their being given a special education at, for example, the Yehudi Menuhin school in London, with an excellent chance of an illustrious career to follow. But this is not discriminatory; it is a response to their interests and their ability to make the most of them. Similarly, someone with aggression and the gift of prophecy ought to be allowed to earn a lot of money without fear of moral rebuke.[1] But musical aptitude or aggression are not grounds for giving *priority* to the interests of their possessors nor for providing for them at the expense of those of less gifted people. This is why the alleged genetic differences in ability or character traits between either the races or the sexes, even if sustained, is not a justification for unequal treatment.

Singer's principle is at its most persuasive when we are talking about very general and basic human interests: having a sensible amount of food, a reasonable place to live, employment within one's capabilities, some leisure for pastimes and the chance to make friends and enjoy company, and so on.

Now the fact that the principle of equal consideration applies to all human beings irrespective of the differences between them will have a crucial role in its being adapted to a defence of animals. That it does might seem to be best illustrated by my previous example of Einstein and the Ethiopian tribeswoman. Despite the differences in sex, colour, ethnic origin, cultural background and, above all, intelligence, they are both entitled to their very different interests being treated equally seriously. For someone to object that Einstein is a genius whose discoveries are of far greater value to the human race than anything that the woman might conceivably achieve and that his interests should therefore take precedence is to enter a minefield. Indeed the notion is more than ambiguous, it is ideological. Is the present President of the United States or the British Royal Family pre-eminently useful to society? Answers from left field will tend to contradict those from the right. Or, more blatantly, to argue that men are superior to women or whites to blacks (Einstein winning on either count) is no less partial.

Infants, permanently retarded humans, and John Rawls

Let us grant that, in the sense proposed, Einstein and the tribeswoman are equal. It is now asked if Einstein and the oak tree, under which he happens to be sitting, are similarly equal. The question would probably be met with incredulity. The oak tree, it will be said, although living and deserving of preservation is just not the sort of being capable of equality with a human being. The tribeswoman, as any anthropologist will tell us if we do not know already, is a complex individual. She will speak a language of some sophistication and will be experienced in the ways of nomadic or village life. In particular she will know what is due of her social class and that of her family. She will thus have a sense of local *justice*; of what is done and not done. These attributes she shares with Einstein, he in *his* own way, and it is this sense of justice or 'moral personality', as the philosopher John Rawls (1972) calls it, that is the necessary and sufficient condition for equality. The oak tree fails these tests despite its beauty and value.

But Rawls' proposal clearly is divisive and the liberationists are united in their opposition to anything like it. Singer's objections (1979: 16–17) are typical and will serve as preliminaries to the fuller treatment in Chapter 7. He argues, firstly, that moral personality will not always be undeniable. Even within so-called primitive peoples

17

there are contrasts of grasp and sensitivity and it will be difficult to know where to locate the minimal qualification. Secondly, it is not 'intuitively obvious why, if moral personality is so important, we should not have grades of moral status, with rights and duties corresponding to the degree of refinement of one's sense of justice' (16–17). Thirdly, and it might seem conclusively, however low we set the minimal requirement of moral personality for equal consideration of interests, there would be large numbers of human beings who would be ruled out of court. The two groups which dominate the debate are infants and imbeciles, namely 'humans with severe and irreparable brain damage'. This strikes him as an unacceptable price to pay since the interests of the individuals in these two groups are often guarded far more intensely than those of normal adults precisely because they are unable to fend for themselves.

However, the proposal that the possession of a version of Rawls' 'moral personality' is central to the argument will not lie down that easily. It would be misleading to proceed to animals without giving some preliminary pointers as to how it might be revived and the objections met. That problems might beset the minimal qualifications for moral personality ought not to disturb us. The exigencies of life require that we must cut Gordian knots to allow for marginal cases; just as a jury's need to be sure beyond all *reasonable* doubt leaves room for genuine dissent. Singer's second criticism raises more basic difficulties at which I will only hint. Rawls' notion, exemplified in the relative sophistication of the tribeswoman, involves the recognition that social life is a matter of 'give and take'. It is the simple grasp of this need for 'give and take', and what properly follows from transgressions, that constitutes moral personality and is the basis of ethical awareness. It is important to note how this view differs from Singer's view of ethics as the 'universal point of view' (1979: 11). The contractualist tends to limit one's obligations to the various groups with which one interacts: family, friends, village, and so on. One's interests will be respected not by being a member of *homo sapiens* but by being a paid-up member of the particular moral club involved. Those incapable of appreciating the importance of obeying the rules will lose moral status. In other words we meet the second objection by accepting a version of what Singer finds repugnant and attempt to justify doing so by showing that it provides a more persuasive account of ordinary ethical thinking.

The third objection, relating to infants and imbeciles, can be answered in several ways. However the two groups do not stand or fall together; indeed they do not stand or fall alone since each admits of significant internal variation. Rawls himself certainly wants to include them and he does so by allowing that the interests of *potential* persons are guarded as zealously as those of actual ones. But how can this be if they are outside the scope of contract and lack moral personality? It looks to be an *ad hoc* device, as Singer claims, to keep up appearances (1979: 17). But a fellow liberationist, Bernard Rollin, unexpectedly comes to Rawls' rescue. He argues convincingly that the criticism ignores the scope of the moral agent's interests. The tribeswoman will be passionately concerned for the health and future of her infants. Community life, as in any society including our own, will be preoccupied with the provision of schooling that meets the needs of its children. So the appeal to the 'potentiality' of infants and other moral patients is rescued from the *ad hoc* by being seen as typical of the justifications given by adults for their own interests in them. Animals command similar respect. As Immanuel Kant, writing in the eighteenth century, puts it: 'A master who turns out his ass or his dog because the animal can no longer earn its keep manifests a small mind' (Kant 1963: 241). Rollin concludes that 'nothing follows from Rawls' theory about excluding animals from the scope of moral concern' (1981: 13), although the obligation will not extend to *all* animals regardless of their place in human affection.

This preliminary defence which I have proposed to meet Singer's rejection of contractualist theory has conservative implications. It provides grounds for holding that even if one makes the possession of something like moral personality a qualifying condition for being a moral agent, the interests of those who fail to qualify are not automatically excluded. David Hume argues not unlike this in *An Enquiry Concerning the Principles of Morals* (1751) invoking 'the laws of humanity' for what I have described as typical justifications employed by moral agents for respecting the interests of moral patients:

Were there a species of creatures intermingled with men, which, though rational, were possessed of such inferior strength . . . that they were incapable of all resistance . . . the necessary consequence, I think, is that we should be bound by the laws of humanity to give gentle usage to these creatures, but should not, properly speaking, lie under any restraint of justice with regard to them. . . . Our intercourse with them could not be called society, which supposes a degree of equality; but absolute

command on the one side, and servile obedience on the other
. . . This is plainly the situation of men, with regard to animals;
and how far these may be said to possess reason, I leave it to
others to determine.

(Hume 1902: 190–1)

(Hume also puts 'barbarous Indians' and 'the female sex' on this
footing. He could have added young children and imbeciles.)

Singer and the other liberationists, including Rollin, would point
out in their defence that what is not automatically excluded by the
defence is not automatically *included* by it. What of moral agents
who show no concern for infants or animals or have interests in
positively harming them? There *are* such; Hume's laws of humanity
are not universal. Are they entitled to act upon these impulses?
Furthermore even those agents who acknowledge the need to give
consideration to the various categories of moral patients, they would
argue, would almost certainly be very restrictive in what they would
acknowledge was due these groups, particularly animals. These
protests could be supported by appeal to the treatment of animals in
contemporary western society (not forgetting the human parallels)
which, even if it is perfectly legal, is regarded by the liberationists as
barbaric. This point was made in the Introduction. They treat
Hume's 'gentle usage', if it be taken as enjoining no more than
kindness to animals, with little short of scorn: 'a Victorian concept
which comes under the heading of "charitable good works" '
(Hollands 1985: 170).

This might be generalised as follows. On contractualist premises
the interests of those people with moral personality are respected in
virtue of what they are themselves as moral agents, whereas the
moral patients who lack this personality are only accorded those
interests which the agents think fit to confer upon them. This,
Singer would argue, is not equality. For the debate to progress we
must proceed to examine the sense in which, it is claimed, interests
can properly be said to attach to animals and what those interests
might be.

Are animals equal?

So far the universal application of Singer's principle of the equal
consideration of interests has been limited to human beings although
it has been implicit all along that animals were waiting in the wings

for inclusion. Many people are enraged by the mere suggestion; it appears either absurdly optimistic in elevating the poodle to the status of its mistress or irritatingly pessimistic in reversing the process. Racial or sexual equality, it will be conceded, is all very well since even the most ardently divisive supremacist will admit that the similarities between the contending groups are considerable enough to keep equality a live issue. But poodles! And what about worms? Where will it end? Now most of these comments, trivial or not, raise points of great interest. For example, if it can be justifiably claimed that trees have interests then perhaps they deserve equal consideration. (It is worth reminding ourselves that some people feel as strongly about the preservation of forests as others do about threatened wildlife such as the barn owl or the greater horseshoe bat, even to the extent of being murdered for their pains.[2])

The 'argument for enragement', if I might call it that, can be met by yet another appearance of Einstein and the Ethiopian tribeswoman. That they could plausibly be thought equal in terms of Singer's equality principle does not imply the promotion of the lady into a mathematical genius nor the diminution of Einstein's intelligence to match that of the lady's peasant husband. To think that it might is due to a confusion over the fact that equality of interests in no way implies that these interests will be the *same*; all that is at stake is that the different interests, whatever they might be, will be given equal respect. (We must not, of course, forget the problems involved in 'weighing' that this heralds.) What is here proposed by Singer, as we have seen, is an ethical principle – it is 'not a description of an alleged actual equality among humans: it is a prescription of how we should treat humans' (Regan and Singer 1976: 152). However if it is possible to unearth an even more minimal characteristic which truly does unite all humans, and which is relevant to their having interests, then Singer seems prepared to accept it as a factual base for his principle which, in a not entirely clear way, supplements its ethical status (1979: 50). The candidate at hand is the capacity for *suffering*. It is invariably presented in a prescient passage from Bentham's *Introduction to the Principles of Morals and Legislation*, published in 1789:

> The day *may* come when the rest of the animal creation may acquire those rights which never could have been withholden from them but by the hand of tyranny. The French have already discovered that the blackness of the skin is no reason why a human being should be abandoned without redress to the

21

caprice of a tormentor. It may come one day to be recognised that the number of the legs, the villosity of the skin, or the termination of the *os sacrum*, are reasons equally insufficient for abandoning a sensitive being to the same fate. What else is it that should trace the insuperable line? Is it the faculty of reason, or perhaps the faculty of discourse? But a full-grown horse or dog is beyond comparison a more rational, as well as a more conversable animal, than an infant of a day, or a week, or even a month, old. But suppose they were otherwise, what would it avail? The question is not, Can they *reason?* nor Can they *talk?* but, *Can they suffer?*

(Bentham 1960: 411n)

Although Bentham's concern for animals is not unique to the period, it demonstrates not only the debt owed by Singer to his classical forerunner but it also takes the next step for him. If we must, as we have seen, forgo intelligence, the possession of language or similar 'advanced' human attributes and move to the minimal criterion of the capacity to suffer in order to allow for the equality of the human 'hard' cases like infants and imbeciles, then consistency requires that we must include *animals* since they too can suffer. The capacity for suffering, to which Singer appends that of enjoyment as a sort of counterweight, is, he adds in a controversial passage,

a prerequisite for having interests at all, a condition that must be satisfied before we can speak of interests in any meaningful way. It would be nonsense to say that it was not in the interests of a stone to be kicked along the road by a schoolboy. A stone does not have interests because it cannot suffer. Nothing that we can do to it could possibly make any difference to its welfare. A mouse, on the other hand, does have an interest in not being tormented, because it will suffer if it is.

(1979: 50)

Thus to the vices of racism and sexism, which received such prominence in the 1960s and 1970s, was added that of 'speciesism' (an infelicitous term, coined by Richard Ryder and taken up by Singer, but one that seems to have staying power). A speciesist is someone who gives preference to their own interests and those of other human beings over those of other species even when the latter are as peremptory as the former and, if called upon to justify it, they do so simply in terms of the primacy of human concerns.

Persons and non-persons

There is a celebrated passage in J.S. Mill's *Utilitarianism* (1861) in which he compares human life with its typical vicissitudes as being nonetheless preferable to that of a contented beast:

> It is better to be a human being dissatisfied than a pig satisfied; better to be Socrates dissatisfied than a fool satisfied. And if the fool, or the pig, are of a different opinion, it is because they only know their own side of the question.

> (Mill 1910: 9)

Despite occasional temptations to envy a pet's life of cosy indolence, Mill's point is that, whatever we might say, nobody would ever deliberately choose to be reduced to the level of the animal whatever the putative delights awaiting them. Now Singer adopts a similar position and for much the same reasons (1979: 89–90). The principle of equal consideration remains intact if we take him to be claiming that in certain specific circumstances of conflict a greater weight of interests support our favouring the being with 'self awareness'.

The concept of 'persons' can usefully surface at this point partly because it is used extensively in the literature and also because it avoids some circumlocutions. (Midgley's article 'Persons and non-persons' (1985) is representative.) A person is a self-aware being who acts in a significant way, is an agent rather than a mere bystander, a distinction which recalls the discussion both of moral personality and moral agents earlier in the chapter. The introduction of moral personality or agency seems to me to be integral to the use of the term. Singer however ignores this way of putting it, despite having said that ' "person" came to mean one who plays a role in life, one who is an agent' and he simply selects rationality and self-consciousness for what he claims 'as the core of the concept' (1979: 76). Although it seems difficult to conceive properly of this 'core' *without* involving a degree of moral agency, Singer has very self-interested reasons for effecting this emasculation, as we shall see in the next section.

By contrast, infants and the most retarded of imbeciles, although human beings and thus 'persons' in the later inclusive sense of *homo sapiens*, are *non*-persons in this exclusive use. Now what is it about persons that gives grounds for claiming a greater weight of interests on their behalf? Singer gives four reasons, of which only two need concern us here, but they will need supplementation:

1. Persons will have specific desires and plans for the future which would be frustrated were they to die. (The objection, which goes back over 2000 years, that once dead it will make no difference, may be food for thought but does not undermine the fact that the possible frustration of such desires would colour a person's *prospect* of death nor does it seem to prevent us feeling pity for Shelley or Mozart at having died so young.) By contrast, infants and imbeciles would not normally be said to have the *capacity* for such explicit desires and plans.

2. Persons are able genuinely to choose, to make decisions to act in a certain way and carry them out aware that they are pursuing their own interests. This is *autonomy*, an attribute involving a sense of being in control of one's own future. Not only is it related to the having of desires, although a person might well have projects without any idea that their fulfilment lay in their own hands, but autonomy seems to require the possession of many other sophisticated attributes which add to the complexity of the person's interests such as intentions, hopes, fears and other emotions like love, pity and guilt. Infants and imbeciles, it is argued, depending upon their lack of maturity or disability, are denied this dimension of experience and the pursuant interests.

Persons and animals

The intelligent reader thinking ahead to animals might have predicted from the previous section that Singer would be giving them the status of human infants or imbeciles. Even this might have appeared to be an ambitious step since it would immediately seem to accord food animals protection against the meat-eater. Meat eating does not justify cannibalism and were a band of devotees to defend the practice on the grounds that they restricted their intake to anencephalics and the newly born, even the most hardened carnivore is unlikely to be impressed. However the meat-eating utilitarian (there are many such!) could circumvent this intuitively knockdown intervention on behalf of vegetarianism by citing the special interests of parents and relations, coupled with cultural and religious sensibilities, which protect babies and imbeciles indirectly from such a fate; animals remain exposed. Whatever the virtues of this defence,

Singer would appear to trump it by his more ambitious claim that some animals at least are *persons*, as he has defined the term emphasising 'rationality and self-consciousness' (1979: 76).

> Some nonhuman animals appear to be rational and self-conscious beings, conceiving themselves as distinct beings with a past and a future. When this is so, or to the best of our knowledge may be so, the case against killing is strong, as strong as the case against killing permanently defective human beings at a similar mental level.
>
> (Singer 1979: 103)

Chimpanzees are his 'clearest case of nonhuman persons' but Singer also includes other apes, whales, and dolphins as clear-cut cases and monkeys, dogs, cats, pigs, seals and bears as probable candidates. If Singer is right then the animals that qualify enjoy very strong protection indeed, since the defectives referred to in the quotation would have to be rational and self-conscious and at least as relatively advanced as mature mongols. Unfortunately Singer's comparison with mongols, or with any other suitably rational and self-conscious defectives, cannot be sustained since they bring with these qualities a degree of moral agency. As maturing children they begin to know what they should and should not do and are praised or censured accordingly; up to a point they become *responsible*. Yet no liberationist would wish to admit this of animals since it would allow them to be punished for *wrongdoing* (rather than for permissible training purposes) of which all are agreed they can have no conception. It is for this reason that Singer emasculates the notion of a person, as I put it in the preceding section, in order to render it suitable for animal use. But in so doing he forfeits profitable comparisons with the treatment of human persons.

This ambitious moral status with which Singer dignifies animals would seem to imply that to kill a nonhuman person would be *more* reprehensible than to kill a human anencephalic. Such is indeed the case: 'So it seems that killing, say, a chimpanzee is worse than the killing of a gravely defective human who is not a person' (1979: 97). (It is worth noting that one could well agree with this conclusion without having to elevate the chimpanzee into a person. To set the death of an elegant and intelligent member of an endangered species against that of a poor human wretch who would probably be none the worse off could be enough to tip the balance in favour of the former.) Singer, however, does not quite have an argument for general vegetarianism since only the pig, of regular food animals, is elevated to personhood. However, as we shall see, his grounds for attributing self-consciousness allow so much room for speculation and sympathetic 'gut reaction', coupled with his urging the benefit of the doubt in difficult cases, that cattle and sheep can be included by those so inclined together with much else, including rats and mice (much favoured by researchers for their adaptability). Fish and reptiles fail the test. However, the specifics of Singer's argument do not matter very much. His point is that some animals are capable of considerable sophistication in addition to being merely sentient: they possess self-consciousness and can have hopes, fears, and desires, be capable of acting with intention, of making plans, of using simple abstract reasoning and even, in exceptional cases, some grasp of rudimentary language. When considered in the light of the equality principle their interests relating to the mere avoidance of suffering will be enhanced by others stemming from these abilities as persons. Even so, those creatures that do not qualify as persons continue to earn consideration of their interests in virtue of being merely sentient, as having the capacity to suffer.[3]

Animals and pain

How does Singer come by these conclusions some of which, to the average reader, will seem exaggeratedly optimistic on behalf of animals? A part cause of initial scepticism will stem from his use of the term 'person'. Clearly if the higher mammals can properly be so designated it would constitute a powerful weapon in the armoury of their equality with *homo sapiens*. However, as we have already seen, his concentration upon rationality and self-consciousness as the alleged 'core' of the concept and neglect of the implications of associated moral agency tends to compromise any solidarity with humans at this level. But identification at a lower level, that of sentience (in the special sense inclusive of the capacity to feel pain) will be untainted by such sleights of hand and it is with this that Singer begins in *Animal Liberation*. Indeed in that book he restricts himself to the claim, in support of Bentham, that animals can suffer pain, which he clearly thinks is enough to convince many people that the treatment of animals in factory farms and experimental laboratories, his main targets, is akin to deliberate exploitation and torture. Strategically this is the right medicine. Successful campaigns for the more humane treatment of animals, if they are to involve the general public have tended to succeed if the rallying cry is one of maiming and cruelty. In his article 'Fighting to win' Henry Spira provides graphic evidence of this from his battles with Revlon, Avon, and Proctor and Gamble (1985: 202–5). That dolphins might or might not be persons makes less stirring copy.

The initial battles have long been won. The legal requirement to anaesthetise research subjects wherever possible is not just to ensure that they remain comatose but to prevent pain, and nobody reading of youths stretching a mouse over a candle flame could doubt the animal's discomfort. The argument is still conducted in part for historical reasons since there have been sceptical thinkers and experimentalists, particularly in Renaissance times, who have appeared to regard animals as noisy automata with no more feeling than a harpsichord. (We will return to these in Chapter 4.) Ironically, however, and most unpromisingly, Singer begins in a manner reminiscent of sixteenth-century scepticism in depicting what we understand by pain; human or nonhuman.

> Pain is something that we feel, and we can only infer that others are feeling it from various external indications. . . . It is conceivable that our best friend is really a very cleverly constructed robot, controlled . . . by a brilliant scientist so as to give all the signs of feeling pain, but really no more sensitive than any other machine. We can never know, with absolute certainty, that this is not the case.
>
> (Singer 1983: 11)

But, he continues, we do not really doubt that other humans feel pain and nor do we doubt it of animals; the inference is a reasonable one.

Now this way of putting things shows a breathtaking disregard for much philosophical thinking in the present century. (We will discuss this in Chapters 5 and 6.) It is enough to point out here that if such doubt is 'conceivable' then, in principle, it must be *possible*; it must make sense. In certain cases we *may* infer that someone is in pain (if for example, they are reaching for a bandage) but if my young son falls heavily from his climbing frame, screams, and I run to him, the case is different: I *see* that he is in pain. Pain is a far more complex phenomenon than the experience of certain sensations, although it is bound up with these, and is in part a product of our *instinctive* reactions to other creatures; instincts we share with some other animals. However, we can agree with Singer that the grounds for attributing pain to animals are as strong as those for attributing them to human beings, whilst leaving in abeyance the nature of these grounds.

Pain and problems

At least two difficulties arise at this point. Although we might make the mistake of thinking that the dog struck by the car was badly injured and in pain, since we reach it only to see it wander away with apparent unconcern, what of the young girl's concern at the wriggling of the worm chopped in half by her father's spade? Is the child mistaken, as were we with the dog, or are we at fault in not sharing her distress? An adult who ignores the screeching of an injured dog is regarded as inhumane but the gardener who casually divides a worm a second time is normally not; despite a child's protests. As we progress away from dogs and the higher mammals, down the zoological scale, both sides agree that the attribution of pain becomes more hazardous but they diverge in their understanding of what pain *is*. Singer would side with those who acknowledge the diminution in similarity of nervous systems and 'pain behaviour' (worms wriggle much of the time) but would still allow that the presence of pain is an open question. Indeed he would be encouraged towards a more positive conclusion by Rollin's account of the Swedish research in 1979, reported in the prestigious journal *Nature* (29, 1979: 805), of the discovery of endorphins and enkephalins in earthworms. These chemicals have powerful pain-killing effects in human beings, are also released by acupuncture, and are involved in the process of thanatosis. Rollin concludes: 'In any event, the presence of these chemicals in invertebrates strongly suggests that these creatures do feel pain' (1981: 31).

But this is a hazardous argument. The mere presence of chemicals is inadequate grounds for attributing *pain* to creatures so distant from ourselves. The limiting case might well be plants. The view that pain really is a private and internal state known only to observers by its behavioural and chemical correlates allows the possibility (Singer's 'conceivability') that cucumbers might, just might, feel it. Clark, with reservations, allows this very point: 'Some plants may be individuals, as trees probably are; some plants may have points of view. Some plants may feel' (Clark 1977: 171). Singer's emphatic disclaimer, 'None of the grounds we have for believing that animals feel pain hold for plants' (1979: 61), is insufficient to rule it out as *conceivable* in his terms. Indeed his denial is undermined by the lively debate over a 'Primary Perception' in plants.[4] The Wittgensteinian alternative is to deny that attributing pain even makes *sense* in such contexts. The concept of pain is seen to have primacy in its application to human beings and is gradually attenuated as it descends the spectrum of animal life until a point is reached, perhaps with worms and certainly with protozoans and plants, where it is diluted beyond recognition and loses any usefulness.

The second problem concerns the relation between pain and suffering. Singer, quite properly, allows that because of their 'superior mental powers' and greater awareness of the implications of being in pain, human beings in many cases *suffer* more than animals: 'A human dying from cancer is likely to suffer more than a mouse' (1979: 53). He has in mind the possibility that the mouse's cancer might be of a type that involves more pain than that of the human being but that the mouse would *suffer less* because it was incapable of knowing what it had, what the prognosis was and the probable end. Two points need to be made about this apparently straightforward distinction:

1. Humans can of course suffer greatly when there is little or no pain; other perhaps than the pain of suffering, if such can be spoken of. For example, lumps that do not hurt when pressed can nonetheless have catastrophic consequences and reduce people to the depths of despair. Are animals capable of this? Mary Midgley, for instance, mentions that 'social birds and mammals are upset by solitude, or by the removal of their young' (1983: 90). This is suffering without pain. Are these descriptions misleadingly specific in attributing to the animals concerned the mental competence of human beings?

2. The 'stiff upper lip' is integral to the myth of the English gentleman. To give way to pain or distress by complaining, moaning, and above all by crying, is the stuff of which lesser breeds are made. They lack, so the myth goes, the ability to 'contain themselves'. What of animals? Are they capable of it? Infants certainly are not; mothers, almost intuitively, diagnose their cries and whimpers as symptoms of needs of which the babies are unaware. As children grow up they slowly learn to conceal their aches and pains in certain ways; they begin to regulate their behaviour for this or that *reason*. Even the most optimistic liberationists are wary of attributing this sort of rationality to animals. The problems are similar to those, raised in the Introduction, over the dog's possible *simulation* of pain. So if we claim that the animal can inhibit its pain we seem to be implying that it knows the reasons why it is doing what it does, which seems excessively anthropomorphic, but if we deny it this capability there

are unpalatable implications of another sort. The denial renders it difficult to sustain the claim that animals which have appalling injuries, but which are nonetheless comatose, such as the laboratory specimens described by Pacheo and Francione (1985), must be *in pain*.

Beyond pain to self-consciousness

So much for Singer's defence of the capacity of animals to feel pain whilst allowing that as one descends from the higher to lower species doubts intrude. He also allows that the greater mental powers of human beings permit of a potential for more profound suffering. But the questions which are raised by this disparity – for example, Can animals suffer without pain? Can they inhibit it? – will not easily be settled against the background of the claim that animals are *persons*. He may be wary, as I have suggested, of attributing to animals the capacity for having *reasons* for acting but might well be unable to avoid some such conclusion in elaborating the extent to which they are 'rational and self-conscious beings, aware of themselves as distinct entities with a past and a future' (Singer 1979: 94).

Readers confronting these issues for the first time are to be forgiven for finding them numbing. The question 'Are animals self-conscious?' brings with it an intellectual cramp not so much because of its difficulty, indeed it seems as if it ought to be relatively simple to answer, but because of the absence of knowing where to begin. 'What is pain?' has been an even more notorious source of the same discomfort. St Augustine, in his *Confessions*, an unsurpassed depiction of the intellectual trials of conversion written around the close of the fourth century AD, focussed on this phenomenon in a celebrated passage:

> What, then, is time? There can be no quick and easy answer, for it is no simple matter even to understand what it is, let alone find words to explain it. Yet, in our conversation, no word is more familiarly used or more easily recognized than 'time'. We certainly understand what is meant by the word both when we use it ourselves and when we hear it used by others.

> What, then, is time? I know well enough what it is, provided that nobody asks me; but if I am asked what it is and try to explain, I am baffled.

> (St Augustine 1961: 263–4)

Augustine has located a psychological mark of *philosophical* confusion which menaces what often appears at first sight to be a
relatively straightforward factual matter. Although it may not be the
case that claiming that it is midday or midnight when the clock
chimes twelve requires an answer to 'what is time?', we might well
wish to resist jumping to conclusions about whether animals suffer or
are self-conscious without pondering what these key terms mean.
Singer, as we have seen, assumes that pain is a private mental event;
rightly or wrongly. The zoologist Marian Stamp Dawkins, in like
manner, assumes that suffering 'clearly refers to some kind of
subjective experience' which must both be 'unpleasant' and 'extreme'
(1985: 29), apparently forgetting that it is quite proper to describe
someone as ignorant of the fact that they are suffering from dyslexia;
or a benign fox from rabies. Rationality and self-consciousness
conceal similar pitfalls; so does language.

Attempts by scientists during the 1960s and 1970s to teach
American Sign Language ('Ameslan') to great apes, mainly
chimpanzees, is one of the few areas of animal research to have
captured public interest. The most famous of these chimpanzees was
Washoe, a household name among liberationists, whose teachers Alan
and Beatrice Gardner first published their results in 1969. Ameslan is
one of the many gestural languages, transmitted by rapid hand
motions (or signing), developed for use by the deaf and dumb. Later
investigators have used other systems such as plastic counters or
keyboards. No speech is used (itself a problem since that is the feature
common to all natural human languages) because of the intractability
of the ape's vocal chords. The Gardners seem to have been as
successful as any subsequent trainers in teaching Washoe over a
period of four laborious years to use appropriately about 130 signs.
Typically she would produce, say, the banana sign when shown
pictures of one, or the eating or giving sign if her trainer mimed the
action in question. More significantly, most of the apes, including
Washoe, used two-sign combinations and longer, but only repetitive,
strings (for example, 'Me Washoe' when shown her reflection in a
mirror). This is the specific piece of evidence advanced by Singer for a
primate's self-consciousness. He continues with the more interesting
question: do these primates possess self-consciousness because they
can use the relevant language or 'is it merely that language enables
these animals to demonstrate to us a characteristic which they, and
other animals, possessed all along?' (1979: 94). Now the Ameslan
apes *are* of great interest but the extent to which their signing can be

said to be language, rather than an innovative extension of mere animal communication, has been a matter of fierce debate from the beginning. Some eminent theorists, for example, dismiss practically all of the claims as wishful thinking by enthusiasts. (The merits and demerits of this debate will be discussed in Chapter 6.)

What is of immediate interest however is that even if it is granted that the utterance 'Me Washoe' *is* a piece of language it is nonetheless doubtful evidence of self-consciousness and for two reasons. Firstly, it is not clear what is involved in this concession. When the equivalent occurs in young children, what is called by linguisticians 'holophrastic' speech, it is part of a relatively rigid schedule of language development. It has been preceded by a predictable progression: crying, cooing, babbling and word-like mimicking, and is followed by the swift mastery of appropriately used sentences, the proper stringing together of which is syntax. The end result is unambiguously language: the still developing ability to use grammatical formations to perform a variety of so-called 'speech acts': asserting, reporting, demanding, questioning and so on. The holophrastic 'No play' or 'Allgone Dada', to use J.C. Marshall's examples (1970: 237), which would be infant analogues to the ape's 'Me Washoe', tend to be *assumed* by researchers to be forms of the cognate assertions 'I am not playing' and 'I know my father has left' (and thus language proper) because of the rapid addition of such speech acts to the child's repertoire. The problem is that with Washoe, and all similar nonhuman subjects, we do *not* progress *beyond* holophrastic speech, so that in allowing that it *is* language the cash value of the allowance is unclear.

In the second place, it is still not clear what Singer's 'characteristic' of self-consciousness consists in (1979: 94). There is an inclination to think it too obvious for words. One looks out of the window at distant trees and murmurs, 'Of *course* I'm self-conscious and so is the dog sitting by my side gazing at me!' But this is to confuse seeing and perhaps hearing, which are certainly evidence of consciousness, with *self*-consciousness. At this rebuttal exasperation tends to creep in, a sign of the onset of Augustine's 'bafflement', and one might explicitly call attention to oneself: 'I know who I am!', 'This is me!' (slapping one's chest). These expostulations will prompt further enquiries: 'Well, *who* are you?' which will produce either a pocket autobiography or a more esoteric reply along the lines that 'I am a being that sees, hears and so on'. Or the breast beating might be countered with 'Are you sure that's you - isn't it your *chest*?' and we now seem to be

32

in pursuit of the 'owner' of the chest. This might well turn out to be something like a *person*; a concept we have already encountered. There is a twofold moral to draw from this exchange (to cut a long story short). In the first place, the self-seeker does a lot of *talking* and, after giving up initial window-gazing, seems to restrict the search to the production and manipulation of concepts such as 'person' or 'being that sees and hears'. The suspicion is aroused that consciousness of self, remembering Singer's question in the preceding paragraph (1979: 94), is not just aided by a grasp of language but is impossible without it. The intuition that prompted the fruitless window-gazing was that the self, not unlike Singer's view of pain or Dawkins' of suffering, was some sort of primary mental experience inaccessible to all but its possessor. This is now in doubt. As if to underline this, the second moral is that the *dog* in our vignette was lost to the proceedings right at the start. If the short debate has taken the speaker some way towards self-realisation, it has not helped the dog presumably because of its inability to contribute its views, or at least to agree with those of its owner. And what of 'Me Washoe'? Even upon the most charitable interpretation, giving it 'missing link' status and unscrambling it as the grammatical 'I am Washoe' or 'This is me, Washoe!', it seems no more advanced than the self-seeker's breast beating which, as we saw above, was an inadequate response even from a language user. This scepticism is reinforced if we bear in mind that what is involved here is not speech, even of a child, but Ameslan gestures involving frequent pointing to the body.

Animal 'signals', however interesting as a subject of study, are sharply different from *speech*. The philosopher Max Black puts it trenchantly:

Man is the only animal that can talk (*homo loquens*). More generally, he is the only animal that can use *symbols* (words, pictures, graphs, numbers, etc.). He alone can bridge the gap between one person and another, conveying thoughts, feelings, desires, attitudes, and sharing in the traditions, conventions, the knowledge and the superstition of his culture: the only animal that can truly *understand* and *misunderstand*. On this skill depends everything that we call civilization. Without it, imagination, thought – even self-knowledge – are impossible.

(Black 1972: 2)

Animals and rationality

Max Black, with whose views I substantially agree, goes much further than denying self-consciousness (what he terms 'self-knowledge') of animals. However, his use of the adverb 'truly' shows how far he is from a position of total scepticism about them. He is not proscribing much of our everyday talk about the higher mammals in particular which is shot through with what they think (that it is time for bed), feel (frightened that you'll beat them), want (a walk) and understand or misunderstand (when you say 'Sit!'). But Black is warning against the false anthropomorphism of assuming that these terms are always used univocally of animals and human beings; much as, in more extreme fashion, the scientist's claim that the rabies virus is extraordinarily clever is seen to be perfectly in order if limited to its context of adaptability. It is not a tribute to its intellectuality. Nor is Black denying the obvious fact that animals are sentient; although *of what* they are sentient, in terms of seeing and hearing, will become a bone of considerable contention in Chapter 6; much as we have already found grounds for ambiguity in what they properly can be said to suffer. Now Singer understandably objects to the conclusion of the preceding section which ties self-consciousness indissolubly to the capacity to speak a language and he counters the argument of Stuart Hampshire, similar to that of Max Black's, which appears to undermine the attribution of a whole range of mental attributes relevant to the claim that animals can be persons. Singer's method is classic and sets the fashion. It does not surface in *Animal Liberation*, where the exclusive emphasis is upon the capacity for suffering, but is developed in the later writings. This is from *Practical Ethics*:

> There is nothing altogether inconceivable about a being possessing the capacity for conceptual thought without having a language and there are instances of animal behaviour which are difficult to explain except under the assumption that the animals are thinking conceptually.
>
> (Singer 1979: 95)

The method to be employed therefore is that we are presented with segments of animal behaviour, either from the experimental laboratory or in the form of anecdotal description, for which the most plausible explanation will be that the animals are 'thinking conceptually'. Without preliminaries Singer plunges the reader into consideration of the implications of well-known experiments carried out in the early 1970s where chimpanzees were faced with an odd number of up to eleven objects from which, after suitable training, they were able to select the middle one. Not surprisingly, Singer's conclusion is that 'the most natural way to explain this is to say that the apes had grasped the concept of the "middle object" ' adding that this is beyond the competence of many children of four years of age. This experiment, by Rohes and Devine cited by Donald Griffin (1976), is typical of a vast accumulation of data gathered from experiments on animal learning over many years. Griffin, in his two books on the subject (1976, 1984), the most recent suggestively entitled *Animal Thinking*, and the psychologist Stephen Walker's *Animal Thought* (1983) provide numerous examples. Similar to Singer's example are the pigeons of Delius and Habers trained to discriminate between symmetrical patterns and asymmetrical ones. Once taught they were able to pick out *different* patterns depending on whether they were symmetrical with each other or not. Bowman and Sutherland discovered that goldfish trained to swim towards a square with a small triangular irregularity projecting upwards from the top side, whilst avoiding the regular square, then preferred the *circle* with a small semicircular indentation at its apex (Griffin 1984: 141). These sorts of experiment typically isolate the hungry animal or bird, although not goldfish for obvious reasons, from all stimuli irrelevant to what is at issue, in a 'Skinner box'. The animal, say a pigeon or rat, pecks at or pushes upon devices appropriate to it that deliver food if successful. In one such case pigeons, trained by Straub and Terrace, were required to peck at illuminated spots on the wall of the Skinner box in specific colour sequences in order to be rewarded; for example, red, blue, yellow, green but not blue, red, yellow, green. Not only did the spots change colour, as the conditions were varied, but they also changed their position on the wall. Griffin concludes:

> Several pigeons learned to perform this task at a level far above chance, indicating that they had learned a sequential rule that guided their decisions about which spot to peck. It seems possible that they thought something like 'I must peck at red first, then blue, next yellow, and then green'.
>
> (Griffin 1984: 142)

Before commenting upon this conclusion of Griffin's I want to return briefly to Singer's passage from *Practical Ethics* (1979: 95). He describes the possession of conceptual thought without language as not 'altogether inconceivable'. This isn't very promising and suggests that it might at least strike readers as highly improbable. It seems strange then that we are so precipitately hurried into assessing concrete situations and invited to accept that it is indeed *the case* without any theoretical preamble to at least sugar the highly improbable pill into some degree of plausibility. The examples do not speak for themselves. As Walker points out, if abstraction means neglecting particulars in favour of some quality which they all possess such as colour, number, shape, or sequence, which these experiments seem designed to demonstrate, then 'it is easy, not difficult . . . a Pavlovian experiment could easily show monkeys salivating to anything white' (1983: 109). Furthermore, K.J. Craik, discussing this as early as 1943, pointed out that simple devices involving photoelectric cell beams could achieve this degree of abstraction (our contemporary electronic scanners exceed it) and that the fact that animals can do likewise loses its force unless the question that is asked is 'Do animals abstract like men?' (Quoted by Walker 1983: 109). This is indeed the crux. That electronic scanners and their computer cognates can 'abstract' does not elevate them into conceptual thinkers.

I am not attempting to undermine the value of the various experiments, and many others like them, which extend our knowledge of the discriminatory powers of animals. They are of immense worth both theoretically and in practical applications like space science and missile technology. But what is the nature of the 'conceptual thought' that they are alleged to reveal? Is it different from other sorts of thought? If so, what other sorts? Griffin's comment in the above quotation is even more perplexing. How might a *pigeon*, far below an ape like Washoe with her signing dexterity, conceivably think even *something like* 'I must peck at red first, then blue', and so on? What are the limits of the phrase 'something like' in a context like this?

From Skinner box to anecdote

Singer's other example is of the more popular anecdotal variety. Jane Goodall, an internationally known naturalist, lived for many months among wild chimpanzees in Africa studying their habits meticulously. *In the Shadow of Man* (1971) recounts these experiences and makes compelling reading. In the following passage, Figan, a young chimp, covets the last banana of a bunch that Goodall had secured in a tree as a lure to bring the apes closer. Unfortunately, the adult Goliath, far above him in the group's pecking order, is resting beneath the tree:

After no more than a quick glance from the fruit to Goliath,

Figan moved away and sat on the other side of the tent so that he could no longer see the fruit. Fifteen minutes later, when Goliath got up and left, Figan without a moment's hesitation went over and collected the banana. *Quite obviously he had sized up the whole situation*: if he had climbed for the fruit earlier, Goliath would almost certainly have snatched it away. If he had remained close to the banana, he would probably have looked at it from time to time. Chimps are very quick to notice and interpret the eye movements of their fellows, and Goliath would possibly, therefore, have seen the fruit himself. And so Figan had not only refrained from instantly gratifying his desire but had also gone away so that he could not 'give the game away' by looking at the banana.

(Goodall 1971: 107, my italics)

Singer, perhaps predictably, takes this agreeable and intellectually relaxed account as unequivocally true to the letter. Figan has a set of interrelated intentions and expectations which project into the future. These are encapsulated in his having 'sized up the whole situation'. Indeed the animal was able to 'devise a careful plan' taking account of Goliath's presence, his probably moving away without seeing the booty, his own (Figan's) liability to betray his hand, and his hoped-for success (Singer 1979: 96). If this is taken as a literally true account of what is going on then one would be forced to conclude that we have self-consciousness and, certainly, rationality of a very high order indeed. I doubt that my averagely intelligent 10-year-old daughter would be capable of such cunning and astuteness.

Rollin gives us another intriguing example; although calling it and others 'stories' is not without its unintended irony. A police dog had been trained to hold miscreants by the arm and only to bite if escape was attempted. On its first patrol two men were disturbed in a robbery attempt and the dog pursued them. But they took separate paths, banking therefore upon a better-than-evens chance of escape. The dog, trained only to seize by the arm, 'chased one suspect up the left fork, apprehended him, *disabled his leg*, left him, proceeded up the right fork, and held the second man by the arm, unharmed' (Rollin 1981: 24). Common sense, he thinks, requires us to say that the dog reasoned. Presumably this is not an invitation to consider the dog's response to its training but rather to imagine a deliberate departure from it by the animal to take account of the unique circumstances of a double pursuit and the need to apprehend two quarries. Again, this would be reasoning of some complexity. (Hearne is encyclopaedic when it comes to such anecdotes. See, for example, the incident involving Officer Beem and Fritz (1987: 207–8). Hearne's analysis of such events is no less generous to the creature's reasoning powers than Singer's or Rollin's.)

Rationality is not always what it seems

It will be enough, at this stage, to make three comments; partly to give a sense of the complexity underlying these apparently transparent episodes and, in the process, to sow seeds of doubt:

1. What is at issue in these examples is not just intelligence. Some species are far quicker than others at adapting to Skinner box techniques (chimps, cats, dogs), or are preferred by circuses as being easier to train and tame (horses, seals, porpoises and, again, chimps and dogs) and these variations are replicated between individuals within a species. Figan appears to have been a very *intelligent* chimp and Rollin's police dog a special one. The claims of Singer and Rollin that the animals are *rational* must be of a different order or all animals, birds, and insects that show a degree of adaptability (which is most of them), will qualify. Thus their accounts must be *literally* true and persuade us, to adapt E.J. Craik's question about abstraction, that 'animals reason like men' (see above, p. 36). But might not Goodall be romancing without realising it? I referred earlier to her account being 'intellectually relaxed' to indicate that it caters to a traditional and affectionate way of speaking about animals but one which is not closely scrutinised. We do not observe Figan and Goliath; we *read* Goodall's account unaware perhaps of a hidden agenda. In Rollin's case we are encouraged to think in this traditional but non-literal way in the name of commonsense.

2. But if this idea of a sub-text is rejected, as it would be by Singer and Rollin, and we take the accounts as being definitive, then it must be pointed out that alternatives are possible and, except perhaps to those determined to make the case for rationality at all costs, more plausible ones.

Lorenz, writing of the pecking order of chickens, wolves, and jackdaws in *King Solomon's Ring* (1964: 147–52), uses the example of a Javanese monkey to show how deeply rooted and matter-of-course the deference to a superior can become (148). Now Figan, seeing Goliath in close proximity, was scared out of his sight and with nothing better to do just hung around more or less losing interest in the banana. He sees Goliath leaving, interest in the banana is rekindled, and he takes it; no sizing up, nor careful planning, just class-consciousness and opportunism. Were Figan in the *habit* of using such wiles, adapting them to different circumstances, then explanations of the less ambitious sort I propose would be unconvincing. The lack of a settled habit, the one-offmanship, also makes way for substitute accounts of the police dog's exploit. It was admitted that it was his first job. He might well have become disoriented by the conflicting urges to run in two directions at once, a common phenomenon in both humans and nonhumans, and as a result bypassed his training and reverted to type by biting the first man in the leg, the most convenient place, and deeply enough to disable. Aberrant on two counts due to confusion, the dog resumed the chase of the remaining suspect unencumbered by the previously warring impulses; his training therefore reasserted itself and he completed the capture as prescribed by the manual. As with Figan, one might be more impressed if the attribution of rationality were backed by claims of apparently inspired behaviour on the part of the same dog on other occasions and preferably not just in the capture of felons. Researchers have to be on their guard for the occurrence of luck. If a 7-year-old throws a dart and hits the bulls-eye it occasions only mild congratulation but if he or she does it seven times out of ten we sit up and take notice.

3. However, to offer competing explanations is only partly persuasive. One is then pushed to weighing up probabilities rather than considering what might be wrong with the account that is to be supplanted. Singer's and Rollin's interpretations are persuasive because both portray the animals as doing things, behaving in this or that way, in order to achieve relatively long-term ends. Furthermore, Figan, in particular, must be taken as having grasped that this is what he is doing and why he is doing it or he could hardly be described as having 'sized up' the situation (Goodall) or being able 'to devise a careful plan' (Singer). We have moved from Figan's hiding himself in order to avoid Goliath, as the cat runs to its dish to get its food, to something very different, namely Figan's considering *that* he is hiding in order not to alert Goliath so that he can secure the banana. The problem is, to adapt the same point made by Anthony Kenny about dogs, that lacking language there is nothing that Figan is able to do to express the difference between the two states of affairs (Kenny 1975: 5). Saint Thomas Aquinas, in the thirteenth century, made the

same point in distinguishing two different ways in which one might be said to know the end or purpose of one's action:

> Perfect knowledge of an end involves not merely the apprehension of the object which is the end, but an awareness of it precisely qua end, and of the relationship to it of the means which are directed to it. Such a knowledge is within the competence only of a rational creature. Imperfect knowledge of the end is mere apprehension of the end without any awareness of its nature as an end or of the relationship of the activity to the end. This type of knowledge is found in dumb animals.
>
> (Quoted by Kenny 1975: 19)

Thus the cat sees the food towards which it is running and because of which it is running. But this fact does *not* permit us to claim that the cat is aware that the reason why it is running is to get its food. This is St Thomas's point. But it is only with this latter achievement, which is a commonplace of *human* action, that we can begin to talk in terms of rationality or reasoning – so the argument will go!

Beyond mere rationality

Armed with the conclusions he draws that the higher mammals, and possibly many other species as well, are rational and self-conscious *persons*, it is easy for Singer to add other human traits to the list: intentions and memory, hopes, fears, and other emotions like love and sorrow. These considerations enormously expand the range of interests that can be claimed for animals beyond those relating to their mere capacity for suffering. If Figan is as self-aware as he is depicted it might plausibly be argued that he has as emphatic an interest in remaining alive as any human being and to kill him, *even painlessly*, for food or medical research would only be permissible in the rarest of circumstances. Such claims are indeed made and not by obvious cranks. A symposium in Cambridge (UK) in 1977 published a 'Declaration against speciesism' which concluded as follows:

> We do not accept that a difference in species alone (any more than a difference in race) can justify wanton exploitation or oppression in the name of science or sport, or for food, commercial profit or other human gain.
>
> We believe in the evolutionary and moral kinship of all

animals and we declare our belief that all sentient creatures have rights to life, liberty and the quest for happiness. We call for the protection of these rights.

(Paterson and Ryder 1979: viii)

This completes my account of Singer's important and seminal account of animals. Some readers will feel that I have unduly laced it with reservations and criticism. The reason for this has been, of course, to give an immediate sense of the debate which his views engender and it is a tribute to Singer that they have been and doubtless will continue to be so prolific in this respect. He moves from the spotlight but will continue to hover in the wings.

2

R.G. FREY: THE CASE AGAINST ANIMALS

The varieties of interest

Much was made in Chapter 1 of the problems involved in the weighing of interests since practical decisions of any complexity involve conflicts. Animals give rise to particular problems as Bentham's criterion of their capacity to suffer was gradually augmented by claims that some of them, the higher mammals, were both self-aware and capable of rational thought. This accumulation of capacities brought with it an expansion of possible interests: Figan, if we take Goodall at face value, might now be claimed to have an interest in outwitting competitors and even in living for as long as possible with an indefinite right to life. But this all seems very unsystematic. Is it just a matter of what people or animals *want*? Goodall, generously interpreted, gives us grounds for thinking that Figan wants the banana, but are there any for supposing that he wants to live out his natural span? These problems require that we hark back, beyond our acquaintance with Figan and Goliath, to the controversial quotation involving Singer's afflicted mouse:

> It would be nonsense to say that it was not in the interests of a stone to be kicked along the road by a schoolboy. A stone does not have interests because it cannot suffer. Nothing that we could do to it could possibly make any difference to its welfare. A mouse, on the other hand, does have an interest in not being tormented, because it will suffer if it is.
>
> (Singer 1979: 50)

Now Singer might be implying that the mouse *wants* not to be tormented. But, analogous to the doubts surrounding Figan's wanting to live a long time as a ground for his interest in so doing, this would sound *odd*. Why? Because if the comparison is made with typically

42

human wants, a comparison which is legitimate (on utilitarian grounds) since the interests of the mouse are to be put into the same scales as those of people, then people are aware of what they want and why they want it. In this sense wants are *desires*. These desires generate interests. But the mouse is not human and the claim that it has *desires* sounds supererogatory if not downright implausible. So in what sense does it have an interest in not being tormented?

It is at this point that Frey makes his first contribution to our thinking about animals by invoking the jurist's usage that, for example, a lady can have a legal interest in the contents of a distant uncle's will whilst being totally ignorant of the fact. Joel Feinberg relates such interests to the legal notion of *harm*:

> The rich man is harmed at the time his home is burgled, even though he may not discover the harm for months. ... An undetected adultery damages one of the victim's 'interests in domestic relations,' just as ... an undetected trespass on his land can damage his interest in 'the exclusive enjoyment and control' of that land.
>
> (Feinberg 1973: 27)

Now this 'lawyer's usage', as Frey calls it, is not reflected in common parlance where to have an interest in something carries the implication of wanting or desiring; hence the confusion over Singer's claim on behalf of the mouse. However, there is a cognate claim available to us which *does* reflect the spirit of the legal concept when, let us say, the obsessive financier is urged by his doctor that it is *in his interests* to take an early retirement. The doctor's claim, assuming he is averagely competent, is not undermined by his patient's refusal to acknowledge what is *in* his interests by preferring to return to matters of money-making, in which he *has* interests. It was an interest in the former sense that the law was protecting in the earlier example of the lady discovering that she was an 'interested party' to her uncle's will. Now this distinction will be fruitful in overcoming some of the confusions we encountered in deciding what interests animals can properly be said to have and whether and how they differ from those of human beings.

The scope of welfare interests

Animals certainly seem to qualify for 'welfare interests', even the lowliest species. If one is attempting to catch a common moth and release it from the house unharmed then we allow ourself to be guided by what is thought to be 'in its interests'. Sometimes an animal will need to be killed on similar grounds. But Frey, having granted a substantial clutch of such interests to animals, of the type catered to by veterinarians, only *appears* to be in agreement with the liberationists who would see them grounded in the capacity for suffering and, for those like Linzey and Regan, as providing a qualification for moral (or perhaps 'natural') *rights*. Frey would, I think, object to the use of 'welfare' as misleadingly implying that the essence of these interests was that they were exclusive to sentient creatures.

Frey prefers the more generous formula that they attach to anything 'having a good or well-being which can be harmed or benefited' (1980: 79). This form of words is more inclusive in that it applies not only to unicellular organisms and the vegetable world but to man-made artifacts such as paintings and machines. Frey argues for this in a variety of ways (79–82). Just as it is not good to deprive a dog of warmth so it is bad to expose a valuable oil-painting to strong sunlight, implying that they both *have a good* which can be compromised. It is perfectly proper to claim that it might not be *in the interests* of a new Rolls Royce to be driven as if it were a Dodgem car. For human beings and animals the same sorts of standards are set. They benefit from exercise and proper food and are harmed by neglect and disease. Although terms like 'harm', 'benefit' and 'good' are used of sentient creatures, it is Frey's contention that they are not solely applicable to them. This is particularly so with an important characteristic which might, at first glance, appear to be restricted to animals; they have *needs*. But one is only inclined to restrict the exclusivity of needs to animals by assuming that the subject must be aware of them. But if this is no longer a necessary condition then plants and machines can have needs. This clearly accords with normal usage; trees need water and sunlight, and cars need fuel and coolant.

The interesting details of Frey's argument are liable to obscure its point. In the preceding section doubts were expressed about the sense in which the tormented mouse has wants particularly if it involves awareness; which is to talk of wants as conscious *desires*. But it is now open to the liberationist to argue for a diluted sense of wants as *needs* which generate what Regan calls 'welfare interests'. Frey is attempting not so much to block this move, for he allows such interests, but to dissipate its significance by showing that such needs of animals (those *in their interests*) are on all fours with those of plants and cars. But if we wish to *exclude* these interests of plants and artifacts, and one certainly would not wish to make way for 'machine rights', then it would seem that we must also exclude those generated by animal needs; unless they can be said to have wants as desires. Human beings obviously do fall into the latter category and their needs *can* generate significant interests because people generally desire that their needs, even if they don't know what they are, be safeguarded. Frey now moves to demolish this remaining possibility, namely that animals have desires, and in the process despatches a lot else besides.

Assessing Frey's distinction

Although Frey's preceding analysis does not yield quite the mileage he claims of it, as I will show, its usefulness is obliquely demonstrated by the confusions which result when it is ignored. It is worthwhile to look briefly at both sides of the coin before continuing. Bernard Rollin discusses these issues in some depth. He compares the claims to 'moral concern' of, respectively, a rock, a spider, and machines. The choice of creatures low in the evolutionary scale, whose susceptibility to pain is questionable, and might be denied entirely, is deliberate since he does not wish to deny due consideration to animals, human or otherwise, who might lack this capacity. Rollin is thus immune to the many counter-intuitive implications that Frey draws from Singer's position that the susceptibility to pain is a 'prerequisite' for having interests (Frey 1980: 139–67).

Rollin begins by dismissing the rock as of no concern; it lacks 'real intrinsic unity' and is dead matter. Singer, you will remember, similarly discounts the stone kicked along the road by a schoolboy as lacking interests because it cannot suffer. However, it must be noted, were the stone a priceless fragment of the Elgin Marbles it would be proper to object that it was not *in its interests* to be so treated and, following Frey (and Kenny, despite his calling it a 'zoomorphic extension' (1975: 49)), that it *needed* careful keeping in temperature-controlled conditions. But Rollin is right that some sort of unity must be present for such claims to get a toe-hold and he invokes the Aristotelian *telos* (a function, set of activities or nature proper to the object). I instantiated such a *telos* by turning the rock into a fragment of the Marbles. This is why animals, vegetable life, and machines unambiguously have needs; they have functions, conditions 'proper' to them.

Confusions creep in when Rollin comes to the spider. He rightly argues that it has needs pursuant upon its *telos* but denies that it 'or any animal need be conscious of its nature and of all of these needs, any more than a man need be conscious of his need for oxygen' (Rollin 1981: 39). But this comparison confuses needs and desires. When the man who is not conscious of his need for oxygen becomes so, perhaps by reading about it in the newspaper, he would be aware of it *as* a need and certainly be expected to desire it. But if the spider is not conscious of *all* of its needs then the implication is that it is conscious of *some*; but this cannot be as the man is aware of *his* needs unless Rollin is attributing desire to the creature. Yet this seems to have been ruled out by his denial (above) that an animal needs to be 'conscious of its nature'. He then states that the needs it has 'to live its life as a spider' are interests, and whilst allowing that machines too can have needs but *not* interests, arguing that the crucial difference is that the need giving rise to the interest 'matters' to the spider (1981: 40). But this claim seems similarly to be bedevilled by the implications of desire. If I have a pain, even an intense one, it might not *matter* to me. Whether it does or not depends upon how I judge its implications. Valetudinarians let every itch matter but they are the exception. Surely a spider, or any animal, is incapable of such obsessions. But if, in Rollin's defence, we retreat to a sense of 'matters' simply as adversely affecting the animal in question, then we are back with a 'lawyer's usage' which carries with it no presupposition of consciousness.

Finally, Rollin attacks the comparison of animal needs and those of machines on the grounds that whereas the *telos* of the animal is its own, intrinsic to it, that of the car or thermostat is 'imposed by the mind and hand of man' and is extrinsic to it. But he fails to bring out the relevance of such a claim. Why should we therefore take animal needs more seriously? Furthermore it is not even clear that the distinction in *telos* is that marked. What is in the interests of animals is increasingly decided by human beings. A good guide-dog, sheep-dog, circus, zoo or farm animal, thoroughbred colt or pet siamese is treated on the basis of criteria proper to the different roles imposed upon them by human beings, and not necessarily to the creatures' detriment. But perhaps the most serious implication of Rollin's point is that even if we grant it and demote the needs of machines from equal consideration with those of animals, he is committed to maintaining the equality of the needs of *plants* to those of animals since their *telos* is no less intrinsic. Nonetheless I do think that there is the germ of a valid criticism of Frey in this discussion of *telos* which I shall now attempt to elaborate.

Animals, artifacts and plants

Frey's position is that human beings, animals, and machines have needs. So do other things. Humans can desire what they need, or otherwise acknowledge it, and, in so doing, 'have an interest' in it. Interests, in this sense which involves desire or acknowledgement, are important for Frey in the moral scheme of things, but in ways that are not always clear. In arguing against Singer's contention that the capacity for suffering is a necessary and sufficient condition for interests since it excludes those rare brain-damaged and comatose individuals who lack it, Frey contends that such unfortunates *do* have interests (for example, in good health) on the grounds that it is 'one desire typical of human beings' (1980: 157). To accommodate this he makes the additional distinction between 'having an interest' and '*taking* an interest', the comatose (such as Karen Quinlan) satisfying only the former.

Now what of animals? Frey's claim is that we will not wish to accord the needs of animals the status of interests because it would commit us to doing the same for those of machines and plants. But if we can drive a significant wedge between animals, on the one hand, and machines and plants on the other, then the argument that they stand or fall together will be weakened. Rollin's resort to Aristotle provides a clue. If I were able successfully to produce a tractor which saw to all of its own requirements, totally without aid or supervision, then I would probably earn a great deal more money than I do at present. Clearly such an invention would be approaching the state of most animals who are capable, under certain conditions, of not only satisfying their own needs but of carrying out prolonged activities necessary for survival. None of this implies that the animal must know what it is doing or why it is doing it, anymore than would my super-tractor. With this considerable reservation, animals more nearly approach the human condition than the most sophisticated machine; particularly if one adds their propensity to reproduce. The similarity is reinforced in two other related respects, both of which facilitate the efficiency with which animals see to their needs, indeed without which it would be impossible for them to do so. They suffer and are sentient. My wedge has become a trident discriminating between the needs of animals and those of machines; plant life occupying a middle ground since it satisfies many of its own needs without, most would agree, being sentient or able to suffer. The trident is *significant* in that it reinforces the similarities between animals and human beings.

Now since Frey was prepared to relax the requirement of desire to allow the Karen Quinlans of this world to have an interest in good health and other entitlements, then he has made a case for someone like Rollin to claim that the needs of animals deserve similar upgrading. The three similarities to the human condition displayed by animals are invoked only as *sufficient* conditions. This would by no means be fatal to Frey's position. He can continue to insist that the mere membership of *homo sapiens* gives a morally relevant edge to the interests of a Karen Quinlan such that they might take precedence over any conceded to animals. But that we might wish to concede *some*, more lowly, interests to animals in virtue of their greater similarity to us than plants or machines certainly reflects commonsense morality. This amendment to Frey's position would also, of course, provide grounds for giving superior status to the needs of plant life and the wider environment over those of artifacts. But none of these considerations would alter the possibility that in a desperate situation, faced perhaps with the threat of no electricity or an environmental crisis, we might decide to cater to the needs of machines or plant life before all else.

Wants and belief: the background

Frey now moves to counter the assertion that animals can possess wants in the sense of desires; a capacity obviously attributable to all but the most marginal human beings. The contention that animals share this power is a vital component of the liberationist argument – a fact which cannot be overemphasised. Human beings may, as we have seen, have interests of which they are unaware (the lawyer's usage) but our propensity to 'take an interest' in subjects extending far beyond our bodily needs provides an even more fertile breeding ground for them. If animals are seen to have a share in these then it may indeed be more than wishful thinking to accord them rights, for example, to life, liberty and the pursuit of happiness with much that these imply for us. Jane Goodall is explicit in describing Figan as having 'refrained from instantly gratifying his desire' and, in so doing, accords him the additional and closely associated ability of *choosing* (to refrain from is to choose not to). Singer, of course, approves 'despite the fact that Figan cannot put his intentions or expectations into words' (1979: 96).

The background to Frey's argument is a tradition in philosophical thinking stretching back, like so much else, to Aristotle. Fully to understand a whole range of typically human activities, including the present cognate ones of wanting, desiring, wishing, and choosing, requires that they be seen necessarily to point to the subject's having *certain* beliefs. It is a mistake therefore to construe desire, let us say, upon the model of sensations like itches or dull aches although these might well initiate attendant desires.

If a woman in search of a piece of string, let us suppose, is rummaging in a drawer and it is claimed that she wants (in the sense of desires) it to tie up a parcel, then at least these conditions must be met:[1]

1. The woman believes that a piece of string will satisfy her desire.
2. She also believes that something which is not string will not satisfy her desire better or as well. (To rule out perhaps that she really wants sticky tape but would make do with string.)
3. She is able to provide an answer to the question, 'What counts as getting a piece of string?'. (So that she would presumably reject a hangman's rope or a mere snippet.)
4. She is also able to answer the question, 'What do you want the string for?'
5. The woman does not believe that she already possesses a piece of string adequate for the task.

The five conditions, as Kenny (1963: 100–26) points out, all involve the lady in having beliefs, some explicitly and some implicitly; for example, in being able to answer certain questions. How do these beliefs manifest themselves? It will be enough to point to three factors to introduce Frey's attack. Firstly, the woman will do certain things and refrain from others. She might, for instance, seize a ball of twine with a flourish of satisfaction having pushed a roll of adhesive tape to one side. She might then proceed to secure her parcel but, it is important to note, she need not. Secondly, she must be able to provide appropriate answers to relevant questions and give explanations if her behaviour is ambiguous or problematical. If she does *not* extract the twine we might well ask why; the answer 'It is not strong enough!' would probably satisfy us. If she does extract it but puts it in her handbag we might again ask why. Her answer, 'I'm not buying the present until next week', brings us to the third point. In acknowledging the debt to Aristotle it was pointed out that the intrusion of belief into the analysis of activities like desiring, wanting, and wishing marks a departure from a view of them as quasi-sensations. The lady's last reply begins to substantiate this important insight. If she is sincere then her desiring commits her to doing *something in the future* unless she changes her mind in the interim.

Here is a more dramatic instance. Ever since his ordeals in Hitler's concentration camps, the indefatigable Nazi-hunter Simon Wiesenthal has wanted to bring as many war criminals to justice as possible and he continues to think this way. His supporters have therefore been entitled to expect continuing confirmatory behaviour from him for over forty years. Gilbert Ryle called this entitlement an 'inference ticket' (1949: 121). But however dominated by his search, Wiesenthal must sometimes do other things, if only to go to sleep at night, and the lady with the present to purchase would have to live a life of unbelievable monotony were we not to assume that the presence of the string in her bag was banished from her mind until the time came to use it. Yet the wanting is not cancelled during periods of sleep or banishment as an itch or a dull ache might be. It is more accurately seen as giving meaning to a temporal pattern in behaviour. Kenny makes a similar point by describing both wants and beliefs as mental *states* 'but not causally explanatory ones'; the contrast being with mental events like sensations (1975: 119–20). Wiesenthal asleep is still the relentless Nazi-hunter but he no longer has the toothache with which he went to bed.

Beliefs, animals, and the importance of language

Frey's own example, which will be attacked by Regan, is of his supposed desire to own a Gutenberg Bible (GB); a landmark of early German printing, copies of which are of singular rarity and value. (The differences of emphasis between the concepts of 'desire' and 'wanting' need not concern us here.) The account in the preceding section will have prepared us for Frey's next move. It is that without the belief that his collection lacked a GB he could not possibly be said to have the desire for one. Of course, he might want to own a second copy but that would depend upon a similar, slightly amended, belief. The next step is to argue that what he believes, therefore, is that the particular sentence 'Frey's collection lacks a GB' is true. This is, of course, a minimal claim. He would need to believe other things as well, comparable to those required for the lady's wanting a piece of string, but the point is that the alleged belief would be negated if the subject did *not* believe that the relevant sentence were true. The relevance to animals should now be clear. To say of the cat, 'It believes that the laces are tied' is to hold,

> that the cat believes the sentence 'The laces are tied' to be true; and I can see no reason whatever for crediting the cat or any other creature which lacks language, including human infants, with regarding the sentence 'The laces are tied' as true.
>
> (Frey 1980: 87)

Frey supplements this with two observations. In the first place, his argument is not side-stepped by the claim that it trades upon the complexity of the content of the alleged animal belief – a cat, an opponent might object, knows nothing of GBs, or of laces, or of their being tied. His reply is that the same problem crops up in the most straightforward circumstances of the cat's desiring the dinner which its mistress is spooning from the tin. Lest this be thought to be counter-intuitive, remember that Frey is not denying that the cat will be attracted to its dinner and will *want* it. (These are wants-as-needs which, as he has been seen to argue, cats share with plants and even machines.) Frey's target is the more complex claim that the cat *desires* its food. This implies the presence of the belief that it is indeed its dinner which is in front of it, which, in turn, involves the cat's believing that the sentence, 'My food is in the bowl' is true. Frey's concern is to highlight the nature of *belief*. Secondly, beliefs demonstrate a grasp of the relationship of language to the world (to put it rather grandly). Volumes in a bookcase, laces tied or untied, are not themselves true or false; they are states of affairs which can give rise to beliefs which may be true or false. But now the grasp of truth or falsity involves the manipulation of the language with which we engage with the books, laces, or whatever. We need to be able to distinguish, say, the false belief expressed in the sentence 'The laces are not tied' from the true one expressed in 'The laces are tied' and the generation of both from, in this case, the laces actually *being* tied rather than untied. But if this is so then in claiming seriously that the cat believes that the laces are tied (above) we are committed to the implication that it is capable of distinguishing this true belief from the false one that they are untied. But if truth and falsity arise from the engagement of language with states of affairs and not from the latter (books, laces) in isolation then, unless we attribute to cats the grasp of a complex language, Frey asks, 'what exactly is it that cats are being credited with distinguishing as true or false?' (1980: 90).

Now Frey's argument so far will not convince a determined

objector who argues that the complexity of animal behaviour alone not only permits us to grant beliefs to them but requires that we do so as the only feasible hypothesis. Frey needs both to address himself to this reply and also to provide an alternative account of the intricacy of animal conduct, such as that of Figan or Rollin's police dog, which will be both plausible yet not involve beliefs.

Behaviour without beliefs

Frey's positive explanation of the complexity of animal behaviour, which gives rise to apparent but not genuine desire and rationality, leans heavily upon the interaction of a creature's consciousness, appetites, drives and instinctive reactions in catering to its admitted *needs*. He concentrates upon the example of his dog's allegedly desiring its evening meal. Its opening foray into the kitchen is sparked off by the activity of its gastric juices initiating well-reinforced and pleasing fixed-action patterns. Detecting its master by sight and smell, it moves unerringly to his side and begins the standard ritual of prancing and whining. As the meat is emptied into the tray the further reinforcement of savoury odours and familiar sights impels the creature to bolt the contents. Satiated to the brim, the dog promptly falls asleep, unless dominated by a conflicting impulse to relieve itself; in which case its toilet training takes over and it waits at the garden door barking until it is opened.

> Nothing is required to 'fit between' his reaction and his behaviour, with the result that there is no place for belief to be inserted into the account; my dog simply has an inherent propensity to behave this way or that, depending on whether the reaction set off in him is pleasing or painful.
>
> (Frey 1980: 128)

Nor is there room for *reasons* on the dog's part for what it does. If its master, in similar circumstances, were asked why he was raiding the refrigerator, he would cite his hunger as his reason for so doing; the implication being that he was aware of alternatives open to him. But Frey's account rules out alternatives in this sense. The dog's behaviour was the outcome of its conflicting impulses and it could only have been different had other urges dominated.

Human beings also can be dominated by their impulses when, for instance, they are startled by a flash in the night sky, or unwittingly fall asleep over a book. In such cases, if asked why they so reacted, they disclaim reasons: 'I didn't mean to – it was the whisky!', 'It just happened!' Frey's position, it seems clear, is that *all* animal behaviour is to be accounted for in this way whereas for *homo sapiens* it is an occasional occurrence. The total inability of cats and dogs to master any sort of language, and the failure of the trained chimps like Washoe even to approach a response of that complexity, simply underlines the impossibility of any appeal to their reasons. But animals might nonetheless be said to act reasonably, but not for a reason, to mark the obvious fact that some species, or individuals within a species, are more intelligent than others. Figan and the police dog would be cases in point. An example lower down the evolutionary scale is provided by sidewinders and Mojave rattlesnakes which elegantly tailor their predacious habits to their poisonous resources. The smaller ones have a highly toxic venom which acts instantly upon lizards and newborn rodents. They kill these almost exclusively; holding on to them until dead. But their biggers and betters develop a venom which although more effective in breaking down mammalian tissue is far slower to act. These older rattlers (cleverly, one is tempted to say) use a strike-and-release tactic upon their larger and potentially more lethal prey, which they leave to die slowly, returning later without danger of retaliation from the animal in its death throes.[2]

Is believing behaving?

The liberationist alternative to Frey's causal account imports beliefs into the explanation. Now, with the doubtful exception of Washoe and her Ameslan friends, animals neither talk nor use linguistic signs. Any beliefs allegedly claimed for dogs, cats, birds and other creatures would therefore have to be extracted entirely from non-linguistic behaviour. Frey provides three arguments against this possibility.

1. His example is that of the cat, which rears up on its hind legs, scratching at a ball stuck in the cleft of a tree. We mark this by saying that it believes the ball is stuck. Lacking language it cannot have our sophisticated understanding of the spherical plaything so the claim must amount to its having a feline equivalent. But cats are rearing up and scratching at all sorts of unlikely things: reflections, stockings, books and bookcases, jets of water, labels on wine bottles. Do cats have feline 'notions' of all these? Are they distinguishable one from the other? If this is not the case we have the prolific implication that a

limited segment of behaviour 'suffices to endow animals with count-less numbers of concepts, including, it would seem, some highly complex ones' (Frey 1980: 113).

2. We may well wish to use the form of words 'The cat believes the ball is stuck in the old oak' and justify it against a background of a way of talking about animals which does not carry the force of the dog's actually having the belief as stated. There is no mystery here. It is a normal device of, for example, parliamentary reporters who some times quote verbatim but more often compose their own third-person accounts of what politicians thought and said (the actual words used are *oratio recta*, the latter *oratio obliqua*). More interestingly, *oratio obliqua* can be used by a mother to say of her 4-year-old child, 'She wants to mess about with the jewellery in the drawer', where the infant has little grasp, if any, of the central concepts used. D.M. Armstrong has defended the ascription of beliefs to animals on the same grounds (1973: 24–7, 113); with the support, incidentally, of Kenny (1975: 51).

This defence is highly dubious, Frey argues. The accuracy of the reporter's account can be *checked* (for example, by consulting Hansard). The mother's comment is confirmed by the child's saying 'Play janglies' or somesuch. The MP and the child had beliefs which were correctly described; the original *oratio obliqua* could properly be contested. But with animals lacking language we have only overt behaviour to go on. This is too imprecise to provide the tight connection necessary to establish whether a belief (or whatever) *is present* in the animal and, if so, what its content is. Such imprecision is a charter for wishful thinkers. So behaviour may connect with the ways we *attribute* beliefs to animals but not therefore with their literally having the beliefs in question. If we confuse the two then we encounter the problems in the first, and main, objection. Frey's example here is that of his dog's tail-wagging which has been observed to be compatible with the attribution of at least three beliefs: that its master was at the door, that lunch was imminent and that an eclipse of the sun was in progress.

3. Frey's objections so far have centred upon the hazards of attempt-ing to extract beliefs from behaviour which is, perhaps paradoxically, too fertile. If however there is a species of desire which does *not* involve belief, then it might be a more appropriate candidate for attribution to creatures which lack language. That there *is* such a candidate was hinted at in Chapter 1 when discussing the allegedly

purposive actions of Figan's hiding from Goliath in terms of the distinction of St Thomas Aquinas between the 'perfect knowledge' of such ends, as humans are aware that they are employing them, and 'imperfect knowledge', which is possessed by dumb animals, being 'mere apprehension of the end without any awareness of its nature as an end'.

Now even Frey's account of his dog's dining contains many instances of the creature doing one thing to achieve another by means of its senses; for example, it smells the food and rushes to the dish to get it. This is enough for it to be an instance of 'imperfect knowledge'. The dog has a *sensual* desire' for its food; to use Kenny's term (1975: 49). This is the sort of desire, what Frey calls a 'simple' desire, upon which he now sets his sights.

Frey will have nothing to do with simple desires. This is perhaps odd because they will be seen to be anything but the rainbow's end for the liberationist. His attack is as imperious and ingenious as it is, I will argue in Chapter 6, ultimately flawed. 'Suppose', he argues, 'my dog simply desires the bone: is it aware that it has this simple desire? It either is not so aware or it is' (1980: 104). He then proceeds to rule out both possibilities. If, on the one hand, the dog is *unaware* of its simple desires whilst nonetheless desiring, then it seems that we must allow it to have unconscious desires. These perhaps make sense for human beings but only because in their case they are posited against a background of mainly conscious ones. But if, as in the case of the dog, it is unaware of *all* its simple desires, then it seems no different from a creature that has none at all. The alternative is that the dog is *aware* that it simply desires the bone. Frey's reasons for rejecting this possibility should be predictable. Standard questioning can elicit from a normal human being, enmeshed in the commerce of language, that a simple desire, possibly betrayed by their behaviour, is one that they are indeed aware of. Such a reply would also be a guarantee of a reasonably lively self-consciousness. But the dog's overt behaviour, which is all it is capable of, might tempt us to credit it with a simple desire were it not that this alternative requires that in addition it be aware of the fact. But nothing in the dog's behaviour can possibly express this further requirement. Whatever else it might do, lacking linguistic wherewithal, is consistent with its *not* being aware that it desires.

Frey's contribution to the animal debate is refreshingly critical. In the first place he forces us to re-think received views about the very nature of animals. They seem to lack beliefs, desires, and wants (other than as needs), at least in the senses in which these terms are normally used. He will be seen, in Chapter 6, to wield his rejection of belief to further effect in denying emotions, like love and fear, to animals and even to attempting to undermine the sense in which they can be said to *see*. In the second place, Frey has ethical fish to fry. The psychological and sentient attributes which his arguments put at risk have been fertile sources for animal interests, and even rights, which are to that extent compromised.

3

THREE CONTRIBUTIONS
FROM TOM REGAN

Introduction

Liberationists tend to be polemicists; a term which has its etymological origins in the Greek for war, *polemos*. They see themselves as writers with a mission; keen, in large part, to impress their readers with the cogency of their arguments, but even keener to convert them to the cause. The price paid, higher in the case of stump orators, is a temptation to cut intellectual corners even to the extent of deriding a sincere opposition. Mary Midgley, who is sensible to this, calls it howling: 'Howling does have a point, and I do sometimes do it. But it has the drawback of making people react – more especially academics – by providing them with something to contradict' (1986: 196). Stephen Clark is perhaps its most colourful exponent. *The Moral Status of Animals* (1977), less so his later work, is littered with derision; the chemist who 'is a fool' and the US biologist who is 'worse than a fool' (38); beliefs that are 'pathological' (39), 'pitiable nonsense' (42 fn.), 'embarrassed squawks' (87), 'obviously inane' (94) and 'a mere conceit of whoremaster man' (104). But it is entertaining, and Clark's style of persuasion, in particular his weaving together of science, literature and religion, has at least one supporter of note in Cora Diamond, with whose views on the nature of moral argument I am inclined to agree (1982: 23–41). Tom Regan, upon whom we now direct attention, is no less passionate for the cause:

> There are times, and these not infrequent, when tears come to my eyes when I see, or read, or hear of the wretched plight of animals in the hands of humans. Their pain, their suffering, their loneliness, their innocence, their death. Anger. Rage. Pity. Sorrow. Disgust. The whole creation groans under the weight of the evil we humans visit upon these mute, powerless creatures.

It *is* our hearts, not just our heads, that call for an end to it all, that demand of us that we overcome, for them, the habits and forces behind their systematic oppression ... The fate of animals is in our hands. God grant we are equal to the task.

(Regan 1985: 25–6)

Conscious problems

Regan arrives at the point of needing to contest Frey's denial of beliefs to animals after having established, in reasonably secure fashion, that animals are conscious and wishing to move beyond this to establish what he sees as the full complexity of their awareness. But there are three aspects of Regan's treatment of consciousness which are instructive for what follows it and I shall begin by touching upon these.

Firstly, the main plank of his so-called 'cumulative argument' is that imputing desires, emotions, and beliefs to animals is not only a normal way of speaking but is the only possible one. He quotes the findings of an experimental group headed by the psychologist D.O. Hebb who in the mid-1940s attempted to describe the moods of chimpanzees without resorting to 'anthropomorphic' terminology. Hebb reported as follows: 'All that resulted was an almost endless series of specific acts in which no order or meaning could be found' (Regan 1983: 26). Needless to say, when normal talking was resumed, Hebb's staff were once again able to communicate with each other; agreeing on the nervousness, fury, placidity or inordinate desire of the respective creatures, having previously been restricted to the language of pulse rate, food intake, vocal sounding, facial contortions, leg movement, and so on.

Now one could comment upon this from a variety of angles. Scientifically, for example, it tells us little more than that if you are engaged in the 'study of temperament' (Hebb's words) then you are not going to get very far if you do not use the *language* of temperament. But equally distinguished researchers like Hull and Skinner interested in, for example, operant conditioning have found no difficulty in translating a cat's pursuit of a mouse into the vocabulary of inherited reflexes (Walker 1983: 85). But, for our purposes, it is Regan's almost touching faith in the univocality of language that is noteworthy. Previously discussed cases like that of the clever rabies virus illustrate the power which context wields over familiar terms and to which we adjust almost without realising it.

Rivers 'seek' their own level. The clever virus *is* clever; but what we therefore expect of it is not the performance of a Harry Houdini. Leaves and roots have 'purposes'; but as *functions* not goals, whereas the reader's purpose in persisting with this book is to sample the plausibility of an attack upon animal liberation. Yet it is easy to *forget* these conceptual niceties. (Clark warns of the dangers lurking in the confusion of 'goals' and 'purposes' (1982: 10).) Now Regan thinks it obvious that everyone 'understands perfectly well what it means to say that Fido is hungry, or that a mother lion is annoyed by her overly playful cubs' (25). This may or may not be so; I seriously doubt it! But Regan does not say *what* it is that everyone is supposed to understand when they say these things. Most intelligent pet owners, breeders or dog-handlers that I've spoken to would be keen to stress the different aura that terms like 'angry' or 'hungry' assume when used of dogs or race horses, or creatures in zoos or circuses. This is not to foist a theory of the inherited reflex upon them; merely to emphasise that 'ordinary language' has depths of subtlety that only reflection makes apparent. (There will be more to say about this in discussing Wittgenstein's notion of *language games* in Chapter 5.)

The second point is a salutary one. In seeking to decide how far consciousness descends the evolutionary scale, it is we who are the touchstone. Regan agrees: 'It is human beings that provide the paradigm of conscious beings' (1983: 29). But the same must apply to the many other capacities that he allegedly attributes to animals: desires, beliefs, emotions, intentions, rationality, self-consciousness, and so on. This second point connects with the first. If our ordinary talk about animals sometimes conceals subtleties of implication that distance it more or less from its application to the human paradigm then we must accept that the force of the attribution, which will draw its ethical implications from the human connection, will be diluted and perhaps dissolved entirely.

The third problem pursuant upon Regan's discussion of consciousness is more complex. What Regan *means* by 'consciousness' is by no means clear. For a start, his examples are all sufficient conditions for its presence, but not necessary ones, and are summed up as the possession of a 'mental life', to use his ubiquitous but far from enlightening terminology: being hungry or annoyed (1983: 25), fearful, nervous, or shy (26), wanting, or feeling pain (30). They are sufficient conditions in that one would normally expect a person or animal to be conscious if they were in one of these states. The real difficulty lies in Regan's examples not providing *necessary* conditions;

a creature can be conscious without being hungry, fearful or in pain. Consciousness is a *minimal* notion involving only a sensuous awareness of the external world (sentience). Thus the anaesthetist asks the patient if they can hear her voice or, in desperation, tests for signs with an ophthalmoscope. Any of the five senses is able to provide a sufficiency; and a necessary condition is that *at least one* operates. Did Regan mean this and just neglect to say so? The suspicion aroused by his constant use of 'mental life' is that he did *not*. Consciousness for him, it seems, is some sort of inner awareness of whatever *experience* is held up as an example of it, such as hunger or fear. Three bits of evidence reinforce this suspicion which, if sustainable, will have serious implications for his philosophy of mind.

The first clue is that Regan approvingly cites Donald Griffin's use of the phrase 'mental *experience*' as addressing the same issue: 'The possibility that animals have mental experiences is often dismissed as anthropomorphic' (Griffin 1976: 85). Yet if to be conscious were satisfied by sentience (as I use the term above) then one would be hard pressed to deny it of Figan, the police dog, and similar healthy mammals whose eyes and ears are obviously in good order. So Regan, assisted by Griffin, must be after something less accessible. This is borne out by the second clue which is that Regan will not unhesitatingly grant consciousness even to *human beings*: 'Human beings, we shall assume, are not "thoughtless brutes" . . . but are creatures who have a mental life. This is a necessary assumption for any work in moral philosophy' (1983: 17). This seems like shameless neo-Cartesianism which, despite its conclusive defenestration by Ryle (1949) and subsequent critics, is quite popular with enthusiastis of the if-you-don't-know-what's-in-other-people's-minds-how-can-you-be-sure-about-animals school of thought. This is Marian Stamp Dawkins, like Griffin, an animal psychologist:

> Much of our behaviour towards other people is thus based on the unverifiable belief that they have subjective experiences at least somewhat like our own. It seems a reasonable belief to hold.

> (Dawkins 1985: 27)

Views of this sort, as we will see, obscure what it is to think sensibly about our own species let alone casting any light upon members of other ones. The requirement of an unverifiable subjective awareness for consciousness will also be seen to vitiate Regan's defence of 'simple desires' against Frey. This is the third clue.

Finding fault with Frey: simple desires

Regan sets out Frey's argument schematically as follows (1983:38):

1. Only those individuals who can have beliefs can have desires.
2. Animals cannot have beliefs.
3. Therefore, animals cannot have desires.

Earlier in this chapter we traced the background to Frey's support for (1) initially to Aristotle but, in more detail, to A.J.P. Kenny. Human desires, and these are the paradigm from which we begin, presuppose the presence of beliefs which, if necessary, can be tested by asking appropriate questions. The possible counter-example of a desire which appears not to involve belief was the scholastic notion of 'imperfect knowledge' which Aquinas attributes to animals: the dog sees its food and rushes towards it, thus manifesting a *sensual desire*. Frey, however, rejects this by confronting the Thomist, or his contemporary representative, with his elegant dilemma: if we allow that a creature has this desire, it is either aware of it or not? A sticky end, as we saw above, awaits either answer. Regan (1982) disagrees.[1]

If the animal has the simple desire but is not aware of it, then, Frey argues, it must have it unconsciously. Regan claims that the inference is invalid 'since it fails to take account of and, indeed, exploits the distinction between being-aware-of and being-aware-that-one-is-aware-of one's desires' (1982: 278). The dog can be aware of desiring its food without being aware *that* it desires it. Most of the time, Regan argues, we simply 'have' desires: 'I am *aware of* them, and I do not fret much over this fact.' But, for various reasons, we sometimes need to 'reflect upon rather than just have (experience) them' (1983: 278). It is only at this reflective level that we are aware *that* we desire. Regan also uses this ploy to discredit Frey's dismissal of the other possibility which is that the animal *is* aware that it has its simple desires. Frey's reason was that it implies self-consciousness but that, in any case, there is nothing in the behavioural repertoire of a creature lacking language which could express this additional awareness. Regan's retort is that it is not necessary for any individual, human or non-human, to be aware *that* it desires in order to be aware *of* desiring. So the issue of self-consciousness doesn't arise.

But *is* there a distinction between being aware of desiring and being aware *that* one desires? Is Regan unwittingly deceiving us with a conceptual sleight-of-hand? How can the lady with the string in her bag, who wants to tie the parcel next week, be *aware of* this desire when she is asleep or busy making love? Regan would seem to be committed to the view that she does not then desire to tie the parcel despite the fact that were she woken up, or her lover unchivalrous enough to delay the proceedings to quiz her about it, she would undoubtedly confirm that she did want the string for this purpose. But this confirmation would demonstrate the fact *that* she so desired it and did so *when otherwise engaged*.

It can only be because Regan thinks that the presence of desire (and belief) is of the same order as experiencing sensations of pain or hunger, thereby confusing mental states with mental events, that he is tempted to believe it possible to be aware *of* them without necessarily being aware *that* they were present. Part of the confusion results from Regan's concentration upon human examples where sensations and reactions so quickly become the subject of diagnosis and reflection. But an *animal's* behaviour on spying its food does give substance to a sense of simple desire implicit in the insights of Aristotle and Aquinas. Newly hatched chicks react to visual clues by pecking at any bright round dot or similar object that contrasts with its background. I.P. Pavlov's dogs varied their own fixed action patterns and learned to react to bells as they would to the sight or smell of bones. A cat sees a bird, or a lion a hyena, and either pounces if it is nearby or begins to stalk it if it is not. In every case the animal is urged or driven or attracted by the evidence of its senses to adopt a means to some end but without any awareness of what it is doing, other than its sense perception, without which it would not even be alive.

Regan is right to have called Frey's apparently decisive little dilemma into question but his diagnosis of what precisely is wrong with it seems just as decisively to have missed the boat.[2]

Finding fault: sentences

Regan next attacks Frey's understanding of belief as requiring the conviction that certain sentences are true. He cites the example of a Portuguese speaker, ignorant of English, surprised by a boy wielding a rubber snake. We rightly say, 'he believes the snake will harm him' but cannot characterise him as therefore agreeing to the truth of certain *English* sentences. Therefore, 'it is very unclear what sense it can make to persist in claiming that what is believed is that *a* sentence is true' (Regan's italics, 1983: 41).

Now Regan does his best to be fair to his opponents. But one's faith in this is shaken by the perversity of this reading of Frey who, admittedly, fails to sketch in the background to the sort of theory that he is proposing. Frey's example, we have seen, is that of his belief that he lacks a Gutenberg Bible (GB) and he continues, in the passage quoted by Regan, 'that is, I believe that the sentence "My collection lacks a Gutenberg Bible" is true'. But surely any number of sentences could follow 'I believe that' and satisfactorily fill the bill: 'My collection of books lacks a GB', 'My library is devoid of (without, unpossessed of, unblest with) a GB', and the translations of these in any written language the speaker might be master of. Frey is certainly committed to holding that 'what is believed is that *a* sentence is true', as Regan accuses him, but this is consistent with its being any one of an appropriate range.

Finding fault: deviant cases

Regan now adapts his example from the previous discussion where a boy with a rubber snake startles a passer-by. He now supposes that the stranger 'happens not to be able to speak or comprehend any language' because of severe mental impairment, it would seem (1983: 42). We have all the overt manifestations of fear: bulging eyes, frantic expression, shying away; but no language. Regan believes it to be perfectly natural, using his 'cumulative' argument, to say that the afflicted stranger believes the snake will harm him. Frey, Regan alleges, is committed to the view that not only 'does he not believe anything, he *cannot* believe anything' (42).

Now this argument of Regan's is certainly more to the point. By positing something approaching a wolf in human clothing, Frey's denial of beliefs would be seen at its most implausible. But Regan develops this in a strange way. He assumes that Frey would simply have no time for such oddities and depicts him as holding that, 'If a proposed analysis fits the "normal" cases, *then that is enough*, and it is quite improper to contest its adequacy by dredging up this or that "deviant" case' (Regan's italics: 43). The implication is that Frey is being pig-headed by refusing any relevance to such cases. This is not borne out by the discussion however. Frey's point is an application of the jurist's principle that 'hard cases make bad law' and is of general logical interest. Such 'hard cases' are of considerable importance because they tend to test the limits of the law's precise application; the exception 'proves' the rule. The same problems can arise with the informal use of everyday language. If you've been instructed to weed the garden do you remove the poppies and buttercups?

Regan has unwittingly raised the important question: What are we to make of apparent counter-examples based upon allegedly deviant cases like that of his afflicted stranger? Some advocates of a Frey-like view might think the matter to be open-and-shut; if no language then no belief – end of argument! Liberationists, wary of the implications for animals, might just as peremptorily go the other way: appropriate fear reactions, therefore belief – end of another argument! Regan, predictably inclining to the latter view, accuses Frey of not having shown that 'alternative accounts', presumably those deducing beliefs directly from behaviour, 'are deficient' (43). This is not true. Frey not only provides three arguments against the sole reliance upon behaviour (as we have seen) but also substitutes his own causal account of animal behaviour which avoids the importation of beliefs. The ball is clearly in Regan's court; he may not like the look of it but he cannot deny its presence. It is, furthermore, ironic that Regan's support for the liberationist view relies wholly upon his own 'cumulative' argument which has as its main support the appeal to our ordinary ways of speaking about animals. But to attempt seriously and sensitively to imagine oneself confronted by the unfortunate creature depicted by Regan would surely test one's emotional reserves rather than intellectual ones. As it stands the case is *too* deviant and inadequately elaborated. The example raises such deep problems about our reactions to, and assessment of, *human imbeciles* that, whatever our views about animals, we would do better to bemoan the sparsity of plausible detail before venturing to attribute or deny beliefs. Of course one could stand back and pronounce from the open-and-shut standpoint either way but that would be to simplify out the implicit complexities of such a case by begging the question in one's own favour. (We will return to this example in Chapter 5.)

Further faults: pre-verbal beliefs?

Regan provides two related arguments to support the existence of pre-verbal beliefs. Clearly if such beliefs occur then Frey's position is seriously breached.

The first is a *modus tollens*. If we rule out pre-verbal beliefs then children cannot be taught a language. But since the consequent is clearly false then the antecedent cannot be true. Regan argues that prior beliefs are a prerequisite for language learning in the first place. This is how he sees the process:

> We begin by holding up or pointing to objects and giving their names – *ball, mother, dog, bottle*. If Baby Jane picks up on what we are attempting to teach, the time comes when she is able to give the correct name: she says 'ball' when the object we hold or point to is a ball. . . . Unless Baby Jane comes to believe that there is a particular thing we are referring to, when we say the word *ball*, all manner of instruction . . . will be for naught.
>
> (Regan 1983: 45)

The scientific study and theoretical discussion of children's language acquisition is very much a going concern backed by a weighty history. Regan's statement is little more than assertion; there is no argument to justify the importation of belief to facilitate instruction. What could a pre-verbal belief *possibly* consist in? Might it be something like a twinge of Baby Jane's colic? One is not denying the attribution but questioning its sense; much as a religious sceptic might wonder at the insistence that the baby was also possessed of Original Sin. Such a depiction of language acquisition is plausible at best only in the context of learning a *second* language. In such a case, belief clearly can antedate the learning process as a function of the pre-existing home tongue.

The acquisition of a first language, however, requires a different explanation and there is no shortage of candidates. Noam Chomsky has argued that children are born with the knowledge of universal principles of grammatical structure. This might appear to give comfort to Regan's pre-verbal beliefs but, upon inspection, does not. Chomsky's principles manifest themselves as innate 'determinations' or 'predispositions' requiring no mediation of belief, a situation not unlike the pecking habits of the newly hatched chicks, although of a different order of complexity. Another, even more plausible, account is that the baby begins randomly to imitate sounds, much like a parrot. When certain utterances are reinforced by rewards it responds to these ever more predicably, much like rats or pigeons in Skinner boxes, but soon outstrips the animals in learning to replace behaviour (like grabbing for its bottle or thrusting it away) with speech acts. Belief, it is argued, begins to enter the picture at this latter stage, when the baby is typically between 18 and 24 months, as a function of its developing ability to improvise beyond its original themes and, above all, in its vocal interaction with others to gain a mastery of the appropriate and inappropriate utterance. It is now seen to be sensible, rather than wishful thinking, to attribute beliefs of increasing complexity to the infant because, in its idiosyncratic lingua franca, it can *talk* about its needs. Self-consciousness is to be understood in the same way. It is not some ill-conceived awareness, present even in the womb, but an emerging *understanding* issuing, in necessary part, from the ability to talk.

None of this, it must be stressed, will be proof against someone like Regan who just insists that pre-verbal beliefs must exist, without giving any substance to them. Such a position has all the dubious merit of that of the believer in fairies, convinced that they *must* exist at the bottom of the garden, despite the lack of any evidence to support the fact. John Wisdom (1953), in his captivating and widely anthologised article, 'Gods', fashions a critique of religion from the logic of such differences.

Regan's related objection concerns not the allegedly pre-verbal beliefs of infants but the non-linguistic performances of adults. The truth of the by now tiresome sentence, 'My collection lacks a GB' will, Frey contends, be 'partly a function of the actual state of my book collection' (1980: 90). This leads him to talk of the difficulty of capturing the 'intimate link between language and the world' (91). Regan seizes upon this. Briefly his criticism is that this link can never be grasped because it involves having beliefs *about this link*, and in the inevitable process of questioning these, having beliefs about the beliefs, and so on *ad infinitum*. But if the link can never be grasped then nobody can believe anything. I will make only two brief comments upon this heady brew since I do not think it bears upon the issue of animal beliefs. In the first place, grand phrases like 'the intimate link between language and the world' suggest an over-simplified view of language on Frey's part. Ironically, it has much in common with Regan's account, quoted earlier in this section, where the emphasis is upon substantives 'standing for' or naming the objects which bear those general names ('ball', 'mother', 'dog'). But naming is not the pre-eminent role of language. (This diversification of language will re-surface in Chapter 5.) Secondly, if given Frey's careless talk of 'links', we allow Regan's claim that this can generate an infinite regress, then the next question is whether it is a *vicious* one; whether, that is, it shows up what gave rise to it as an absurdity. Regan suggests that Frey's regress could be halted were there certain beliefs which did not require the true-or-false criterion, one of which would be that involving the link of language and world. But he sees no way of establishing what these beliefs might be and Frey is certainly far from being able to assist. But Regan does see them as non-linguistic beliefs, for reasons which are not altogether clear, although it will not have escaped attention that the claim materially assists the attribution of similar such beliefs to animals.

A stich in time

Having, to his own satisfaction, disposed of Frey's troublesome objections that beliefs and desire necessarily involve language (apart from the remaining difficulty of the tail-wagging), Regan can now resume his original position that animals are capable of both. He talks of his 'intuitive "belief-desire" theory'; a description used by another writer, Stephen Stich, from which Regan quotes at length and praises as 'especially perspicuous' (1983: 35). Stich writes:

> The theory postulates two different sorts of functional states, beliefs and desires, with normal subjects having a large store of each. Desires can arise in a variety of ways. One way in which they typically arise is as a result of deprivation. An organism deprived of food, water or sexual release, will acquire a desire for food, water or sexual release, the strength of the desire generally increasing with the length of time the organism has been deprived . . .
>
> If our canine's master puts a meaty bone in the dog's dish . . . then the dog will form the belief that there is a meaty bone in its dish. It will also, no doubt, form a variety of further beliefs.
>
> (Regan 1983: 35-6)

A reader who has read, with any sympathy at all, the criticism of Singer's account of animal rationality and self-consciousness, or Frey's treatment of these problems, will see immediately that Regan, in endorsing Stich's view, has saddled himself with a theory that raises more questions than it answers. Firstly, desires are confused with needs, and like needs, both desires and beliefs, being depicted as *functional* states, act like drives with the strongest winning out. Furthermore, this allows for a lack of *awareness* of the desire or belief. However, the price paid is that all contact with the paradigm use of these notions, namely of human beings, has been lost. Secondly, since plants are organisms that can suffer 'deprivation' they too would seem to qualify for desires and belief. Thirdly, there is no recognition that paradigmatic desires and beliefs provide *reasons* for action unless the idea is that animals also have their reasons. Stich's original notion of 'functional states' is inflexible in this respect, unless it be taken as including linguistic behaviour. But it would then be of no use to animals. Fourthly, and above all, one needs to know the difference between the dog that forms the belief about the bone and another, in similar circumstances, that does *not*. That one eats the bone and the other doesn't will not do since the abstainer might be operating on the basis of a different belief.

Although Stich is certain that animals possess beliefs and desires, he denies that we can specify their content; we can say *that* they believe but not *what* they believe. (His doubts concern the concepts that it is proper to attribute to animals such that we can couch their beliefs in forms proper to them.) Regan parts company with Stich at this point by claiming that animals have 'preference-beliefs'. That dogs recognise a 'connection between bones and satisfying desires *is* to have a belief about bones . . . the belief that a bone is to be chosen if a given desire is to be satisfied' (Regan 1983: 58). It relates sufficiently closely, he claims, to our concept of a bone which the animal can therefore be said to share. Moreover its having the preference-belief 'can be fairly judged by attending to the only thing we have to go on – namely, his non-verbal behaviour' (58).

The amphiboly of tail-wagging

It is at this point that Regan considers the example of Frey's dog which, it will be remembered, wagged its tail in precisely similar manner when its master was outside the door, when lunch was immanent, and when the sun was eclipsed by the moon. Non-linguistic behaviour, Frey argued, cannot '*show* that my dog possesses the belief *that p* unless that behaviour is connected with the belief *that p* in such a way that that same piece of behaviour is not compatible with the belief *that q* or *that r* or *that s*' (1980: 114). The context of this criticism must be borne in mind. Frey is querying Armstrong's attempt in *Belief, Truth and Knowledge* (1973) to account for our being able to say, 'The cat believes the ball is stuck' when the animal lacks the concepts involved. Such attributions, Armstrong argues, are 'referentially transparent'; a perfectly legitimate device used when fitting the words or thoughts of other people into third-person reports. A missionary could say of a bushman, 'He wants me to take my watch from its chain' despite the fact that the native knows nothing of watches and chains and speaks no English; this is *oratio obliqua* (reported speech). But problems arise in using this stratagem of animals where all we have to go on is overt behaviour; whereas the bushman will be master of a complex language from which, it is fair to assume, native equivalents will be forthcoming.[3]

Regan's whole position is threatened if he is unable satisfactorily to meet this challenge. The derivation of preference-beliefs from behaviour alone is an important first link in a lengthy chain. His reply is that the objection only appears plausible because it isolates the tail-wagging too peremptorily from its context; Frey does not have 'a sufficiently rich understanding of behaviour' (Regan 1983: 68). If we know enough about the dog's social life, that it gets on well with its master, regularly breaks into a song-and-dance at the inimitable knock on the door and leaps up to him as he enters, then we *will* be in a position to say confidently that it believes its master is at the door. Presumably Regan would be prepared to say the same *mutatis mutandis* of the other contexts of an eclipse or impending lunch. But Regan makes an important addition: 'When we say that the dog believes his master is at the door, we imply that the dog has certain *expectations* ... manifested by the dog's future behaviour.' He continues:

> We are right to attribute this belief to him if we have reason to believe that he now has those expectations he would have if he believes that it is his master, just as we would be right to attribute to Mary the belief that her friend Nora is at the door if we have reason to believe that she has those expectations she would have if she believed it was her friend at the door. But just as we cannot say that Mary believes this solely on the basis of her walking to the door when a noise has been heard, so we cannot say *what* Fido believes just by viewing his tail-wagging as a piece of isolated behaviour.

> (Regan 1983: 69)

Regan can now employ the notion of the animal's expectations, as he sees it, very prolifically. Firstly, if they are manifested after our attribution of the belief then they provide a check on its accuracy (69–70). Secondly, he claims that it illuminates the sense in which we talk of animals acting with intentions; for instance, when the animal is digging to retrieve its long-concealed bone it has certain expectations which enable us to ascribe the belief, among others, that it will find it. If it fails to do so, its evident disappointment will be because its belief was false and this, he believes, counters Frey's denial that animals can distinguish true from false beliefs (Regan 1983: 70-1).

Finally, the dog's preference-beliefs are predicated on the basis of its expectations about bones or whatever else it might be said to want or not want. But expectations involve beliefs about the future and if an animal can act so as to bring about its own satisfaction then it must be 'self-conscious' (74–5). Furthermore, it is capable of holding the necessary beliefs to enjoy a full perceptual and 'emotional life', in the sense, for instance, that to fear something is to believe that in some way it poses a threat (75). It is hardly surprising that after all this Regan concludes that animals are 'individuals who, like us, have beliefs and desires' (78) and, of course, the additional attributes discussed above; although doubts about whether to include fish or insects incline him to restrict the candidates to 'normal mammalian animals aged one or more' (81).

It will not be a surprise to learn that, in my view, Regan's argument does little more than ruffle the surface of perhaps an augmented version of Frey's basic position. But it will be more fruitful to locate what has gone wrong against the background of Wittgenstein's contribution to the analysis of the central psychological notions so far on offer. This will form the substance of Chapter 5. But an impatient reader, needing to get to grips on their own behalf with the suspicion that Regan's ambition outstrips his justification of it, might care to dwell upon the following two points:

1. The above, somewhat convoluted, quotation from Regan (69) compares the dog to a human being, Mary. The dog's 'expectations' consist in its excitable behaviour at the appropriate time (he '*now* has those expectations', but note that the 'now' is omitted of Mary). Can the dog be said to have expected its master an hour earlier when, say, it was contentedly washing itself in front of the fire? Surely not; there is no song-and-dance or even the intimations of one. Yet it makes perfectly good sense to say of Mary that she was expecting Nora *all morning* despite her being totally engrossed in washing herself in front of the fire. Mary's expectation is a mental *state*, possibly dating back months to the original appointment, which gives rise to manifestations, instanced by her checking her watch or peering around her lace curtains. Even Mary asleep expects Nora the next day. Now unless we can specify a sense of the dog's expectation that is logically separable from its manifestations, we cannot call its song-and-dance a manifestation *of expectation*. Were Mary suddenly to get

in a fluster as the bell rang, it would be quite different since in her case we have the requisite mental state. The cases are not analogous.

2. Regan is presumably committed to the view that the animal *has* the beliefs and expectations and that we are not just attributing them for purposes of our own. The latter position is, in part, that of Armstrong for whom it is consistent to hold that the use of these terms of animals differs from their implications for human beings. Now Regan imports both terms in their *human* sense, albeit with manifestations limited to non-linguistic behaviour. With what justification? Belief, we are told, is justified by the dog's having expectations. Now is the dog *just* making a fuss with its tail-wagging and so on? No, it is *expecting*; and what makes it so is the dog's beliefs. Each supports the other but neither has support independent of the other. Were procedures of this sort able to legitimise the proliferation of controversial entities they would indeed have a bright future; to begin at the beginning, both God and the Devil might have reason to be grateful to them.

Beyond utilitarianism: inherent value and Singer

Many devotees regard Regan's most significant contribution to the cause of animals to be his ethical principle of *inherent value*. It is certainly the most peremptory basis for a defence of animals from which follows equally categorical practical considerations. Any account of Regan's views would be lop-sided without it.

The need to postulate inherent value is forced upon Regan because of the uncompromising nature of his commitment to the reform, as he sees it, of present practice: a *total* ban on the use of animals in science, agriculture, sport, hunting, and other types of alleged exploitation. Alternative moral theories seem unequal to the task. Traditional religious doctrine, as we shall see in later chapters, can be lukewarm. Regan shares with Singer a distaste for contractualist theory, such as that of John Rawls, since (as we saw in Chapter 1) full membership of the moral club is restricted to those capable of appreciating its obligations. It is for this reason that Regan calls the concern of its moral agents a source of 'indirect' duty whereas, he argues, our moral intuitions require that moral patients deserve guarantees in their *own* right to protect them. The duty to be kind and avoid cruelty to animals is better, he argues, in that it is at least a 'direct' duty, but it does not assure treatment that is comprehensive enough. Vivisectors and steak fanatics can be souls of benevolence.

It is, however, Regan's reaction against utilitarianism which occasions the most interest. Singer, albeit somewhat reluctantly, allows the painless killing of 'non-self-conscious' chickens or seafood, and 'for overriding utilitarian reasons' perhaps self-conscious creatures as well (Singer 1979: 104–5). But Regan, well aware of the vagaries of assessing interests and the capriciousness inherent in weighing them, correctly fears this concession as the thin end of a significant wedge. Stephen Clark, who is as categorical in his views as Regan, is so scornful of the allegedly mitigating effects of killing being painless that he is forced to a redefinition of death:

It is surely extremely paradoxical that death should not be recognized as the greatest of single hurts, the final pain for fear of which all other pains are intensified. If death is no hurt, what ill is done by those who have their cats 'put down' for not matching the new decorations?

(Clark 1977: 76)

The thrust of Regan's argument is that although Singer's moral intuitions against hunting, the fur trade, and the use of animals in science, and in *favour* of vegetarianism and so on, are commendable, his moral theory is inadequate to sustain them. Thus, for example, Regan is particularly severe on the attempted utilitarian support for vegetarianism which, depending upon the strengths of the various interests brought to bear on the issue might well, as we saw earlier, be out-gunned:

respect for the equality principle is no guarantee that animals will be treated equitably. ... That animals are raised intensively, for example, while human beings are not, provides no distinctively *utilitarian* arguments against raising animals in this way. For it may be that treating animals in these ways brings about the best consequences, all considered.

(Regan 1983: 228)

Something stronger is needed.

Inherent value as antidote

Regan's task is formidable. The moral patients that he is so keen to protect must be seen to possess some quality that is non-negotiable. Their experiences of pleasure or other interests fail to meet this test, given utilitarian criteria. Inherent value (IV) has nothing to do

72

therefore with the value of the life or the experiences of the individuals that possess it. Regan begins by attaching IV to moral agents. All possess it equally; the alternative would signal a return to the inequities of traditional meritocratic or 'perfectionist' ethical theories which measure moral worth by sex, class, race or ability. IV cannot vary in strength dependent upon what one does: 'A criminal is no less inherently valuable than a saint' (1983: 237). Regan can easily bring animals, infants and imbeciles into the fold. If justice is not satisfied by moral meritocracy or utility then 'it must look to a different kind of value'. He continues: 'If moral agents have inherent value, we cannot ignore that value when attempting to determine what treatment is just or unjust' (238). Since moral patients can suffer wrongs and injustice similar to those of moral agents it would be arbitrary to exclude them from IV (239).

What both groups have in common is Regan's *subject-of-a-life criterion*; which is satisfied by a level of consciousness which he has contentiously attempted to establish for adult higher mammals: individuals with beliefs, desires, perception, memory, a sense of themselves and of the future, as initiators of action with preference-interests and 'an individual welfare in the sense that their experiental life fares well or ill for them' (243). Given its significance, justice must take account of IV. This generates the 'respect principle'; that individuals are 'to be given their due' (248-9). Now it seems naturally to follow that the many ways in which subjects, human or non-human, can be harmed (presumably whether they are aware of it or not) is to *fail* in this. Thus is derived the 'harm principle' (262) from which it is a short step for Regan to argue that all who possess IV can make valid claims, or have them made on their behalf, against being harmed; which is to say that they have moral *rights*. These rights imply duties, typically for human agents, not only to forbear from inflicting harm upon those with IV but, if necessary, to come to their aid if they are threatened.

Regan's case is, in essence, complete. But it is not free from obscurities which even critics like Mary Anne Warren, in sympathy with the rights movement, think to be damaging (1986: 165-6). Of crucial importance is the role of sentience; in the form of the subject-of-a-life criterion. It seems, for a start, to contradict Regan's initial claim that IV is independent of the intrinsic value of the creature's experiences. He is clearly aware of the pitfalls of sentience being possessed to a greater or lesser degree, contrasting say horses with chimps, whereas IV cannot be. His solution is to force sentience into the unsuitable role of an all-or-nothing affair: 'One either *is* a subject of a life . . . or one is *not*' (245). Secondly, Regan's unease about his sentience criterion is underlined by its only being a *sufficient* condition for IV. Thus those that *fail* to satisfy it, for example 'permanently comatose human beings', can nonetheless possess IV (246). Even plants and 'cancer cells' are not debarred from IV; and surely only the pressure of some varieties of extreme feminist ideology can account for Regan's incredible omission of the human foetus. So why bother with the subject-of-a-life criterion at all if it isn't necessary: if concern for lower animals and 'a genuine ethic *of* the environment' requires that frogs, crabs, sea-anemones, trees, mountains and the sea itself be invested with IV? All Regan can do is to wring his hands over the difficulties of making the more peripheral attributions stick (246). But, thirdly, *locating* IV is quite unlike the detection of sex-attractant pheromones in moths requiring ever more sophisticated gas chromatographs to isolate the minute traces involved. IV is not obscure in this sense. It is disarmingly straightforward. It is a 'postulate' (236, 247–8); in geometry something taken for granted – a 'theoretical assumption' but 'not one made without reason' (247).

That the justifying reasons are Regan's intuitions is made quite clear in his refusal to allow IV to admit of varying degrees. His view, he writes, 'is rationally preferable' since the alternative ushers in a form of perfectionism which 'is unacceptable' (236–7). But it is open to him to postulate IV of anything he wishes if he is prepared to bear the consequences; and he almost seems prepared to do so. In a paradoxical way this provides a defence of a postulate like IV as well as being its weakness. Regan has not located some interesting pheromone-like characteristic, or even a moral quality, uniting a proliferating membership of IV holders; his vacillation over the subject-of-a-life criterion rules that out. He has simply *invented* a quality and invested it with significance. Such creations can be powerful weapons of rhetoric and persuasion in the hands of the converted; witness the charisma of Original Sin, a notion with which inherent value has many, if reverse, affinities.

4

THE HISTORICAL
PERSPECTIVE: ARISTOTLE
TO DARWIN

Introduction

In *Animal Liberation* (1983) Singer has a chapter entitled 'Man's dominion'. His aim is to persuade us that western culture, as opposed to much eastern thought, is in the grip of an ideology hostile to animals which is so much second nature to us that it 'resists refutation' (231). Its original twin supports are the Old Testament and the views of the Ancient Greeks, typified by Aristotle. Both provide for man's privilege, being, in the words of *Genesis*, 'in the image of God' and his having 'dominion' over fish, fowl, cattle and 'over all the earth, and over every creeping thing that creepeth upon the earth' (Gen. 1: vv. 26–7). In Aristotle's case the dominion extends to other human beings such as women and slaves. Particularly significant in the development of this ideology was its being channelled through the war-oriented culture of Rome where the grotesque appetite of an otherwise upright and civilised people for the centuries-long institution of the 'games', at which literally thousands of animals, military prisoners and criminals could slaughter each other in a single day, demonstrates the almost limitless possibilities of moral polar-vision; the social decencies existing alongside a craving to witness the improvised agony and death of creatures, human and non-human, totally without status. Christianity's eventual supremacy reasserted the sanctity of *human* life, Singer argues, but did little to ameliorate the standing of animals, upon which the New Testament and the ministry of Jesus is almost totally silent.

Animal fortunes are seen reaching their lowest ebb during the seventeenth-century Renaissance, typified by Descartes' contention that they were mere automata incapable of suffering. The most permissive and least conscience-ridden of open seasons had arrived. However, Singer's plot thickens in considering the spate of animal experimentation which not unpredictably followed. The results, demonstrating the anatomical similarities of the higher mammals and humans, encouraged a revival of the traditional view that animals do suffer. This heralded an era positively sympathetic to animals; initially tentative but accelerating into the Enlightenment's more strident attacks upon what was seen as our abuses of animals, in particular that of eating them. Voltaire, Rousseau, Bentham, William Paley, Henry Salt, Lord Chesterfield, Schopenhauer, T.H. Huxley and, above all, Darwin are cited by Singer. His lament is that although all of these, some quite explicitly, put forward good arguments for its being wrong to eat meat, almost all of them were quick on the draw with a rational justification, such as an appeal to Revelation, for their consuming it nonetheless. This then for Singer is the irony. Our view of animals, which clearly he thinks remains the prevailing one, is ideological in the sense in which it props up what he sees as our corrupt practices of eating meat, experimenting *in vivo*, hunting, and the rest.

My own excursion into the past which follows is differently motivated. Singer concentrates only upon the historical *attitudes* to animals whereas I think it equally if not more important to probe the *reasons for* an attitude. An understanding of the true workings of animal life, particularly along the lines originally proposed by Aristotle and Aquinas which will be seen to anticipate a great deal of contemporary ethology, can provide a firm foundation for treating animals humanely but at the same time eating them, experimenting upon them, and a lot else besides. Singer prefers to give precedence to the theories of his eminent sources whilst deploring their lapses into indulgence whereas, to turn the well-stocked tables, it might be more reliable to accept what they actually practised as indicating less than complete confidence in what they preached.

Aristotle (384–322 BC)[1]

Greek thought in the fifth and sixth centuries BC, preoccupied with the mystery of the universe and man's place in it, contains little of interest on the subject of animals. Even Plato's one passage of any length, at the close of his dialogue the *Timaeus*, is a strange amalgam of fact and fancy based neither upon systematic observation nor dissection. (Anatomy existed in the fourth century BC, as an adjunct to medicine, but was in its infancy as a science.) Aristotle however was a great innovator in scientific method and his treatises on the *History*,

Parts, and *Generation* of animals were products of careful observation and classification. But the more fruitful comparisons between animal life and human beings occur in the less technical works and are surprising in sounding so up to date. Here, in the *Politics* (*P*), he explains the reasons for the social pre-eminence of *homo sapiens*:

> The reason why man is a being meant for political association, in a higher degree than bees or other gregarious animals can ever associate, is evident. Nature, according to our theory, makes nothing in vain; and man alone of the animals is furnished with the faculty of language. The mere making of sounds serves to indicate pleasure and pain, and is thus a faculty that belongs to animals in general: their nature enables them to attain the point at which they have perceptions of pleasure and pain, and can signify those perceptions to one another. But language serves to declare what is advantageous and what is the reverse, and it therefore serves to declare what is just and what is unjust.
>
> (*P*, 1253a 8-13)

Basic Aristotelian themes interweave in this passage. The natural world is to be understood as an organic whole; everything in it serves a purpose (although the purpose is inherent in nature itself and not that of a transcendent being like the God of Christianity or of Plato's *Timaeus*). In this sense human beings are 'meant' to be social; it is part of their natural function. They are nonetheless part of the natural world, being animals, yet superior to the rest of it in benefiting from the advantages of language. There is a clear sense of living beings existing in a hierarchy.

In his treatise *On the Soul*, usually referred to by its Latin title *De Anima* (*DA*), Aristotle analyses this hierarchy naturalistically. It is based upon biologically based psychic faculties which living beings manifest and inanimate ones do not. (The Greek term *psyche* is used by Aristotle as a catch-all for the proliferations of this *life principle*, its literal rendering, which tends to confuse the English reader in its usual translation as 'soul'.) Thus plants and animals have souls, as well as ourselves, in that they are living; which is simply to say that they have certain capacities. He puts it graphically and famously: 'For if the eye was an animal, then sight would be its soul . . . so that when sight leaves it it is no longer an eye except homonymously' (*DA*, 412b), much as we might say of a dead body that it is our friend; in one sense it is but in a very different sense it is not. Such a soul is clearly 'not separable from the body' since sight can only exist as the capacity of an eye in working order.[2] The soul of a plant is its capacity to nourish itself, a feature of all life, but this 'nutritive soul' is the *only* potentiality of the vegetable. Thus we properly explain the action of roots in terms of the role they play, given them by nature, in furthering this function of the plant (*DA*, 416a). Living beings cannot properly be understood in the absence of such *teleological* explanations.

Plants are stationary (at least they were to Aristotle's knowledge) but animals are not. Animals move around. They need *perception*; most basically the sense of touch, of which taste is a species, because of its role in nutrition (*DA*, 434b). Thus primitive creatures like starfish make do with touch and taste alone. But the presence of other senses allows for behaviour of increased complexity, promoting in the hierarchy the creatures that have them.

This gives rise to the force of Aristotle's contention that animals can be said to have *desire*; the minimal sense in which they are 'set in motion' by nourishment and can be said to have appetites: 'Those living things that have touch also have desire' (*DA*, 414b). Thus the starfish or sea anemone has *epithumia*; the 'simple' or 'sensual' desire previously discussed. The fox, whether seeking, catching, or consuming, has a more complex variety of it.

The implications of Aristotle's account of animal experience is best brought out by contrast with that of human beings. We bring rationality, in the form of thinking and understanding, to bear upon the psychic faculties we share with plants and the lower animals. (That we *do* share this inheritance ought not to need emphasising.) But rationality brings with it language and the possibility of being correct and incorrect; 'thinking admits of being false and is enjoyed by no animal that does not also have rationality' (*DA*, 427b). Now this affects even what animals can be said to *perceive*. The 'evidence of the senses' can notoriously be mistaken. But not for animals. Thus Aristotle restricts their perception to what he calls 'special sensibles' proper to each sense (except touch): colour is what we *really* see, sound what we hear, flavour what we taste (*DA*, 418a). The feature of these 'sense objects' is that they are incorrigible, they cannot be false. The judgemental aspect of seeing is thus stripped away for animals: 'For the perception of special sensibles is always true and is enjoyed by all animals' (*DA*, 427b). (This statement of the position by Aristotle is slightly misleading since the animal, lacking thought, has the potential for neither falsity *nor* truth.) Yet animals *are* accorded imagination; by which Aristotle means a sort of passive experience without belief or conviction, since these would bring with them possibilities of being correct or incorrect. So animals lack beliefs: 'The conviction that accompanies all belief is produced by persuasion, a task of reason, and while some of the beasts have imagination none has reason' (*DA*, 428a).

Aristotle puts this another way in the *Nicomachean Ethics (NE)*, where he denies that animals can do wrong by acting 'incontinently'; as, for example, a person confused by drink or madness will nonetheless do something foolish yet knowing it to be so. It is 'because they have no universal belief but only an impression and memory of particulars' (*NE*, 1147a 37). They are aware only of wanting what is perceived *here and now*.

So animals can satisfy their appetites; they perceive, pursue or take flight. Young children behave similarly and even adults when, for example, they reach out for support if suddenly made dizzy, or shield their eyes from the sun, or lash out in sudden frenzy. To this extent, all mammals can do what they want when prompted by *epithumia*. This behaviour is voluntary. But they are incapable of other sorts of wanting peculiar to human beings; specifically *wishing* or *choosing*, which involve rationality and a grasp of language:

> Both children and animals have a share in voluntary action, but not in choice. . . . Choice is not shared with man by irrational creatures as desire and temper are.
>
> (*NE*, 1111b 7–9)

It is purposive choice (*prohairesis*) of which animals are incapable. As Aristotle puts it, 'An object of choice is something within our power at which we aim after deliberation' (*NE*, 1113a 11). Deliberation is not within the power of animals. Nor is incontinence, as we have already noted; indeed vice and virtue in general are beyond animals. Yet brutes certainly *appear* to exhibit virtues like courage; 'beasts charging those who have wounded them, are also considered to be courageous' (*NE*, 1116b 29). But the appearances are misleading:

> Courageous people act for a fine motive, and their spirit is an accessory; but beasts act under the influence of pain: it is because they have been injured or frightened; this is shown by the fact that in a forest they do not attack. . . . They rush into danger, blind to the risks they run.
>
> (*NE*, 1116b 32–4)

This is a point of first importance which was alluded to in Chapter 2 in sketching the background to Frey's views. Aristotle is ruling out a purely behavioural account of courage in terms of 'spirit' (*thumos*); certain motives and beliefs are also necessary factors. Motives involve beliefs and since, as we have seen, animals lack these (*DA*, 428a), they are incapable of true courage. In his *Rhetoric(AR)*, Aristotle treats the emotions more systematically but along similar lines. Two examples must suffice. Anger is defined as 'a longing, accompanied by pain, for a real or apparent revenge for a real or apparent slight . . . when such a slight is undeserved' (*AR*, 1378a). Fear is 'a painful or troubled feeling caused by the impression of an imminent evil that causes destruction or pain' (*AR*, 1382a); it is 'accompanied by the expectation that we are going to suffer some fatal misfortune' (*AR*, 1382b). The cognitive elements of belief and assessment necessary for both anger and fear would, given Aristotle's analysis, be beyond the competence of animals and the implications are similar for his accounts in the sequel of love, hate, shame, benevolence and pity. But, as with courage, the brute's behaviour would *resemble* that of a human being similarly situated and can be marked by an appropriate turn of speech which is why 'we do not speak of the brutes as temperate or licentious (*except metaphorically* . . .) because they possess neither choice nor calculation' (*NE*, 1149b, my italics).

Aristotle's sensitive and acute account of animals will not commend itself to liberationists despite its being perfectly consistent with duties of kindness. Admittedly it does not *force* such considerations upon us and Aristotle himself is not inclined to grant any although he does admire the natural instinct for mutual affection in 'birds and most animals' (*NE*, 1155a 18). He argues that 'there can be no friendship or justice towards inanimate things, and not even towards a horse or an ox, nor yet towards a slave qua slave'; going on, typically precise, to permit familiarity with a slave as human being (*NE*, 1161b 1–4). Indeed the social status of tame animals is that of irrational slave; wild ones being less well regarded (*P*, 1254b): 'Plants exist to give subsistence to animals, and animals to give it to men' (*P*, 1256a 28). This legacy passes to Aquinas.

St Thomas Aquinas (1225–74)

Aquinas was, of course, a Christian and the foremost theologian of his, or probably any other, age. Although influenced by numerous writers, as diverse as the neo-Platonist Avicenna and the Jewish Maimonides, his main debt was to Aristotle, referred to in his writings as simply *The Philosopher*. His theology is a subtle synthesis of the Greek inheritance and traditional Christianity, the Old Testament in particular.

His remarks on the nature of non-human animals are scattered thinly throughout a vast and often inaccessible corpus and his eclecticism renders him liable to misreading. Aquinas retains Aristotle's *psychic hierarchy* of plants with 'vegetative' soul, animals with 'sensitive' soul, and human beings with 'rational' powers, to which he adds intelligences without body (angels) of which God is supreme (Gilby 1951: 182–3). Animal souls, being no more than sensitive, are mortal (corruptible) but human souls are immortal because rational (Pegis 1948: 288). However an intriguing wrinkle here is that the human soul is vegetative and sensitive as well (whilst retaining its unity) and, in *its* case, these inferior powers achieve incorruptibility on the coat tails of rationality; hence the 'resurrection of the body' in the *Apostles' Creed*:

> When, therefore, a soul is sensitive only, it is corruptible; but when the intellectual is joined to the sensitive, then the sensitive soul is incorruptible. For although the sensitive does not give incorruptibility, yet it cannot deprive the intellectual of its incorruptibility.
>
> (Pegis 1948: 306)

Appropriately, in *Summa Contra Gentiles*, Aristotle's comparison of animals and slaves is recalled; the order of nature being personified as divine providence which 'makes provision for the intellectual creature for its own sake, but for other creatures for the sake of the intellectual creature . . . every other creature is naturally under slavery' (Regan and Singer 1976: 56–7). This is echoed in *Summa Theologica* (*ST*, I–II, 91, 6), his masterpiece, where animals are ruled by sensuality: 'various natural inclinations, so that what is . . . a law for one, is against the law for another. Thus . . . fierceness is, in a way, the law of a dog, but against the law of a sheep or another meek animal', whereas the 'law of man . . . is that he should act in accordance with reason' (Pegis 1948: 626).

The lack of a rational soul does not, of course, deny some sort of mental life to the lower animals; the question is of *what* sort. Aristotle, as we have seen, asserts that animals (and children) are capable of voluntary action but not deliberative choice (at *NE*, 1111b 7–9); a passage Aquinas quotes with approval. But he refines the analysis (*ST*, I–II, 6, 2) in terms of his own distinction between perfect and imperfect knowledge (quoted in Chapter 1). The human being can give reasons for what he or she is doing; for example, looking for string to tie a parcel, whereas, in the case of animals, we have 'the voluntary in its imperfect nature, inasmuch as the [creature] apprehends the end, but does not deliberate, and is moved to the end at once' (Pegis 1948: 483). Aquinas is simply making a point about the appetitive power of an animal to be attracted to what it perceives; it 'desires the thing seen, not merely for the purpose of seeing it, but also for other purposes' yet is unaware of these 'other purposes' (Pegis 1948: 324). For example, a cheetah chasing a gazelle can rightly be said to intend to catch it, meaning that if we do not interfere and it is not diverted elsewhere then this is what it will probably do; but, if Aquinas is right, it does 'not act intentionally, intending a goal which is the reason for [its] actions' (Kenny 1975: 21). Further implications of this, along Aristotelian lines, are developed (in *ST*, I, 78, 4):

> As nature does not fail in necessary things, there must needs be as many actions of the sensitive soul as may suffice for the life of a perfect animal . . . The animal needs to seek or to avoid certain things . . . because they are pleasing or otherwise to the senses . . . just as the sheep runs away when it sees a wolf, not because of its color or shape, but as a natural enemy. So, too, a bird gathers together straws . . . because they are useful for building its nest. Animals, therefore, need to perceive such intentions, which the exterior sense does not perceive.
>
> (Pegis 1948: 333)

Thus animals *perceive* much as we do. They also appear to have the 'estimative' power to manifest 'intentions' to behave fittingly or otherwise, information not directly given by the senses, and the 'memorative' power to store and recall appropriately. But Aquinas adds an important qualification to these latter powers:

> Other animals perceive these intentions only by some sort of natural instinct, while man perceives them also by means of a certain comparison. Therefore the power which in other animals is called the *natural estimative* in man is called the *cogitative*. . . . As to the memorative power, man has not only memory, as other animals have, in the sudden recollection of the past, but also *reminiscence*, by seeking . . . for a recollection of the past by . . . individual intentions.
>
> (Pegis 1948: 333–4)

In addition to perception, nature has equipped the lower animals with suitable instincts, only *apparent* intentions, which reveal themselves as sudden familiar attraction or repulsion; and that is all. *Homo sapiens* shares these powers but 'perfects' them in its ability to mull over the merits of alternative courses of action, summoning the past to aid its cogitations.

That animals intend and remember *imperfectly* is because they are unable to bring judgement to their performances. This is underlined by Aquinas in his restriction of truth and falsity to beings capable of the intellectual operations of affirmation and denial (*ST*, I, 16, 1–8 and 17, 1–4). Judgements, like beliefs, must be capable of being true or false. He explicitly invokes Aristotle's doctrine of the incorrigibility of the 'special sensibles' proper to each sense; thus, in a sense, the animal sees an object as it truly *is* but it is incapable of *knowing* this because it cannot make judgements.

> Sight is not deceived in its proper sensible. . . . But in affirming and denying, the intellect may be deceived by attributing to the thing . . . something which is not consequent upon it, or is opposed to it.
>
> (Pegis 1948: 188)

These activities of the intellect seem, for Aquinas, necessarily to require the possession of language; at least for terrestrial creatures. This lack would be nature's outward sign of other animals' inward deprivation by comparison with human beings: 'The truth of enunciations is nothing other than the truth of the intellect' (Pegis 1948: 179, 182).

Given that the natural order disposes animals to the uses human beings see fit to put them, it is hardly surprising that the ethical conclusions drawn by Aquinas are fairly uncompromising:

> It is not wrong for man to make use of them, either by killing or in any other way whatever . . . And if any passages of Holy Writ seem to forbid us to be cruel to dumb animals, for instance to kill a bird with its young: this is either to remove a man's thoughts from being cruel to other men . . . or because injury to an animal leads to the temporal hurt of man.
>
> (Regan and Singer 1976: 59)

Given that Aquinas was quite explicit that animals *are* sensitive to pain these conclusions will strike contemporary ears as being harsh. Singer, not surprisingly, regards such 'indirect' grounds for prohibiting cruelty, relating as they do to *human* suffering, as paradigmatic speciesism. (The validity of such defences is discussed in Chapter 7.)

René Descartes (1596–1650)

An otherwise appreciative letter from the English philosopher Henry More to Descartes, written in 1648, rebukes the by then internationally known scholar on one particular topic:

> But there is nothing in your opinions that so much disgusts me, so far as I have any kindness or gentleness, as the internecine and murderous view which you bring forward in the *Method*, which snatches away life and sensibility from all the animals
> (Williams 1978: 282)

Descartes replied in conciliatory fashion:

> There is no prejudice to which we are all more accustomed from our earliest years than the belief that dumb animals think. Our only reason for this belief is the fact that we see that many of the organs of animals are not very different from ours. . . . Since we believe that there is a single principle within us which causes these motions – namely the soul, which both moves the body and thinks – we do not doubt that some such soul is to be found in animals also.
> (Kenny 1970: 243)

Against the background of Aristotle and Aquinas this might strike us as unexceptional. Descartes, an admirer of both, appears to be doing no more than denying animals a rational soul. But the stakes are far higher; as More's letter implies. As Descartes puts it in his celebrated scientific treatise the *Principles of Philosophy* (1644), 'By the word thought I understand all that of which we are conscious as operating in us. And that is why not alone understanding, willing, imagining, but also feeling, are here the same thing as thought' (Haldane and Ross 1970: I.222; H & R). Perception, in the form of seeing, and sensation are subsumed by thought in the same passage. If Descartes has indeed unmasked a mere prejudice, then its significance puts the views of his predecessors in the shade; animals not only do not think, they do not perceive, choose, nor feel. They are not conscious. So what *are* they? Descartes' answer is deceptively simple. They are *automata*, akin to the ever more ingenious mechanical toys with which the leisured classes of that time used to amuse themselves; but of a superior sort.[3] 'It seems reasonable', he continues in the same letter to More,

> since art copies nature, and men can make various automata which move without thought, that nature should produce its own automata, much more splendid than artificial ones. These natural automata are the animals.
>
> (Kenny 1970: 244)

Descartes' view is *deceptively* straightforward. It isn't crazy; although its implications aroused the ire of an Englishman like More, with his horses and hounds, and were later ridiculed by Voltaire (1694–1778). The view that animals are automata crops up frequently, although not obsessively, in Descartes' writings. The most instructive source is his first published work (1636), referred to by Henry More, the cumbrously entitled *Discourse on the Method of Rightly Conducting the Reason and Seeking for Truth in the Sciences*. Here, as we shall see, the context is important. The passage in which animals are described as 'automata' and then 'machines' follows immediately upon a detailed physiological account of the *human* body in which it is summed up as 'a machine which, having been made by the hands of God, is incomparably better arranged . . . than any of those which can be invented by man' (H & R, I.116). Given the full title of the *Discourse*, it is now possible to see that his account of animals is not some insidiously motivated apologia for slaughtering the furred and feathered but follows naturally as part of his overall metaphysical programme which was to integrate revealed truth (religion), calculative method (philosophy) and the external facts of animate and inanimate existence.

At the heart of the problem lies Descartes' dualism. He divides reality exhaustively into *res cogitans* (thinking substance) and *res extensa* (extended substance). The former includes human and divine minds; it is incorporeal and, to put it baldly, in no way competes for space with *res extensa*, which is everything else including organic bodies. *Res cogitans* is consciousness; and from the omnipresence of this, Descartes derives the certainty of the statement for which he is most famous, *I think, therefore I am* (H & R, I.221). The strategy here is to establish the true essence of the person as being a function of consciousness, which is quite separate from the fact that it inhabits a body.

Nonetheless the consciousness, the soul or mind, *does* find itself within a body with which it is intimately connected, 'from the fact that pain and other of our sensations occur without our foreseeing them; and that mind is conscious that these do not arise from itself alone' (H & R, I.255). But, in a significant way, the body is self-subsistent. However, the relatively straightforward bodily machine of the *Discourse* is much complicated, in the case of human beings, by the addition of soul since the relationship is one of mutual interaction. Clearly I become conscious of states of my body if I stub my toe or when the purely physical reaction of the eye to light is translated into my seeing a rainbow. Conversely, my courage and pity give rise to the gymnastics of climbing a tree to rescue a cat. But it must be remembered that this cosy interosculation is of *res extensa* (the body) with an incorporeal *res cogitans*, whose contents (thoughts, choices, desires, wishes, perceptions) do not have spatial dimension. So how *can* changes in one bring about changes in the other? Descartes' attempt to square this particular circle in *The Passions of the Soul* turns out, not surprisingly, to be an exercise in controlled obscurity. He explains in great detail that the main seat of interaction is the pineal gland, or conarion (Article 31), and in Article 34 states that its mobility permits it to be agitated by the bodily animal spirits and 'that it may also be moved in diverse ways by the soul' (H & R, I.347). But the *possibility* of interaction is never questioned.

The problematical nature of mind–body interaction is of direct relevance to Descartes' explicit discussion of animals. Clearly the culprit is his *dualism*, specifically the mutual exclusiveness of the two parties. Yet if dualism is put at risk then Descartes will also be deprived of his most destructive weapon against animals. This is demonstrated by a passage from a letter written by Descartes in 1647 to the Abbé Claude Picot:

> The brute beasts who have only their bodies to preserve, devote their constant attention to the search for the sources of their nourishment; but men, in whom the principal part is the mind, ought to make their principal care the search after wisdom.
>
> (H & R, I.205)

An Aristotle or Aquinas may well be joined by the intelligent reader in commending such sentiments. Urging the pursuit of wisdom upon even intelligent chimpanzees like Washoe would be a waste of breath since their possession of 'sensitive' souls limits them to conscious appetitive endeavours. Nor would theological difficulties ensue for such souls are not incorruptible. But Descartes' dualism forbids such a view. *Any* consciousness involves the presence of *res cogitans*; it cannot exist in an attenuated form. One either has a soul or one doesn't; animals do not. The brute beast's search for nourishment must be a non-conscious search; like that, perhaps, of an electronic scanner. Bernard Williams (1978) makes a similar point:

> It is one product of his 'all or nothing' account of mind and consciousness: either a creature has the full range of conscious powers, and is capable of language and abstract thought as well as sensation and feelings of hunger, or it is an automaton, with no experience of any kind.
>
> (Williams 1978: 284)

Thus Descartes can hold that the language test is absolutely conclusive. It is employed in the *Discourse* as the first of 'two very certain tests' to detect counterfeit human beings; ones with machine bodies like our own but lacking souls. Such human automata might 'emit some responses' to specific stimuli but it could never happen, he argues, 'that it arranges its speech in various ways, in order to reply appropriately to everything that may be said in its presence, as even the lowest type of man can do' (H & R, I.116). Descartes' second test is that our reason provides for a flexibility of response to complex demands far surpassing the stereotyped reactions of a machine; the animal analogue that he has in mind here is clearly instinct. The human automaton would fail both tests but the difference between man and animal is that a machine 'possessing the organs and outward form of a monkey or some other animal without reason' would be indistinguishable from the real thing (116).

The argument in the letter of 1646 to the Marquess of Newcastle goes into more detail on the man–animal differences revealed by these tests. 'Words, or other signs that are relevant to particular topics without expressing any passion' are the only outward mark of inward thought. 'These signs must be relevant, to exclude the speech of parrots, without excluding the speech of madmen . . . even though it does not follow reason' (Kenny 1970: 206). The refusal to countenance words or signs that express a 'passion' is particularly intriguing. Descartes' aim is to rule out,

> Not only cries of joy or sadness and the like, but also whatever can be taught by training to animals. If you teach a magpie to say good-day to its mistress, when it sees her approach, this can

only be by making the utterance of this word the expression . . . of the hope of eating, if it has always been given a titbit when it says it.

(Kenny 1970: 206–7)

There is an acute insight here and similar arguments are often used to discredit the Ameslan apes; the objection being that the correct sign-response is cued not by grasping the *meaning* of what was originally signed but by the reinforcement effect of rewards. But the apes are nonetheless conscious. Descartes wishes to *rule out* such quasi-verbal performances because, in his view, they do not necessarily require any awareness whatsoever; they are just physical effects of the nervous system. He has clarified this in an earlier passage of the letter in referring to a whole clutch of *human* actions which 'are not guided by our thoughts'; walking or eating absent-mindedly, parrying blows, and sleep-walking. Most importantly in this context, he includes the movements of our passions which,

> even though in us they are accompanied with thought . . . it is none the less very clear that they do not depend on thought, because they often occur in spite of us. Consequently they can also occur in animals . . . without our being able to conclude from that that they have thoughts.

(Kenny 1970: 206)

It is true, as Williams points out, that Descartes' examples are a mixed bag. (There is, for example, a considerable difference between walking without thinking about it and doing it in one's sleep.) But what is more important, in clarifying his position, is that he *believes* such human behaviour is literally thoughtless. So the 'cries of joy or sadness and the like', in the earlier quotation, probably refer to human outbursts of passion that we simply find ourselves giving voice to. But the then becoming aware of the passion does not, Descartes thinks, require that consciousness was required to mediate at its onset.

In some ways, Descartes' view of animals is made that much more plausible by his taking account of marginal human behaviour which, as he sees it, being simply that of the bodily machine and not involving the soul, is identical with that of the lower animals. There is, at least, the acknowledgement that in significant respects we *are* animals, something which Darwin was to emphasise, and it would be possible to conclude that we share a common ancestry with them (a contention that Descartes, for theological reasons, would not have been prepared to concede). Yet this coin has another side. His insistence that we may use the terminology of human mental experience of animals, yet requiring that it be disinfected of any taint of consciousness, might serve to undermine his view from an unexpected direction. We have already seen that in this special sense the magpie expresses a passion, in its case the hope of eating, and a few lines further on he writes of dogs, horses, and monkeys which give expression to 'their fear, their hope, or their joy' (Kenny 1970: 207). In a letter of 1637 he discusses the sense in which animals *see*: 'My view is that animals do not see as we do when we are aware that we see, but only as we do when our mind is elsewhere. In such a case . . . we too move just like automata' (Kenny 1970: 36). In the next paragraph he allows that there are souls of animals but 'they are nothing but their blood, the blood which is turned into spirits by the warmth of the heart'. In writing to the Abbé Picot, as we have noted, Descartes mentions the brute beast's constant preoccupation with the search for nourishment and, in the famous letter to Henry More, he does not deny *life* to animals, 'as consisting simply in the heat of the heart; and I do not deny sensation, in so far as it depends on a bodily organ' (Kenny 1970: 245). It is no surprise to learn from an earlier work that this is the lowest grade of sensation, to which 'belongs the immediate affection of the bodily organ by external objects; and this can be nothing else than the motion of the particles of the sensory organs'; it isn't until the mind is involved that we get *perceptions* of pain, hunger, colours and the rest (H & R, II.251).

The question is whether Descartes can speak this way yet still maintain the view that animals are *machines*:

> Doubtless when the swallows come in spring, they operate like clocks. The actions of honey bees are of the same nature . . . and of apes in fighting, if it is true that they keep discipline. Their instinct to bury their dead is no stranger than that of dogs and cats who scratch the earth for the purpose of burying their excrement; they hardly ever actually bury it, which shows that they act only by instinct and without thinking.
>
> (Kenny 1970: 207)

It is easiest to fault Descartes' remarks about the *visual* powers of animals. Let us grant his point that animals *see* as a human being does when 'our mind is elsewhere' (Kenny 1970: 36). But this is not failing to *see*. A walker does not cease to see the obstacles negotiated just because her mind is wholly preoccupied with the demands of the day ahead, nor is her walking transformed into that of an automaton. Descartes is wrongly taking our normal state of vision to be that which is accompanied by the relatively rare act of reflection *that* we are seeing. So by his own admission animals see very well. Furthermore, his very reasonable observation about the obsessive appetitive conduct of some animals is precisely what we do *not* observe in machines and (as we noted in the criticism of Frey's comparing the needs of animals with those of tractors) can serve as a ground for morally distinguishing the two.

To reply on Descartes' behalf by citing nature's power to create perfect automata, which replicate obsessional appetition, is to overlook the obvious fact that such creations, were they indistinguishable from the 'real thing' in every respect, would qualify *as* the real thing; as he himself admits in the *Discourse* (H & R, I.116). In like manner the special senses that Descartes gives to the *life* and *sensation* of animals have a hollow ring to them. It may well make more sense to say that the heart's heat, rather than the action of an incorporeal soul, is the *source* of life but then it will be the complexity of the resultant behaviour which is *life itself*. In similar vein we could argue that Descartes' lowest grade of sensation results from a confused conflation of what is admittedly a necessary condition for sensation or perception, namely a healthy organ (for example, a light-sensitive retina and optic nerve), with what it gives rise to in the organism (the dog's screeching when struck or leaping to catch a ball in its mouth). It is only Descartes' doctrinaire assumption that consciousness is a sort of inner light, shed by an incorporeal source, which is exclusive to an apparently arbitrary range of beings, which necessitates his resort to the special senses of mental predicates. Yet, even on this cardinal point, the two letters contain passages betraying Descartes' unease. In that of 1646, noting the likeness between the bodily organs of animals and our own, he rather lamely allows that 'it may be conjectured that there is attached to those organs some thoughts such as we experience in ourselves, but of a very much less perfect kind' (Kenny 1970: 208). And to More he is prepared to grant that although we cannot prove that animals think, nor can we be certain that they do *not*, 'since the human mind does not reach into their hearts' (244). A reader could be forgiven for thinking that Descartes' opening charge of prejudice, against the belief that animals share a consciousness in some respects like our own, might more justly be levelled at his own dualism.

Nonetheless, whatever its faults, Descartes' bold and acute account of animals as automata, although rarely in their best interests, has been highly influential; which is why no account of animals is complete without it. The quotation above, from the letter to the Marquess of Newcastle, juxtaposing the alleged clock-like behaviour of the swallows, bees, apes, and dogs, yet in the same breath referring to their *instincts*, is a microcosm of the debate over the merits of behaviourism which has dominated twentieth-century ethology. Descartes, arguing from a mainly theoretical rather than experimental basis, anticipates the late nineteenth-century physiologists like Ebbinghaus and Thorndike for whom the basic tool with which to explain animal behaviour was the reflex. The problem was whether the discovery by Pavlov that such reflexes could be conditioned, for which he earned the Nobel Prize in 1904, provided the explanatory wherewithal to account satisfactorily for animal learning and instincts. Here is W.H. Thorpe's description of behaviourism which might well have been written for Descartes:

> This school prided itself on being purely objective, inclining to a rigid mechanistic outlook and dispensing with any vague and unnecessary concepts involving mind. In short, it implied that it was a physiological rather than a psychological system.
>
> (Lorenz 1964: xi)

Empiricist reactions: animals revived

Descartes' influence was considerable upon his immediate followers for whom the cutting up of myriad animals, in ways that would now strike us as barbarous, became something of a vogue. But what exasperated the critics, and the Cartesians were not short of them, was the impossibility of eliciting any remorse for what the experimenter claimed was no worse than machine-breaking.

Voltaire, unencumbered by preconceptions about *res cogitans*, reverted to the observed similarities of anatomy and sympathetic behaviour such as a pet's faithfulness and, in his *Philosophical Dictionary* published in 1764, pours scorn upon such intellectual gymnastics:

> What a pitiful thing, what poor stuff it is to say that animals are machines deprived of knowledge and feeling. . . . Barbarians seize this dog who so prodigiously surpasses man in friendship. They nail him to a table and dissect him alive to show you the mesenteric veins. You discover in him all the same organs of feeling that you possess. Answer me, mechanist, has nature

arranged all the springs of feeling in this animal in order that he should not feel? Does he have nerves to be impassive? Do not assume that nature presents this impertinent contradiction.

(Voltaire 1971: 64–5)

Views consonant with those of Voltaire, typified in the letter from Henry More to Descartes, prevailed also in England, where Cartesianism had little impact. The writings of its two most famous philosophers of the period, John Locke and David Hume, continued in this vein of generous common sense and form a backdrop to the views of Darwin.

John Locke (1632–1704): Locke was a speculative psychologist. He sets out to explain, most notably in *An Essay Concerning Human Understanding* of 1690, how the mind, which he depicts as a sort of internal theatre of *ideas*, comes by the knowledge that it has. Secondly, however, his method of proceeding is not by way of the dissecting scalpel nor the Skinner-box but by elaborating and building upon principles of his own devising. Although such methods are often derided by contemporary practitioners as 'armchair' theorising, the history of the natural sciences shows, even in areas like particle physics and astronomy, that speculation can be prophetic in anticipating what research will later confirm. In the field of animal consciousness, where a mountain of experimental data is useless without proper philosophical analysis, the armchair is even less to be despised.

The acquisition of knowledge is a sequence, Locke argues, the first step of which is perception being 'the inlet of all the materials of it' (1965: I.117). He has no doubts that animals do perceive: '*perception* seems to me to be that which *puts the distinction betwixt the animal kingdom and the inferior parts of nature*', plant life being 'all bare mechanism' (I.115–16). Perception is present in all sorts of animals, the only limitation being the state of the senses. Thus 'an *oyster* or *cockle*' will have fewer and more sluggish senses than other animals, as benefits its limited lifestyle, but is little different, he adds, from a human being afflicted with extreme decrepitude. This ominous aside is typical of his strategy. Locke is at pains to point to the continuum of all animal life, human and otherwise, even reminding us of 'what is confidently reported of mermaids or sea-men', observing that there are 'some brutes that seem to have as much knowledge and reason as some that are called men' (II.50).

The 'simple' ideas introduced into the mind by perception are then processed in various ways. They are kept in mind by contemplation and then 'laid aside out of sight' and, with varying degrees of success, revived again in the absence of the objects which initiated them. This is the power of memory, 'which is as it were the storehouse of our *ideas*' (I.117). 'Several *other animals*' seem to have it to a great degree, as well as man, and Locke supports this with the curious example of birds learning tunes (I.122): 'It cannot with any appearance of reason be supposed . . . that birds, without sense and memory, can approach their notes nearer and nearer by degrees to a tune played yesterday', unless they retain an *idea* of it. (The contexts that Locke must have had in mind are hardly everyday occurrences and he might have been better served by something more mundane, such as the agitations of a dog prompting its master to take it for a walk. But his point is clear enough.) Now ideas perceived or revived must be *discriminated* between, such as sweet from bitter or red from green, or the mind will be of little use. An associated power is that of *comparing* ideas in various respects ('extent, degrees, time, place'). Human beings, Locke argues, are far more dynamic than animals in these respects since they can 'cast about' and consider fresh bases for estimation whereas, he writes, '*beasts compare* not their *ideas* further than some sensible circumstances annexed to the objects themselves' (I.124–5). His view seems close to that of Aristotle's *epithumia*; the discrimination of brutes is limited to what, in some form, they are directly perceiving: the smell of friend or foe, the sound or sight of prey or predator. Yet even this way of putting it is unduly permissive since 'friend', 'prey', and similar ideas are *complex* ones, and '*brutes* come far short of men' in the ability to collate the several simple ideas necessary for a complex one.

Locke is here anticipating a great deal of recent experimental work on the capacity of various creatures for what is called cross-modal comparison; although he is, of course, just theorising. The dog, let us say, has the simple ideas of a shape, smell and vocal sound whereby (*we* say) it knows its master; yet for the dog they remain, as Locke puts it, 'distinct marks'. It cannot compound the several distinct marks into the one character. And he offers supporting instances, anecdotal but not irrelevant, of animals being far more easily deceived than would be human beings by their reactions to just one of the simple ideas in the absence of the others; such as that of the canine bitch who accepts foxcubs as her own pups 'if you can get them once to suck her so long that her milk may go through them' (I.125).

But the decisive break between the human and nonhuman begins, for Locke, with the child's use of *words*. Language involves *abstraction*, in the sense that, for example, the word 'tree' gives a general significance to the separate complex ideas which a person will have formed of this or that individual tree. The word 'tree' stands for a *general* idea which abstracts from the differences between trees as such. The vocalisations of animals fail to achieve this, Locke contends, 'for parrots and several other birds will be taught to make articulate sounds distinct enough, which yet by no means are capable of language' (II.9). And of the brute creation in general Locke concludes: 'This, I think, I may be positive in, that the power of *abstracting* is not at all in them; and that the having of general *ideas* is that which puts a perfect distinction betwixt man and brutes' (I.126).

Locke's intention is clear enough. Parrots seem to speak but because they lack the power to form general ideas, which give meaning to words, they do not really speak. That an animal reacts to white objects (or spherical, moving or only animate ones) would, for Locke, be a tribute to its powers of discrimination but would in no way be evidence that it was aware of, or understood, what it was doing. That an infant duck unfailingly picks out its mother from a crowd, or the human or other surrogate upon which it might have 'imprinted' instead, provides classic ethological evidence of release mechanisms which may be cued by visual features of the adult in question, but says nothing of the baby creature's grasp of abstraction (Walker 1983: 212). Indeed even to speak of *recognition* in cases like this, without implicit qualification, is misleading hyperbole.

Some commentators, like Walker, put considerable emphasis upon Locke's allowance of some reason to animals since this is so often seen as the power which irrevocably divides the species. But what Locke does allow (Bk 2, Ch. 11, 11–12) is so qualified by his reservations about abstraction as again to recall the arguments of Aquinas. With Descartes' dismission of animals in mind, Locke states that,

> if they have any *ideas* at all and are not bare machines (as some would have them) we cannot deny them to have some reason. . . . But it is only in particular *ideas*, just as they received them from their senses. They are the best of them tied up within those narrow bounds.
>
> (Locke 1965: I.127)

With the denial of any faculty of abstraction he goes on to compare animals with similarly deprived human deficients (of a sort called, rather quaintly, 'naturals') whose defining feature, compared with 'madmen', is that *they are deprived of reason* (I.127). Locke's admission could hardly be less generous; it amounts to little more than that animals *perceive*. This, as we have already seen, is what distinguishes the 'animal kingdom and the inferior parts of nature' (I.115). Indeed his use of the term 'reason' in this context seems almost disingenuous.

David Hume (1711-76): If, as I have suggested, a careful reading of *An Essay Concerning Human Understanding* reveals that far less is conceded to the mental wherewithal of the brutes than appears at first glance, then Hume, Locke's equally illustrious successor, more than redresses the balance. In *An Enquiry Concerning Human Understanding*, published in 1748, and more stridently, in *A Treatise of Human Nature* of 1739, his earlier masterpiece, Hume anticipates Voltaire's argument that the continuum of physiological make-up and behavioural repertoire is enough to establish that any differences between the mental capacities of the human and nonhuman are matters of mere degree.

Hume justifies this procedure, with typical stylistic bravura in the *Enquiry* (Sect. XI), as a paradigm of the only possible way to establish facts by his empiricist methods. It is,

> a species of Analogy, which leads us to expect from any cause the same events, which we have observed to result from similar causes. . . . The anatomical observations, formed upon one animal, are, by this species of reasoning, extended to all animals . . . and any theory, by which we explain the operations of the understanding, or . . . of the passions in man, will acquire additional authority, if we find, that the same theory is requisite to explain the same phenomena in all other animals.
>
> (Hume 1902: 104)

So by 'analogy' we learn the facts of life: that pain follows a punch, nourishment a good meal, that winter gives way to spring, and day to night. But animals too, as Hume observes, learn from experience and (note how he puts this) they 'infer, that the same events will always follow from the same causes'. As they develop, they 'treasure up a knowledge of the nature of fire, water, earth, stones, heights, depths, &c., and of the effects which result from their operation' (1902: 105). Hume is here talking of mammals like horses and greyhounds; the same would not apply 'by analogy' to cockles or termites. Thus will a dog, from experience, answer the call of its name or cower if its master 'lift up the whip to beat him' (105).

Now although the animal is described as having made an 'inference' and as having expectations, Hume appears to qualify the attribution. 'It is impossible', he continues, that its state of mind 'can be founded on any process of argument or reasoning' about causes and effects (106). Is this to be the point at which the human intelligence asserts its superioriority over the animal? Surprisingly Hume is not at all clear. It seems as if the answer is to be Yes, since if the missing arguments *were* available they may well be too abstruse for all but the 'care and attention of a philosophic genius'. He makes this admission but undermines its objectionable implications by the not uncommon strategy of claiming that what appears to demarcate animals turns out to be a human trait. (This recalls the liberationists' appeal to infants and imbeciles.) Animals have 'imperfect understandings'; this is the mark of their not being guided by reasoning. But, Hume adds, children are no better nor, more importantly, most adults in the normal course of events. He even includes 'philosophers themselves, who, in all the active parts of life, are, in the main, the same with the vulgar, and are governed by the same maxims' (106).

Hume employs similar strategies to undermine an appeal to instincts, of which a certain amount had been known and documented since ancient times. He admits that much knowledge is of this sort, 'in which they improve, little or nothing, by the longest practice and experience' (108). But there is nothing extraordinary in this, he reminds us, since the 'experimental reasoning itself, which we possess in common with beasts' (a product of *custom*, as we were previously informed), is itself:

> Nothing but a species of instinct or mechanical power, that acts in us unknown to ourselves. . . . Though the instinct be different, yet still it is an instinct, which teaches a man to avoid the fire; as much as that, which teaches a bird, with such exactness, the art of incubation, and the whole economy and order of its nursery.
>
> (Hume 1902: 108)

The previous discussion should serve to explain *why* Hume makes this claim but it is, nonetheless, highly contentious. He seems to be ignoring the important distinctions we would wish to draw between habitual behaviour, such as going to church or washing up, automatic or unthinking actions, like walking or chewing one's food, and reflexes such as blinking and blushing. Some will be premeditated, some cannot be; others we will justify and yet others be totally unaware of. And which of these types of behaviour does that of Hume's bird most resemble? Would the actions of a man and wife building a shed in their garden be as instinctive, for Hume, as those of the bird and its mate? Is a bird as *aware* of what it does instinctively as a boy, swarming in the branches of a tree, is? To none of these important sorts of question does Hume's analysis in the *Enquiry* offer answers.

The argument in the earlier *Treatise* is more clear-cut and pulls fewer punches:

> No truth appears to me more evident, than that the beasts are endowed with thought and reason as well as man. The arguments are in this case so obvious, that they never escape the most stupid and ignorant. . . . The very first action of the first animal we shall please to pitch on, will afford us an incontestable argument . . .
>
> (Hume 1911: I.173)

He distinguishes the actions of animals which are 'on a level with their common capacities', a dog's avoiding precipices and shunning strangers, and 'extraordinary instances of sagacity', evidenced by the same bird (here ten years younger, of course) busy about its maternal preparations at the proper time, 'with all the precaution that a chemist is capable of in the most delicate projection' (1911: I.174). It is a pity that Hume's analysis of animal reason (in Bk I.3. XVI) in terms of mounting experience of cause-and-effect relationships is entirely upon the model of the first type of behaviour, the dog's, rather than that of the bird. Quite clearly the complex nest-building and incubation repertoire is of more moment because it appears *not* to be based upon anything the creature has learned, and furthermore, as in our response to his argument in the *Enquiry*, it is vital to know how seriously Hume intends the comparison between the 'sagacity' of the bird and the projections of the chemist. Furthermore, unless there is reason to suppose that Hume is speaking idly or metaphorically, and commentators are divided over his proneness to this, then we must ponder the depth and sophistication of what he believes to be plausibly attributable to animals *in the absence of linguistic ability*; a phenomenon that he never discusses.

Charles Darwin (1809–82): scientific rigour and anecdotal optimism

That animals and human beings present a continuum of development, physical and psychical, in some cases including vegetable life, has been mooted by all the thinkers we have discussed (including Descartes, albeit at the level of body). But only Aristotle, in his treatises on the parts and processes of animals (which I did not discuss), attempts any sort of descriptive taxonomy of the process and, in his case, a teleological theory to account for it. His achievement is still the admiration of an esoteric band of historians of science. With Darwin's immensely erudite and detailed evolutionary account in *The Origin of Species* (1859) and *The Descent of Man* (1871), the continuum is not only established experimentally but the supporting theory is anything but esoteric; it is one of the most celebrated pieces of science in the western world.

Darwin's theories deserve some scrutiny, given my concerns in this book, because uncritical readers have a tendency to assume that because of his immense scientific stature, everything that he had to say about the mental competence of animals (and he was by no means silent) carries the imprimatur of that authority. But informed opinion is far more divided than this. His scientific achievement was to develop the physical underpinnings of a psychic hierarchy, reminiscent of Aristotle's, from the known facts of domestic horticulture and animal husbandry. Darwin's most fruitful examples were taken from the flourishing field of pigeon-fancying in which expert breeders had deliberately produced varieties of such individuality that they might be thought different birds, yet all were known to have descended directly from the Indian rock-pigeon (Walker 1983: 42). Darwin posed the seminal question: Why not a similar process, without intentional human agency and over a greater period of time, to generate the even more dramatic variations within the whole animal kingdom?

As is well known, a substitute agency *was* at hand in the form of the much-discussed theories of the clergyman Thomas Malthus (1766–1834) who contended that population growth would render the world intolerable if not checked by war, famine, disease and moral restraint. Since this grave theory gave every appearance of applying with even more plausibility to the uninhibited world of the brute beasts, the idea of nature being a 'struggle for existence' became Darwin's principle of *natural*, rather than human, *selection*. Such an environment, in which creatures increase at a far greater rate than available nourishment, ensures that statistically those fittest to survive will do so for longer, and will benefit from the added opportunities of reproducing themselves, than those less well equipped. The superior will predominate as species unless and until new competition arises. The theory places every facet of behaviour and equipage under the scrutiny of survival value. Of central importance are strategies which contribute to prolific breeding because only thus will adaptations conducive to survival tend to be passed on to future generations at a greater rate than useless ones. This Darwin termed *sexual selection*. Modern Darwinism has incorporated genetic implications into sexual selection, and its use of the term 'inclusive fitness' emphasises 'the degree to which an individual's genes are included in the next generation' (Walker 1983: 44). So the 'survival of the fittest', despite often being used as a slogan to describe the theory in its entirety, is at best only a necessary condition for a species' success. Of equal importance is that it reproduces prolifically.

Darwin's treatment of sexual selection provides an unusual transition to the issue of mental competence. Vocalisation, particularly by birds, plays a key role in many courtship displays and he devised the intriguing hypothesis that the human vocal organs were originally employed for this purpose: 'some early progenitor of man, probably first used his voice in producing true musical cadences, that is in singing, as do some of the gibbon-apes at the present day; and . . . that this power would have been especially exerted during the courtship of the sexes' (Darwin 1909: 133). At best it would have been one of several possible functions of vocal display and soon subordinated to its use as a vehicle for 'long trains of thought' (134) and 'the power of forming general concepts' (135). The account is illuminating in giving further credence to the biological continuity of verbal and pre-verbal vocalisation, observable in the language-learning of human infants, which is stressed in many contemporary theories (and to which Wittgenstein gives support). The more historical implication, which Darwin also seems to have drawn, that language developed in its complexity by minimal steps, is far more contentious (137). It might lead us to expect that the languages of recent so-called primitive tribes would betray this in their structure. This appears not to be the case. In the words of the linguistician, John Lyons, 'there is no group of human beings, in existence at present or known to have existed in the past, which does not possess a "fully developed" language' (1970: 10).

In Chapters 3 and 4 of *The Descent of Man* (1871), Darwin explicitly compares the 'mental powers of man and the lower animals' (1909: 98). It must be borne in mind in assessing his contribution here that the bald scientific fact that something *B* evolved from something else *A* does not, of itself, provide a basis for comparison. The fertilised egg, or zygote, that becomes the 21-year-old Einstein, or the bulb that develops into a daffodil, have nothing in common except perhaps a genetic or similar structure. But the 10-year-old *child* Einstein has a great deal in common with his adult self. Now the Darwin of these chapters of *The Descent of Man* is not the impartial zoologist of *The Origin of Species*, citing his research to support his conclusions, but a man with a mission whose methodology is strongly reminiscent of David Hume's. Furthermore, he was a celebrity who received regular correspondence from naturalists and pet owners and he, and his associates like G.J. Romanes, were prepared to use such testimony to support the case that 'there is no fundamental difference between man and the higher mammals in their mental faculties' (1909: 99). But nonetheless, the details of competence do vary and he admits that in respect of mental power,

No doubt the difference in this respect is enormous even if we compare the mind of one of the lowest savages, who has no words to express any number higher than four . . . with that of the most highly organised ape.

(98)

As if to pre-empt the hopes of the Gardners for their protégé Washoe a century later, he adds that, 'the difference would, no doubt, still remain immense, even if one of the higher apes had been improved or civilised as much as a dog has been in comparison with its parent-form, the wolf or jackal'. But, despite all this, Darwin is hard pressed to pin down the difference. It is beyond the ape to 'follow out a train of metaphysical reasoning, or solve a mathematical problem, or reflect on God, or admire a grand natural scene' (192–3) and Darwin allows it to 'be freely admitted that no animal is self-conscious' (127), but if these are preferred as distinctive contrasts he is ready with the empiricist's appeal to marginal cases: 'At what age does the new-born infant possess the power of abstraction, or become self-conscious, and reflect on its own existence?' (193–4). And, he adds, 'the half-art, half-instinct of language still bears the stamp of its gradual evolution', which is nicely-put but not, as we have just seen, grounds for a pejorative comparison. Even the 'feeling of religious devotion' is not an exclusively human pastime, for 'we see some distant approach to this state of mind in the deep love of a dog for its master . . . Professor Braubach [1869] goes so far as to maintain that a dog looks on his master as on a god' (146). Darwin is finally reduced to the criterion of the *moral sense*, 'summed up in that short but imperious word *ought*, so full of high significance' (148), which 'perhaps affords the best and highest distinction between man and the lower animals' (194).

The comparison with Hume is most marked in Darwin's rugged conviction in simply-drawn analogies. The lower animals 'manifestly feel pleasure and pain, happiness and misery . . . Even insects play together, as has been described by that excellent observer, P. Huber [in 1810], who saw ants chasing and pretending to bite each other, like so many puppies' (Darwin 1909: 104). Fear and similar emotions affect the human and nonhuman in the same ways and both are capable of suspicion and love. He approves of anecdotes 'published on the long-delayed and artful revenge' of decoy elephants and monkeys, and relishes the story of Sir Andrew Smith who was eye-witness to a baboon's retaliation upon an officer, who had long mistreated it, by bombarding him with a hastily constructed mud-pie on his way to Sunday's parade: 'For long afterwards the baboon rejoiced and triumphed whenever he saw his victim' (105). And it comes as little surprise when we are assured that animals can be easily offended: 'Several observers have stated that monkeys certainly dislike being laughed at; and they sometimes invent imaginary offences' (108). Yet what strange attributions these are, given that only a few pages later Darwin grants that it is 'freely admitted that no animal is self-conscious' (127).

The attributions and the anecdotes continue apace and Darwin seems so sure of his sources that supporting argument is thought unnecessary. Those purporting to demonstrate reasoning ability are the most prolific: 'Animals may constantly be seen to pause, deliberate, and resolve' (114). He clearly outbids John Locke in extending this to abstraction: 'But when a dog sees another dog at a distance, it is often clear that he perceives that it is a dog in the abstract; for when he gets nearer his whole manner suddenly changes, if the other dog be a friend' (126-7). (What a curious conclusion to draw from such an event.) Most intriguing of all, however, is the account by a Mr Colquhoun of the sagacity of his gun-dog, a retriever, who was faced with the task of bringing in two ducks who had been winged and come to ground on the far side of a stream. Failing to gather both together, the dog, 'though never before known to ruffle a feather, deliberately killed one, brought over the other, and returned for the dead bird' (118–19). (The reader could be forgiven for fancying that this retriever was 'some early progenitor' of the police dog cited by Bernard Rollin.)

Why this credulousness? Walker's suggestion, and it has support from other sources, is that Darwin's 'quaint, if not slightly ridiculous' methods were 'partly due to a desire to support his contention that human intellectual abilities do not provide an exception to the theory of evolution' (1983: 47). Perhaps so; although it would have been a misconception on Darwin's part since the theory is perfectly well equipped to account for differences of outcome, nor would modern Darwinians cease to be so were they to hold, as they invariably do, that their own mental competence was of a different order to that of the rest of the animal kingdom.

Our conclusion must be that Darwin's contribution to our understanding of animals has something of a Jekyll-and-Hyde character about it. His account of their mental powers, and the Hume-like analogies with those of human beings, quickly came under fire from experimental psychologists and biologists like Lloyd Morgan, E.L. Thorndike and Pavlov. This marked the beginnings of behaviourism. Even modern-day liberationists who, as we have seen, are not averse to their own anecdotal methods, nonetheless find those of Darwin unappealing and seldom enlist his aid.[4] Yet the seminal brilliance of his contribution to the science of evolutionary theory remains as vital as ever. Writing in 1970, François Jacob, a Nobel Prize winner for Medicine, summed up his own view of the modern legacy:

Originally the theory of evolution was based on morphological, embryological and paleontological data. During the present century, it has been strengthened by a series of results harvested by genetics, biochemistry and molecular biology. All the information coming from various fields is combined in what is known as modern Darwinism . . . The chance that this theory *as a whole* will some day be refuted is now close to zero.

(Jacob 1989: 371)

5

LUDWIG WITTGENSTEIN: LANGUAGE-GAMES AND PRIMITIVE BEINGS

Introduction

> I ought to be no more than a mirror, in which my reader can see his own thinking with all its deformities so that, helped in this way, he can put it right.
>
> (Wittgenstein 1980a: 18)

This fragment from 1931, although not published until 1980 in *Culture and Value*, will surprise most readers accustomed to academic theorists anxious only to impose their own conclusions upon anyone prepared to listen. It was written at a time when Wittgenstein was reacting against his own earlier philosophy, notably the *Tractatus* (published in 1921 and the only book to appear during his lifetime), and moving towards a new conception of the subject, the originality of which is still a matter of fierce debate. The mirror image is therefore in part autobiographical. Two years earlier he had put it somewhat backhandedly:

> I still find my own way of philosophizing new, and it keeps striking me so afresh; that is why I need to repeat myself so often. It will have become second nature to a new generation, to whom the repetitions will be boring. I find them necessary.
>
> (1980a: 1)

Devotees argue, with justification, that what the insensitive reader finds repetitious in Wittgenstein's later writings is precisely the source of their power and stylistic appeal; but the issue is not settled by name-calling.[1]

The dissatisfaction with the *Tractatus*, which motivated Wittgenstein's subsequent work, took two related forms. The first was a preoccupation with game analogies, brought about by a change in his view of mathematics. The earlier work suggests that the importance

103

of this discipline lies beyond itself, in its intimate relationship with the logical structure of reality. But Wittgenstein became convinced, influenced perhaps by the logician Frank Ramsey, that the significance of mathematical symbols is simply a function of the rules employed by mathematicians. The comparison is with the fascination of chess where the contrasting value of the pieces is a mere product of rule-following.

Secondly, the apparent diversity and complexity of ordinary language was originally thought by Wittgenstein also to conceal the uniform logical structure of the world although, unlike Bertrand Russell, he did not believe that everyday language was irremediably confused (see Baker and Hacker 1980: 270). Yet, despite this disclaimer, the *Tractatus* was emphatic that the meaning of a word is located somehow beyond language. That people use the same word or sentence in different contexts, for example, when believing, hoping, exclaiming, arguing, questioning, and so on, was treated as of no significance. But Wittgenstein's view in this connection also changed dramatically. He was moved to think it doctrinaire to insist that language fulfils a uniform role independent of the human contexts in which it is used. The contexts provide for the game analogy; a word operates within a series of *language-games*, which alone determine its meaning and value. (A better analogue than chess would now be the contrasting roles, say, of the Ace of Spades, not only within the immense variety of card games but also dependent upon the cards accompanying it in a given hand.) The upshot of this is that in the works from 1930 onwards, Wittgenstein's interest tends to focus on the so-called mental acts which give language its setting.

Norman Malcolm, whose short but engrossing *Memoir* (1958) of Wittgenstein is indispensible reading, depicts graphically the vicissitudes of the last six years of his life following the resignation from his Cambridge professorship in 1947. The artificiality of much academic life repelled Wittgenstein and, in Malcolm's words,

> He believed that a normal human being could not be a
> university teacher and also an honest and serious person. . . .
> Wittgenstein several times renewed the attempt to persuade me
> to give up philosophy as a profession. He commonly did this
> with other students of his.
>
> (Malcolm 1958: 30)

Philosophy should be practical. If it does not engage with questions of everyday life then it is of limited use:

I know that it's difficult to think well about 'certainty', 'probability', 'perception', etc. But it is, if possible, still more difficult
to think, or *try* to think, really honestly about your life and other
peoples lives. And the trouble is that thinking about these
things is *not thrilling* but often downright nasty. And when it's
nasty then it's *most* important.

(Letter of 1944 in Malcolm 1958: 39)

If our examination of the nature of animals eventually involves us in
unpalatable conclusions about what is thought to be their proper
entitlement, these thoughts might provide timely reassurance that we
are not *thereby* misguided.

No more than a mirror

Wittgenstein's writings have an organic unity which belies their
usually fragmentary appearance. It would be alien to his view of
philosophy to address traditional issues in a systematic way. His aim
is to illuminate the way in which common forms of speech and
argument proceed by way of logical connections which render them
perfectly in order in one sense, if we focus upon the context in which
they operate, but which, in another sense, given the complexity with
which these contexts are generated in practical living, frustrate
attempts to grasp an *overall* structure. For example, a term like 'think'
is wielded in diverse situations and profound errors arise if we
nonetheless draw the conclusion that there is one, perhaps mysterious, process of thought to which the term refers in all its
circumambulations:

> You do not understand your own transactions, that is to say you
> do not have a synoptic view of them, and you as it were project
> your lack of understanding into the idea of a medium in which
> the most astounding things are possible.

(Z 273)

Such a synoptic view can be achieved only by a patient sifting of how
expressions are used. Clarification is piecemeal and so are the
implications for traditional philosophical problems where one insight
can illuminate a whole range. This explains not only the necessity and
appeal of Wittgenstein's method but also its strangely provisional
nature. Sensitive readers are impelled to develop and side-track his
quasi-dialogues for themselves. In this sense we are to see him as 'no

105

more than a mirror'. It is therefore no surprise to find that Wittgenstein's remarks about animals are embedded within passages primarily concerned with human beings and are, to that extent, not readily available. It is all too easy to quote, for example, *Philosophical Investigations* (*PI*) 647: 'What is the natural expression of an intention? – Look at a cat when it stalks a bird'; and to conclude that it is Wittgenstein's view that cats have intentions in the sense envisaged by Regan. This would be typical of the errors which result from a neglect of context. Hearne is remarkable in both paying attention to context yet falling into the trap nonetheless. This vitiates what would otherwise have been an intriguing analysis.

The craving for generality

The Blue Book (*BB*) begins by probing the obvious fact that we use words with meaning. Yet the question 'What is meaning?', even if applied to nouns like 'pencil' or 'flower' generates 'a mental cramp' and provides us with 'one of the great sources of philosophical bewilderment: a substantive makes us look for a thing that corresponds to it' (*BB* 1). Wittgenstein makes several direct allusions to St Augustine's similar diagnosis of reactions to the question 'What is time?' (This was quoted in Chapter 1.) The act of *pointing* to the 'thing' (a pencil or flower) fails to isolate the meaning of the terms in question since the act is ambiguous. One might be wishing to isolate either the shape, material, colour, quality or even obstructive nature of the object. So we are tempted to bypass such complications by locating the essence of meaning in a process of *interpretation* which, in cases like these, must accompany an act of pointing. This brings the idea of a *mind* into prominence which accommodates such processes. These, for Wittgenstein, are typical cases of misunderstanding our 'own transactions', being hurried into 'the idea of a medium' (*Z* 273, above), rather than looking calmly at what happens. They are symptoms of an endemic 'craving for generality' (*BB* 17).

Traditional ways of thinking about words as signs (of things, of mental ideas or images needing interpretation) tend to gloss over the complexities of actual usage, as possible explanations of language in themselves, and focus attention upon something *beyond language* to give it significance. The temptation is thus to say, 'in all cases what one means by "thought" is what is *alive* in the sentence. That without which it is dead, a mere sequence of sounds or written shapes' (*Z* 143). Yet the example of a 'configuration of chess pieces' points to what is wrong here. What breathes life into them are the rules of the game of chess. These make possible the popularity and excitement of competition; the significance of chess as a social phenomenon. The dynamism of chess has its analogues in language.

> Think of the tools in a tool-box: there is a hammer, pliers, a saw, a screw-driver, a rule, a glue-pot, glue, nails, and screws. – The functions of words are as diverse as the function of these objects. (And in both cases there are similarities.)
>
> Of course, what confuses us is the uniform appearance of words when we hear them spoken or meet them in script and print. For their *application* is not presented to us so clearly.
>
> (*PI* 11)

Language-games and forms of life

If we know anything about handicraft it would be seen to be a waste of time to look for some one function which all tools perform. But with words and sentences we are misled by surface appearances. We do *varieties* of things with tools and likewise with words. If we combine this activity with the warnings against generality it should be obvious why the term *language-game* is so apt. Games are as multiform as tools:

> But how many kinds of sentence are there? Say assertion, question, and command? – There are *countless* kinds: countless different kinds of use of what we call 'symbols', 'words', 'sentences'. And this multiplicity is not something fixed, given once for all. . . . Here the term 'language-*game*' is meant to bring into prominence the fact that the *speaking* of language is part of an activity, or of a form of life.
>
> (*PI* 23)

It is vital to emphasise the variety of uses of sentences even *within* his specific instances. Thus, for example, the sentence 'Thank you', given the circumstances, could be an insult, a joke, a threat, a question, or even a request. Furthermore, it is a mistake to pick out an apparently paradigm case (saying 'Thank you' for some service or gift, perhaps) as constituting the essence of the concept, for this too fragments under the pressure of context. This would be a typical example of the 'craving for generality', which, as we have seen, Wittgenstein deplores.

> Our craving for generality has another main source: a pre-occupation with the method of science. . . . Philosophers constantly see the method of science before their eyes, and are irresistibly tempted to ask and answer questions in the way science does. This tendency is the real source of metaphysics, and leads the philosopher into complete darkness.
>
> (*BB* 18)

There is no criticism implied here of the proper use of scientific method; only of its *mis*use. The possibilities inherent in a unified theory of electromagnetism, nuclear forces, and that of gravitation is of compelling interest, whether or not the applied potential is realised. Nor is the contribution of neurologists or ethologists to our understanding of animal or human behaviour in any way compromised. Curiosity is satisfied; good causes are served. But philosophers who attempt to capture the diversity of their own nature and the perceived world in some similarly inspired 'theory of reality' explain nothing. The result is an often grotesque parody of science. (Theology can also engender confusions of this sort.) The atoms and molecules of the physicist have fanciful counterparts in the 'ideas', 'minds', and 'sense-data' of the metaphysicians; or the souls, Gods, angels, and devils of traditional religion.

A battle against bewitchment

So what *is* Wittgenstein after? He locates the erroneous need to proceed by way of quasi-scientific models in the mistaken feeling that the philosopher needs to '*penetrate* phenomena' in order to understand it (*PI* 90). Interest can then only focus on the occult entities we invent, without perhaps realising it, as evidence of our discoveries. Our interest in animals, and indeed in other people, is particularly bedevilled by this preconception. We mistakenly assume that we cannot understand them without somehow sharing what is going on behind their eyes, and since we cannot achieve this we feel dissatisfied. Marian Stamp Dawkins, the zoologist, is a spectacular offender; we need, as she puts it, 'to unlock them from their skins' (1985: 28). Hearne is also at fault in similar vein. The dog's knowledge *of* the track (see Chapter 3, p. 61 above) is something, she argues, 'which I can't of course characterize' (1987: 101). This is because she thinks it to be mysterious and hidden; like a sensation. The urge is to penetrate a mysterious *mind*; the rainbow's end. On the contrary; the truth stares us in the face. Now Wittgenstein does not simply dismiss this metaphysical urge; he casts it in a new light to make it genuinely explanatory. Philosophical puzzlement is of a different order to that of natural science. What needs to be explained is what is *not* hidden:

> It takes its rise, not from an interest in the facts of nature, nor from a need to grasp causal connexions: but from an urge to understand the basis, or essence, of everything empirical. Not, however, as if to this end we had to hunt out new facts; it is, rather, of the essence of our investigation that we do not seek to learn anything *new* by it. We want to *understand* something that is already in plain view. For this is what we seem in some sense not to understand.
>
> (*PI* 89)

Yet again he makes use of St Augustine's perplexity about time to exemplify the point: 'I know well enough what it is, provided that nobody asks me; but if I am asked what it is and try to explain, I am baffled' (St Augustine 1961: 264). This could never be a satisfactory response to a scientific question such as 'What is the specific gravity of hydrogen?', except marginally as perhaps a weak joke. 'What is *the* time?' is similar, in being empirical; we consult clocks or watches to find out. The peculiarity of 'What is time?' is that we know that the materials for an answer are ready to hand but they resist our attempts to assemble them. The same will be seen to be true of numerous similarly philosophical puzzles; about thinking, fear, pain, consciousness, language, numbers, and so on. In such cases the need is not to discover something; it is rather as Wittgenstein puts it, 'something that we need to *remind* ourselves of . . . We remind ourselves, that is to say, of the *kind of statement* that we make about phenomena' (*PI* 89, 90). To clarify 'time', for example, we would recall that we speak of the seasons succeeding each other, of well-bred young ladies getting married and having children and not the other way around, of people ageing, of silver tarnishing, and so on. What we are here disarticulating is the 'form of life' that generates the *language-game*, or, more correctly perhaps, an overlapping series of language-games, of 'time' (see *PI* 23, above). This is by no means a straightforward business nor is it a 'merely verbal' matter; a frequent cause of misunderstanding which has, quite misleadingly, given rise to the scornful depiction of Wittgenstein and a whole generation of British and American philosophers as 'linguistic analysts'. His interest is not that of the philologist primarily involved in the dissection and classification of syntax. To locate the concept of 'time' in language-games, themselves inseparable from the hurly-burly of social activity in which they figure, does more than tell us about words – it tells what *time is*. It is no enigmatic flux nor astral river but a deceptive product of 'forms of life' which involves language. That such a deception is unmasked demonstrates a vital purpose:

> Philosophy is a battle against the bewitchment of our intelligence by means of language.
>
> (*PI* 109)

> Our investigation is therefore a grammatical one. Such an investigation sheds light on our problem by clearing misunderstandings away. Misunderstandings concerning the use of words, caused, among other things, by certain analogies between the forms of expression in different regions of language. – Some of them can be removed by substituting one form of expression for another; this may be called an 'analysis' of our forms of expression, for the process is sometimes like one of taking a thing apart.
>
> (*PI* 90)

The vacuity of naming

Wittgenstein spends a considerable amount of time debunking the view that language is primarily a system of signs which stand for, or name, something. There are at least three traditional variants of this view; words stand for objects, mental processes of some sort, or a combination of the two. John Locke, it will be remembered from the preceding chapter, adopted the second. Words signified ideas in the mind and his problem was whether animals were capable of forming the abstract ideas named by general words. Plato and St Augustine are generally credited with forms of the first view although the objects, in each case, differ. The implication of all such positions is that we acquire a complete understanding of a word if we know what it stands for, and of a sentence if we know what its component words signify.

Wittgenstein depicts such a view with some of its attendant difficulties:

We name things and then talk about them: can refer to them in talk.' – As if what we did next were given with the mere act of naming. As if there were only one thing called 'talking about a thing'. Whereas in fact we do the most various things with our sentences. Think of exclamations alone, with their completely different functions. Water! Away! Ow! Help! Fine! No! Are you inclined still to call these words 'names of objects'?

[A]sking something's name . . . is, we might say, a language-game on its own. That is really to say: we are brought up, trained, to ask: 'What is that called?' – upon which the name is given.

$$(PI\ 27)^2$$

The one-word exclamations are, as Baker and Hacker point out, 'a *reductio ad absurdum*' of the Augustinean (or Platonic) picture of sentences (1980: 72). To have mastered them requires a grasp of the part played by such utterances in the practical situations that confront language users. To insist that even so they continue to name objects will be vacuous. For example, to argue in empiricist vein that 'Water!' stands for the mental idea of the need for refreshment, totally misses the point that it might stand for any number of such ideas (the house is on fire, the roof leaks) which only the practical situation can articulate and differentiate.

The assumption that language consists basically of words which refer to or name something is peculiarly insidious because of its apparent innocence. (It is a spy in our midst, not an assassin in uniform.) Much linguistic activity *does* involve referring to or naming. We label for a variety of reasons. But in most of these cases we can validly distinguish between the word and the thing named. To ask for beer does not, in general, raise questions about how the word is used. (Of course it *could*; 'Beer' is a common surname in these parts.) But the historical precedents, be they Platonism or Cartesianism, allied to seductive current idioms (the 'mind's eye', 'he hasn't a thought in his head'), tempt us to adopt the same naming model for *all* substantives; in particular, we find ourselves puzzled by references to vital human activities like thinking, believing, remembering, intending, expecting, being in pain, and so on, and are drawn irresistibly to diagnose the problem as one of discovering what these terms stand for. Aware that it is easier to pat a dog or clutch a glass of beer than handle someone's thoughts, including perhaps our *own*, we

111

resort to their being mysterious inner processes, occurring in a mind, which enjoys the haziest of locations somewhere above the neck. A more modish alternative is to argue that these terms name *brain* processes. This theory is very little better. Brain activity is electro-chemical in nature and to correlate that with, say, my expecting the arrival of my mother on the midnight express, in no way helps to explain what grounds I have for saying that I am looking forward to her arrival, which is what we should expect of such a theory. The claim is almost certainly *true* as a general scientific hypothesis about the importance of the brain, and central nervous system, for *all* human goings-on. But as far as the thought about my mother is concerned, the interest shifts forward to that 'observed linguistic behaviour', which certainly does provide the sort of explanation we are looking for when we ask someone what they are thinking about, or why they think it. We have ceased the search for new facts, supernatural or neurological, and, in this instance, have been forced to acknowledge the centrality of 'something that is already in plain view' (*PI* 89, above).

Hearne spends some time discussing the simple naming games in which some animals can figure (1987: 42–76). But, yet again, she offends this dictum of Wittgenstein's by hypothesising *through* them and convincing herself that they are sustained by a complex yet inscrutable mental life. Such attributions are indeed possible, but only of language-users.

Thinking about thinking

We can never be clear about thought, expectation, or the related psychological activities (pain being a particularly pregnant example of Wittgenstein's) in the straightforward ways sometimes available to us with beer, Beer, dogs, and glasses. The latter readily participate in language-games of naming, pointing to, buying and selling; the former do not. But only by attending to the variety of active situations in which the concept of thought (for let that be our representative example) *does* function will we understand it. It is not reducible to one thing or even type of thing.

> Where do we get the concept 'thinking' from which we want to consider here? From everyday language. What first fixes the direction of our attention is the word 'thinking'. But the use of this word is confused. Nor can we expect anything else. And

that can of course be said of all psychological verbs. Their employment is not so clear or so easy to get a synoptic view of, as that of terms in mechanics, for example.

(*Z* 113)

Wittgenstein is not being defensive in stressing the diverse ramifications of thought, as a theorist who was in the business of providing a unified theory might well be. His method is to *exhibit* it by a series of examples and counter-examples. Animals provide Wittgenstein with intermediate examples between thinking and non-thinking; an important methodological aid to clarity:

A main source of our failure to understand is that we do not *command a clear view* of the use of our words. – Our grammar is lacking in this sort of perspicuity. A perspicuous representation produces just that understanding which consists in 'seeing connexions'. Hence the importance of finding and inventing *intermediate cases*.

(*PI* 122)

Our understanding of words is bound up with the circumstances in which we *learn* them, not necessarily as children, and, if we generalise the process to that of a community sharing these conventions, then the means are available for deciding the proper application of the terms in question. These contexts are 'forms of life'. They are fluid and dynamic; never rigid. Thus, for example, the term 'goal-posts' is only grasped by appreciating the purpose of wooden posts, coats, chalk marks on walls, or whatever, in certain ball games. Even to accuse an opponent of moving them in an argument can, albeit with some difficulty if challenged, be traced to these origins. But it would be a 'hard' case, an intermediate one, precisely because the similarities and differences with the game paradigms need to be mulled over. Totally to lose logical contact with these would be to rob the accusation of its force. We can here claim justifiably to give 'goal-posts' a *use* in somewhat, but not completely, alien fields. What is perhaps easy to see of 'goal-posts' will have momentous implications in the case of 'thinking' and the other psychological verbs; particularly in their application to animals and machines.

One learns the word 'think', i.e. its use, under certain circumstances, which, however, one does not learn to describe.

(*Z* 114)

We learn to say it perhaps only of human beings . . .

(Z 117)

We don't say of a table and a chair: 'Now they are thinking', nor 'Now they are not thinking', nor yet 'They never think'; nor do we say it of plants either, nor of fishes; hardly of dogs; only of human beings. And not even of all human beings.

(Z 129)

'No one thought of *that* case' – we may say. Indeed, I cannot enumerate the conditions under which the word 'to think' is to be used—but if a circumstance makes the use doubtful, I can say so, and also say *how* the situation is deviant from the usual ones.

(Z 118)

But a machine surely cannot think! – Is that an empirical statement? No. We only say of a human being and what is like one that it thinks. We also say it of dolls and no doubt of spirits too. Look at the word 'to think' as a tool.

(PI 360)

Wittgenstein here invites us to consider a series of 'doubtful' uses, as well as establishing the primary one. That children learn to use the term 'think' of human beings, and the same would apply to the constellation of concepts that have implications for thinking (promising, hoping, intending, fearing, and so on), is not intended as merely an empirical statement; it is primarily a grammatical one (PI 360). Were it not, the obvious retort on behalf of tables, chairs, plants, fishes, and dogs, would be that a learning process which seeks to impoverish these beings is simply biased against them. This objection, tempting though it may seem, misses the point. It would only have force if the lesson learnt were of a straightforward nature; for example, if 'only human beings think' had the form of 'only human beings are cuddly' (which the child would doubtless soon rumble when it discovered that teddy-bears and puppies were even more so).

As we saw in Chapter 3, many of the confusions about language-learning are swept away if we distinguish between the acquisition of our native tongue and that of a subsequent one, the learning of which is a function of our mastery of the first. Our objector has made this mistake; 'only human beings think' (the straightforward form, above) would only make *sense* to someone who already had a grasp of the concept (*PI* 32). But it is learned by the infant in the first place as a cumulative spin-off from the very process of learning to speak (itself a thinking activity), and that is achieved by the prolonged adaptation of a developing vocal facility to the everyday concerns of eating and playing and its reaction to the promptings of familiar adults. The word 'think' slowly gains a toehold in the developing mastery of calling for the pot, rejecting the beans, promising to be good, and, above all, in questioning and arguing. It is important to note that these and similar goings-on are, at least in the initial stages, *team* games and in all of them the 'teacher', whether parent or elder sibling, plays a starring role. Not only is it appropriate to depict 'think' as a 'tool' (*PI* 360), and the other psychological verbs with it, since the child is enabled to do all of these things in employing it, but, furthermore, its necessary antagonist or co-conspirator can only be a human being. Even the Ameslan apes show little inclination to 'sign' unless rewarded. But the role of the family pet is nonetheless instructive. The child will soon learn that the dog can be summoned, and thus will spring up an attenuated language-game; a shadow version of the commanding game it plays with its parents. Being parasitic upon the parental game, the animal variant will be what Wittgenstein calls a deviant or doubtful use (*Z* 118, above), because the child will often embellish the situation with replies or objections on the animal's behalf. Why? The explanation is that the child is humanising the animal and treating it as it would an adult who, for some reason, came when called but was unwilling to continue the conversation. Thus many children, and not a few adults, are convinced that animals are trying to talk to us but unable to make us understand. In these cases the psychological verbs are used in the primary (human) sense but deviantly because of the mistaken picture that animals are like a Hottentot in Times Square trying to tell us that he wants to go home. Reading *Adam's Task* encourages one to entertain misleading pictures of this sort. Hearne draws fanciful implications from the mundane circumstances of the utterance; rather as we might if playing football with the dog. The difference is that *we* know it is *not* football.

But not every application of such activities to animals need be deviant, in the sense of being confused. The shepherd who, with appropriate whistles, commands his dog to guard the sheep, unlike the infant with the family pet, knows full well that the animal is not in the business of remonstrating or giving an opinion, although it might well disobey. The dog can be described as having been commanded because its response is *similar* to that of a human being in like circumstances. Yet the dog's response to a command is also *dis*similar to the human paradigm. In particular, the animal's having learned to obey orders without the facilities of speech, differs enough for us to have a language-game *intermediate* between that of the shepherd himself being ordered to guard the sheep by the farmer, at which he might protest or even give notice, and making a joke about ordering the rain to stop. The same account can be given of our talking of the animal's being said to 'guard' the sheep or even to have 'disobeyed' the order. This intermediate language-game certainly recalls the human paradigm but in marking also to mark the *difference*, must be seen as attenuated or 'thin'. It is deviant only in the sense of being divergent; which is, I think, how we are intended to take *Z* 118.

These gradations of thinking and related activities are *not* hypotheses or assumptions about private mental events which provide the true explanations of the observed phenomena. The temptation to think that 'inner' processes really hold the key is a metaphysical item of Cartesian excess baggage: 'A *picture* held us captive. And we could not get outside it, for it lay in our language and language seemed to repeat it to us inexorably' (*PI* p.115). A chess player who insisted that understanding how to play chess was with him an inner process to which others were not privy would have succumbed to the picture: 'We should say that when we want to know if he can play chess we aren't interested in anything that goes on inside him' (*PI* p.181).[3] That certain sensations *accompany* the playing of a game might interest a biographer but say nothing for the player's grasp of that game. The answer lies in looking at our language-games and observing their logical implications: 'Philosophy simply puts everything before us, and neither explains nor deduces anything. – Since everything lies open to view there is nothing to explain. For what is hidden, for example, is of no interest to us' (*PI* 126).

'But – they simply do not talk'

It is sometimes said that animals do not talk because they lack the mental capacity. And this means: 'they do not think, and that is why they do not talk'. But – they simply do not talk. Or to put it better: they do not use language – if we except the most primitive forms of language. – Commanding, questioning,

recounting, chatting, are as much a part of our natural history as
walking, eating, drinking, playing.

(*PI* 25)

The devil's advocate presents the prologue of this important section.
His mistake is to think that the true meanings of the acts we perform
with language (commanding, chatting, and so on) are to be found in
the realm of 'mental' acts. Our 'craving for generality' (*BB* 17)
encourages a false picture which refuses to allow us to accept the
diversity of language-games which these facts 'of our natural history'
make possible. We observe the numerous *manifestations* of thinking
and, seduced by the conviction that they *must* share something in
common, we delve beneath their surface for an answer to the question
'What then *is* thinking?'

But the manifestations are the language-games we play and
Wittgenstein points to them as their *own* court of appeal. Of games in
general he warns,

> Don't say: 'There *must* be something common, or they would
> not be called "games" ' – but *look and see* whether there is
> anything common to all. – For if you look at them you will not
> see something that is common to *all*, but similarities, relation-
> ships, and a whole series of them at that.
>
> (*PI* 66)

The second part of *PI* 25, the authorial voice having taken over,
presents the twofold problem posed for this undertaking in the case of
animals. Animals do not use language. (The switch of expressions
from their not talking is vital for, as Baker and Hacker observe, 'it
emphasises the integration of speaking with the varied activities of
human beings' (1980: 70–1). Parrots talk, but they do not use
language.) Activities like commanding, questioning, recounting, and
chatting, are beyond even parrots but are definitive of many basic
human activities and central to numerous others. If we try to apply
such descriptions to creatures who do not share these features of our
natural history then, to the extent of the divergence, the terms
gradually lose their point. The same would apply *mutatis mutandis* to
similarly deprived human beings; young infants, for example, or the
retarded. Of commanding, in particular, Friedrich Waismann writes:

> If we now try to transfer what we call 'command' to quite
> another realm of being . . . . a particular uncertainty arises. It is as
> if the word has lost its specific meaning, which, after all, clings

to the human world, and in the end it becomes a matter of choice what processes we wish to call commands.

(Waismann 1965: 135)

The 'primitive forms' of communication

However, although animals do not use language, *PI* 25 is explicit in allowing that 'the most primitive forms' of it are within their competence. What Wittgenstein clearly has in mind here are not just the varieties of 'natural communication' by which animals hoot, howl, hiss, gibber, squeak, shriek, stridulate and otherwise make themselves heard, but also the contexts in which these play a part. Thus the dog barks and the cat takes evasive action. Animals also communicate by posture, gesture, and odour. Tail-wagging by the green acouchi attracts females during courtship, by cats it is a repellent threat, yet with dogs it is a sign of a less specific but good tempered agitation which attracts both its fellows and human beings. What is to be made of all this?

Mistakes are what will be made, for a start, if we too readily generalise from the use of phrases like 'natural communication' and 'primitive forms' to crediting Wittgenstein with the view that animals use primitive language. The liberationists would welcome this; the conclusion that animals were primitive *persons* (to recall Singer) would be the next card in the deck. The fallacy here ought now to be apparent. The carpenter who inadvertently strikes his finger and yells 'Curse that hammer!' would be said to have expressed his pain and rage. His utterance expresses his meaning. There are similarities to the dog that cowers and snarls upon being kicked in the ribs. But until we apply the lessons of *PI* 66 and *look and see* we will miss perhaps critical divergences. In what sense does the bark of the dog express its meaning?

'The dog *means* something by wagging his tail.' – What grounds would one give for saying this? – Does one also say: 'By drooping its leaves, the plant means that it needs water'?

(Z 521)

We should hardly ask if the crocodile means something when it comes at a man with open jaws. And we should declare that

118

since the crocodile cannot think there is really no question of meaning here.

(Z 522)

Let us just forget entirely that we are interested in the state of mind of a frightened man. It is certain that under given circumstances we may also be interested in his behaviour as an indication of how he will behave in the future. So why should we not have a word for this?

(Z 523)

If someone makes the gesture of tipping a glass it normally means that they are inviting a companion to join them for a drink. Equally, if a person throws their hands in the air in apparent eagerness, anger, despair, joy, or supplication, then a requirement of any of these 'feelings' applying is that if the subject is questioned then by some means or other they are *capable* of specifying which. (They may, for any number of reasons, decline to do so but that does not affect the capability.) The first two passages from *Zettel* make the point that no sense can be given to tail-wagging nor crocodilian belligerency being meaningful in these ways. The grounds should be clear: animals do not use language. The objection that they *must* know what they are doing or they would not do it, is simply to resort back to the human paradigm again; this is what we might say of the average human being who wagged appendages or came at us with jaws agape. 'There is nothing astonishing about certain concepts only being applicable to a being that e.g. possesses a language' (Z 520).

That animals do not use language will be the end of the matter, if we *look and see* free of assumptions about subliminal 'mental events' being the essence of thought. But it is not the end of everything and Z 523 redresses the balance. The 'state of mind' of a frightened man *is* relevant to his fear, as we shall see later, unless, of course, we persist in identifying it with 'inner processes'. But Wittgenstein is reminding us that as often as not our concern is with what a frightened or angry person *will do next* rather than with their justifying reasons or intentions. Thus if, in my example above, we *were* charged by a drunkard with jaws agape, or upraised knife, it would be a natural reaction to take evasive action and save questions, however pressing and philosophical, for a later date.

We have a similar interest in the behaviour of animals. The observations by ethologists and psychologists about the predictive value of their vocal utterances, facial gestures, tail movements, and body-language generally, facilitate research work, aid commercial interests such as farming and the training of pets and working animals, and are of undying interest to television audiences. Furthermore, *other animals* react to these modes of natural communication in equally predictable ways and, as a result, we have the intricate so-called social life of birds, fish, and the higher mammals. But, again, the absence of the capacity to use language rules out even the possibility of their sociability involving self-conscious debate about territorial boundaries, conservation of food stocks, the peaceable settlement of disputes, or the taming and 'exploitation' of inferior species, which are the features of human society. Scientific evidence for this, if it were needed, is that if the deliberative and self-communing awareness necessary for such attributions *were* somehow available to animals in the absence of language (at, let us suppose *per impossibile*, the level of 'inner' processes) then we would expect that the higher the animal in the evolutionary scale, the more intricate their social organisation. This appears not to be the case. As the Burtons point out: 'Outside human societies, the most complex social life is found in the Hymenoptera, the order containing the social insects, and the Isoptera, the termites' (1977: 221). In attempting to come to grips with international disputes we tend to ask *why* the Americans did this or the Russians that. People have their reasons. With animals, lacking language, this is not the case. The ethologist sees no evidence for its being a relevant question even to raise;[4] Wittgenstein suggests that it cannot even be given a *sense*.

This is given a final twist in the continuation of Z 523 (not quoted). There is no need for a special 'word' which would relate simply to behaviour; the normal word is apposite even under the special circumstances. However, in Z 523 Wittgenstein is talking of human beings. In the next section it is mooted that, 'There might be a concept of fear that had application only to beasts, and hence only through observation'. *It is not ruled out* but some of the implied limitations in the use of such a 'concept' are suggested. The reasons for the ambivalence are not hard to find. The charging drunkard of Z 523, of whom we say 'He is afraid' although our sole interest is in evading him, will almost certainly be afraid (or angry) in the full sense in which he could give us reasons for what he is doing (answering 'Why?'). A new word here would be positively unhelpful. But what of the crocodile with open jaws? It doesn't *mean* anything (Z 522), there is no sense in asking 'Why?' about its motives, and yet its *behaviour* is sufficiently like that of the hostile drinker to need noting, which another word would fail to do. (Whereas we would resort to an alternative were a tree plunging down towards us.) But, it is vital to realise, what we have here are different language-games played with the same words 'afraid' or 'angry'. The need to mark the similarities *and* dissimilarities once again recall *PI* 66. With these glosses in mind Z 526 offers little comfort to the animal enthusiast: 'If someone behaves in such-and-such a way under such-and-such circumstances, we say that he is sad. (We say it of a dog too).'

Expectation and belief

The preceding section should have begun to establish the direction in which Wittgenstein's remarks about animals are guiding us. Regan, in his criticisms of Frey, makes great play with the sense in which the dog Fido has expectations of the arrival of its master comparable to those of the young lady, Mary, waiting for her friend. 'Expecting' is a concept closely related to those of 'believing', 'intending', and 'hoping', and, with these other implications in mind, Regan is attempting to make sense of the dog's expectation from behaviour alone. My attempts, in Chapter 3, to undermine his comparison with Mary's expecting her friend gain support from the previous discussion. But Wittgenstein's remarks *must* be seen in the light of the role given to language-games. Consider the following:

> When I sat down on this chair, of course I believed it would bear me. I had no thought of its possibly collapsing.
>
> But: 'In spite of everything that he did, I held fast to the belief . . .' Here there is thought, and perhaps a constant struggle to renew an attitude.
>
> (*PI* 575)

> I watch a slow match burning, in high excitement follow the progress of the burning and its approach to the explosive. Perhaps I don't think anything at all or have a multitude of disconnected thoughts. This is certainly a case of expecting.
>
> (*PI* 576)

Again, as in Z 523, discussed in the preceding section, the distinction is between varieties of belief and expectation available to human beings. Let us concentrate briefly on the act of sitting down (*PI* 575).

121

The belief or expectation that the chair would bear the sitter consists paradoxically in the absence of a thought. Let us now imagine a potted plant placed upon the chair. In the continued *absence* of a thought would *it* believe in the security of its perch? Obviously not. The difference lies in the potentiality of the human being to harbour doubts. The attribution of belief presupposes this environment which is the *logical grammar* of this language-game. Now we order our chimpanzee to take the chair. It does so unhesitatingly. Does it believe the chair will bear it? As we might expect, if we do make this claim then its logical grammar will be intermediate between that of the human being, where it finds its fullest expression, and that of the potted plant, where it has no part at all to play and will be rejected. There is no mystery about this grammar. What happens, if we *look and see*, is that it is appropriate to make the attribution if we are dealing with a creature that might well have fingered the upholstery, showed a reluctance to take a seat, or otherwise resembled a human being in its overt actions, *but in the complete absence of being able to give reasons* for its actions. We would expect the same limited reaction, and would be playing the same language-game in attributing belief, were we dealing with a young infant or an adult in an advanced stage of imbecility or decrepitude.

'I assimilate psychological concepts'

The diagnosis of the source of the confusion between mental *capacities* like thinking and understanding and the inner sensations, which can but need not accompany them, comes to a head in Wittgenstein's discussion of the connection between language and *memory* (PI p.231):

> When I say: 'He was here half an hour ago' – that is, remembering it – this is not the description of a present experience.
>
> Memory-*experiences* are accompaniments of remembering.
>
> Remembering has no experiential content. – Surely this can be seen by introspection?
>
> I get the *idea* of memory-content only because I assimilate psychological concepts. It is like assimilating two *games*. (Football has *goals*, tennis not.)

Wittgenstein is not denying that there are images that we summon of sights, sounds, and even smells. But memory is not *composed* of these. What gives certain images the status of *memory* images, rather than of fantasy, let us say, is that we locate them in language-games that involve references to the past and present. Simple tense-talk is enough: 'I enjoyed my dinner', or Wittgenstein's example, 'He was here half an hour ago'.

John W. Cook, in a much admired article, 'Human beings' (1969), sums up Wittgenstein's diagnosis of the pervasive error of both Vicki Hearne and liberationists like Regan and Singer:

> Since a person can read or think or remember or understand something without, on the particular occasion, *saying* anything, we are tempted to exclude the mastery of language from consideration when asking what thinking is, what understanding is, etc. Accordingly, in our search for the essence of each of these we gravitate towards a kind of concept, namely *sensation*, that can be applied to a subject that has no mastery of language. (Brutes and infants can have sensations.) Putting the matter in another way, we concentrate on the 'silent' cases of thinking or understanding or remembering and 'look into ourselves' for the essential element, i.e. take notice of feelings, images, words going through our head, and so on. In this way we come to assimilate concepts like *thinking, understanding, remembering,* and so on to sensation words.
>
> (Cook 1969: 138–9)

It is to sensations and to pain, the most notable of these, that we now turn.

Sensations

Properly to understand what memory is, and this goes for the other mental capacities as well, involves something of a balancing act. In the previous section, John Cook, following *PI* p.231, criticizes the assimilation of capacities to sensations. Remembering is a language-game that involves, among other things, the mastery of the language of tense and the past. But this too can easily be misunderstood. Wittgenstein is not saying that remembering is *just* being able to use tense-talk or to rub one's stomach after a hearty meal. That would be a form of not very subtle behaviourism. (And, of course, to argue that the complex of behaviour is the criterion from which we *infer* back to the inner 'state of mind' is a return to the original, and illicit, assimilation: the error of Descartes, Regan, Dawkins, and many others.)

Both mistakes result from a failure to recall Wittgenstein's frequent insistence that our language-games develop as tools to facilitate our interaction with other *human beings*, 'the *speaking* of language is part of an activity, or a form of life' (*PI* 23, above). The infant is encouraged to develop and expand its primitive reactions, instinctive responses, and even spontaneous creativity by using language. The 'balancing act' of memory is that the child learns to talk of the past, let us say, in some contexts where sensations or images or feelings would *naturally* either trigger the comment or be triggered by it. 'Granny died yesterday', says its weeping mother, and the child, invaded by images of the old lady's face and an uprush of sensation, cries too. The here hybrid language-game of remembering and distress is taught in the context of the onset of images and sensation which may well be seen as *characteristic* of it. In which case the language-game would identify them as such: memory images, feelings of distress. But the images or feelings are not the *constituents* of memory or distress since the games may recur not only without any sensations at all, or with very different ones, but certain sensations may be characteristic of a whole series of language-games. The 'pain' of rock-climbing will differ from the 'pain' of angina although phenomenologically they might well be indistinguishable. (More of this later.) So although sensations differ radically from capacities, their conceptual application is involved with the learning of language-games. Wittgenstein puts it in typically gnomic fashion: 'An "inner process" stands in need of outward criteria' (*PI* 580).

Pain and animals

If describing someone as remembering involves the grasp of a fairly extensive language-game and is not simply naming a memory-image, then the presence of pain ought to be amenable to the same analysis. Yet it has been strangely resistant. The conviction that 'pain' must *name* a private sensation could be the result of a concentration upon, and consequent 'bewitchment' by, a too narrow range of cases of the toothache type: 'A main cause of philosophical disease – a one-sided diet: one nourishes one's thinking with only one kind of example' (*PI* 593). The question we must ask is, 'How does a human being learn the meaning of the names of sensations? – of the word "pain" for example'. Wittgenstein continues:

Words are connected with the primitive, the natural, expressions of the sensation and used in their place. A child has hurt himself and he cries; and then adults talk to him and teach him exclamations and, later, sentences. They teach the child new pain-behaviour.

'So you are saying that the word "pain" really means crying?' – On the contrary: the verbal expression of pain replaces crying and does not describe it.

(PI 244)

The primitive, pre-linguistic behaviour of screeching or clutching the affected part, or rushing to a familiar source for comfort, is gradually augmented to become a generic language-game in which precise specifications by means of words, the use of justifying reasons, the importation of associated concepts like those of 'suffering', 'treatment', and 'death', begin to shape the complex social phenomenon we call pain. We learn to *think* about it, worry over it, even simulate it. It is a technique that we can master but it is impossible fully to describe: 'We remain unconscious of the prodigious diversity of all the everyday language-games because the clothing of our language makes everything alike. Something new (spontaneous, "specific") is always a language-game' (PI p.224).

The pain of angina and the pain of rock-climbing, assuming the sufferer is aware of his or her plight, will differ to the extent that the implications of being subject to a weak heart contrast with those of being a mountaineer, despite the similarity of the sensations. Pain is a complex social phenomenon; its sensations private and relatively simple.

The transition to animals is straightforward. It is again a matter of 'finding and inventing intermediate cases' (PI 122), and judging them on the basis of the similarities to, and relationship with, the human paradigm (PI 66). Two adjacent passages from *Zettel* point the way:

It is a help here to remember that it is a primitive reaction to tend, to treat, the part that hurts when someone else is in pain; and not merely when oneself is . . .

(Z 540)

But what is the word 'primitive' meant to say here? Presumably that this sort of behaviour is *pre-linguistic*: that a language-game is based *on it*, that it is the prototype of a way of thinking and not the result of thought.

(Z 541)

It was remarked earlier that the young infant, in the early stages of speech, by talking to the family dog and replying on its behalf, is humanising it, having learnt the relevant language-games in its interaction with adult humans. John Churchill, in a sensitive article central to our topic, emphasises how instructive it is that we so readily accept that plants, machines, and even household utensils, can in fantasy think, feel and speak. A few deft additions by the illustrator or cartoonist, a human face, perhaps limbs, and preferably clothes, are all that is needed (1989: 317). Churchill draws two morals from this. Firstly, and correctly, in Wittgenstein's words, 'Only of a living human being and what resembles (behaves like) a living human being' can one say these things (*PI* 281). Thus we literally anthropomorphise the trees and artifacts. Secondly, 'Because similarities of physical constitution and behaviour are matters of degree, understanding behaviours and confidence in ascribing pain are matters of degree as well' (Churchill 1989: 317–18). The use of 'degree' here is misleading. Thomas the tank engine or the Ents of Tolkein do not feel a lesser degree of pain than human beings, nor is there lack of confidence in attributing it, because given the language-game that is here played, they are in the same boat as fictional people. The language-game of fiction, however, including the child's playing with dolls or trains, is clearly parasitic upon what is fondly called real life; thus Wittgenstein calls it a 'secondary one' (*PI* 282). But children and sentimental adults often do confuse the two and the importance here for talk about animals is to establish what language-game is played in talking about their pain, and other sensations, and the dangers inherent in over-emphasising the similarities to the human paradigm. Churchill's second moral *is* relevant, not when we are faced with recognisable fictions, but when there is an uncertainty about which language-game to play in an 'intermediate case'.

> Look at a stone and imagine it having sensations. – One says to oneself: How could one so much as get the idea of ascribing a *sensation* to a *thing*? One might as well ascribe it to a number! – And now look at a wriggling fly and at once these difficulties vanish and pain seems able to get a foothold here, where before everything was, so to speak, too smooth for it.

(PI 284)

Churchill (1989: 318) comments upon this: 'Yet the fly, in Wittgenstein's view, is an uncertain case', citing a passage from *Remarks on the Philosophy of Psychology*:

Think of the uncertainty about whether animals, particularly lower animals, such as flies, feel pain.

The uncertainty whether a fly feels pain is philosophical; but couldn't it also be instinctive? And how would that come out? Indeed, aren't we really uncertain in our behaviour towards animals? One doesn't know: Is he being cruel or not?

(Wittgenstein 1980b: I. Sect. 659)

Churchill's singling out the fly for comment is liable to obscure the general point being made about *all* animals here. In its case the uncertainty is over whether the 'foothold' (of *PI* 284) is firm enough to bear the weight of an ascription even minimally related to the primary use. (It would be thought almost insane to *weep* for a dead fly.) When Wittgenstein remarks 'One doesn't know' he is not saying that we do not know whether the injured fly is or is not in pain, as we might say it of a dog that runs away after being hit by a car, but that the simplicity of its behaviour coupled with the minimal and ambiguous nature of our instinctive responses leaves us uncertain *what to say*. We might say almost anything and have it justified by what *there is to see*. (This recalls the above quotation from Waismann.)

The case of the dog, as the exemplary higher mammal, is different. For a start it demonstrates the pre-linguistic prototypes of behaviour upon which the primary language-game of pain is based (*Z* 541). It yelps and whines, licks its own wounds and those of others, as a primitive reaction to their distress, and so on. But there are still considerable uncertainties born of the creature's inability to use language. It will lick its wounds but is unable to consider whether this is advisable, or how long they will take to heal, or whether it will be put down if they do not. It cannot be said to decide to inhibit its whining, which may be grounds for refusing to allow that animals could be 'suffering in silence', as humans can; nor will we be able to accuse it of malingering, as we are reminded in *PI* 250, 'Why can't a dog simulate pain? Is he too honest?' The uncertainty referred to by Wittgenstein in the passage from his *Remarks* (1980b) is, in the case of the higher mammals, more radical than that over the fly. The similarities of their pre-linguistic reactions to human responses serve as constant temptations to treat them and speak of them in ways that are perhaps too reminiscent of the human paradigm; being, in part, neglectful of the implications of the lack of language. The infant that talks to the dog, answers on its behalf and congratulates it for being clever, yet half-knows that he is deceiving himself, is in all of us.

The series of attenuated language-games reflects the gradations of animal behaviour. With dogs it has begun to misfire with uncertainty, ants and flies undermine its usefulness still further, and when flatworms and viruses are at issue it is at a standstill. This limit is mentioned in *Culture and Value*: 'It would almost be strange if there did not exist animals with the mental life of plants. I.e. lacking mental life' (Wittgenstein 1980a: 72).

From sensations to emotions

Similar observations emerge from some of Wittgenstein's remarks about other 'feelings', including those emotions often claimed for animals as grounds for affording them special treatment; namely, fear, hope, joy, shame, grief, and so on. These share with pain, and its correlates like itches, tingles, and throbs, three features in particular:

1. They are not used to name private inner processes; although such perturbations frequently, often characteristically, accompany the language-games within which the concepts function. Compare, on the one hand, 'Fear gripped me like an icy hand' or 'My heart stopped when I saw her' with 'I am afraid the interest rates are slipping'. Here the traditionalist's exasperation is countered by Wittgenstein: 'But "joy" surely designates an inward thing.' No. 'Joy' designates nothing at all. Neither any inward nor any outward thing (Z 487). The offending term here is 'designates'. 'Joy' does not serve to point to either inner sensations or simple overt action, although these will frequently accompany it; we see it manifested in the behaviour of human beings, and what resemble them, in suitable circumstances. Sadness is the same (Z 526, above).

2. Appropriate forms of words operate in a variety of contexts. Later theorists, like John Austin (1962) and John Searle, were to coin terms like 'performatives' or 'speech acts' to highlight the fact that verbal utterances only become meaningful language in appropriate social circumstances. 'I love you' can be a complaint, a proposal, a declaration, or a verbal alternative to an embrace or some other pre-linguistic prototype of affection.

We ask 'What does "I am frightened" really mean, what am I referring to when I say it?' And of course we find no answer, or one that is inadequate.

The question is: 'In what sort of context does it occur?' . . .

Is it, then, so surprising that I use the same expression in different games? And sometimes as it were between the games?
(*PI* p.188)

3. Some emotions have characteristic forms of behaviour which frequently accompany them. Wittgenstein gives the example of facial expression, and continues, 'This itself implies characteristic sensations too. Thus sorrow often goes with weeping, and characteristic sensations with the latter. (The voice heavy with tears)' (*Z* 488). We are then warned, not surprisingly, 'But these sensations are not the emotions.' And, we can add, neither is the behaviour either if we isolate it from an appropriate social setting.

But this coin has another side. Wittgenstein is at pains to point out that the feelings which we tend to classify as 'emotions' also *differ* in two important respects from those, typically pain, that are sensations. In the first place, pain is *locatable* within the body by pointing, prodding, or a verbal description such as 'behind the eyes'. This is not so with the emotions unless we confuse them with accompanying sensations:

'I feel great joy' – Where? – that sounds like nonsense. And yet one does say 'I feel a joyful agitation in my breast'. – But why is joy not localized? Is it because it is distributed over the whole body?
(*Z* 486)

The answer is No. Joy, sadness, fear, and the rest, are predicated of the *human being*, the person, or (allowing for the differences soon to emerge) the animal. 'Joy is manifested in facial expression, in behaviour. (But we do not say that we are joyful in our faces)' (*Z* 486).

The second respect in which these groups of feelings part company is more significant so far as their attribution to animals is concerned. We have already noted its origins in Aristotle's *Rhetoric*. The situation in which someone experiences a pain, locates it between the shoulder blades, let us say, but has no idea of the cause is in no way odd. It is the stuff of which doctors' fortunes are made. But someone who announced that they were afraid, or hoping, or feeling guilty, but seemed unable to tell us any more would indeed be a source of perplexity. A person should be able to say what they are afraid of, hoping for, or feeling guilty about. Furthermore, any answer sincerely given will be authoritative, unlike that of the medical diagnostician who is liable to well-meaning error. The emotions, or most of them, are said to be *directed*, and have *objects*:

Among emotions the directed might be distinguished from the undirected. Fear *at* something, joy *over* something.

This something is the object, not the cause of the emotion.

(*Z* 488)

Thus a face which inspires fear or delight (the object of fear or delight), is not on that account its cause, but – one might say – its target.

(*PI* 476)

Some will contend that this is counter-intuitive. But it is too easy to generalise from examples like those of people fleeing from drunken attacks or ravenous lions. One can fear the onset of a war which might never break out, or hope against a million-to-one odds to win a lottery. But a yet-to-be or never-to-be event can hardly function as a cause. What clearly mediate in such cases are various *beliefs* that one has, and the grounds for these are the grounds for the emotion in question. 'A thought rouses emotions in me (fear, sorrow etc.) not bodily pain' (*Z* 494).

Wittgenstein is *not* implying that the thought or belief *causes* an emotion, as a blow causes pain, but that the objects of emotions are amenable to reasons. Why were Americans, after Orson Welles' famous dramatisation of *War of the Worlds* in the late 1930s, so afraid of the Martians? Because they believed that they had heard a genuine news broadcast, that the Martians had landed, and that the omens were on the dark side. Reasons, in such and myriad similar cases, operate in two major ways. Some listeners might well have ridiculed the news as being worth no more than the mildest alarm. (A psychologist might here be interested in the biographical details which would have contributed to the *causes* of the varied emotional reactions to the reasons in question; for Wittgenstein, a matter of scientific, not philosophical, interest.) On the other hand, whilst the original avowal of terror of Martians (its 'objects') by a conventional listener cannot be contested; what happens when (as was the case) the radio stations speedily revealed the true facts? If the retractions are accepted, which means that the inclining reasons are seen to have been based upon a mistake, then the listener is under a logical compulsion to abandon their fear of Martians; unless they have reasons for disbelieving the retraction. Of course, different fears might linger (for example, that of the power of the media so to confuse), and other emotions such as outrage, but the moral is that it is *reasons* which support the original object and, if they are undermined, it falls. The only partial analogue with pain is that if we can reason a sufferer into believing that, for example, the *cause* is not angina but over-exertion, then the sensation is unlikely to go away but the grounds for suffering and despondency assuredly will. But pains do not have objects separable from their causes.

Wittgenstein, in talking of animals, sometimes uses the language of the directed emotions without explicit warning that a special language-game is being played. However, given that his basic method of analysis is one of 'finding and inventing *intermediate cases*' (*PI* 122) it would be tedious and unnecessary were every such case labelled for instant handling. What he tends to do is to draw attention to the most clear-cut cases where the lack of language *entirely* rules out the possession of certain attributes by animals, such as hope, remorse, and grief, whilst leaving his readers to follow through the implications in those cases where the same word, such as 'fear', is used but operates in a different language-game.[5] Here are some, much quoted, lines:

> Why can a dog feel fear but not remorse? Would it be right to say 'Because he can't talk?'
>
> Only someone who can reflect upon the past can repent. . . .
>
> There is nothing astonishing about certain concepts only being applicable to a being that e.g. possesses a language.
>
> (*Z* 518–20)

> One can imagine an animal angry, frightened, unhappy, happy, startled. But hopeful? And why not?
>
> A dog believes his master is at the door. But can he also believe his master will come the day after tomorrow? – And *what* can he not do here? – How do I do it? – How am I supposed to answer this?

Can only those hope who can talk? Only those who have mastered the use of a language. That is to say, the phenomena of hope are modes of this complicated form of life . . . .

'Grief' describes a pattern which recurs, with different variations, in the weave of our life. If a man's bodily expression of sorrow and of joy alternated, say with the ticking of a clock, here we should not have the characteristic formation of the pattern of sorrow or of the pattern of joy.

'For a second he felt violent pain.' – Why does it sound queer to say: 'For a second he felt deep grief'? . . . .

But don't you feel grief *now*? ('But aren't you playing chess *now* ?') The answer may be affirmative, but that does not make the concept of grief any more like the concept of a sensation.

(*PI* p.174)

There is a mixed bag of examples in these passages and a great deal at issue which creates ripples beyond the surface comment.[6] It is appropriate therefore that the quotations follow my fairly lengthy account of Wittgenstein's general position. It will be enough, in conclusion and with Chapter 6 still to come, to comment upon the implications of some of the key attributions to animals made in them: remorse, grief, compassion, anger, fear, hope, and, involved in all of them, belief.

Remorse, hope, grief and compassion

It is an endearing trait in quite a few types of pet dog, and observers claim as much for certain other mammals as well (apes and perhaps horses, but rarely cats), that they react in ways not unlike children, and some adults, when they have committed some misdeed which merits punishment. A dog will retreat beneath a table, be difficult to extricate, and fail to meet its master's eye. Wittgenstein would agree, I think, that to attribute to the animal either remorse, repentance, or guilt in such circumstances would be unnecessarily anthropomorphic. It could be equally misleading if said of an infant in the earlier stages of language learning; although in both cases there might be a playful point to make by emphasising the human or adult resemblance. It would be undue anthropomorphism, jocular or not, for two reasons. In the first place the behaviour itself is ambiguous, even in context, since it would be consistent with the animals being either fearful, ill, or just plain agitated. Even more conclusive, however, is the fact that remorse or guilt requires a grasp of wrongdoing and the need for reparation. Clearly a being unable to learn to talk of the past, to know what the past *is* and that it can be atoned for, ought not to be said to be remorseful. What seems to be important for Wittgenstein in the case of remorse, like that of hope also, but *un*like that of fear, is that there is an absence of *characteristic* pre-linguistic prototypes which would provide grounds for attributing remorse or hope to creatures that do not use language. Each of them is 'a transaction that is made in language', as Churchill puts it (1989: 314). Wittgenstein would wish to emphasise, I think, that it is the only possible arena in which these feelings operate.

If remorse and hope are linguistic transactions, remembering that they frequently will occur with accompanying sensations and behaviour, although perhaps not characteristic ones, then *grief* will need to be seen in this light. Again, grieving will occur against an often contradictory background of sensations and behaviour (weeping, poring over photographs, and so on) but, not unlike a game of chess, it is itself neither sensation nor behaviour. It is, if anything, closely related to hope (as its obverse perhaps), but involved with an intense awareness of past disaster. It is a sophisticated emotion and the grasp of language is certainly a necessary, if not perhaps sufficient, condition of it. Animals can, of course, manifest relatively short-term distress at, say, the loss of a mate, but it shows itself only in a disruption of behaviour. Without language it cannot *consider* its plight. Furthermore, as with hope and remorse, there are not characteristic prototypes: pulling a long face or weeping frenziedly would be inadequate simulations of grief.

Compassion, which is related to hope and grief, serves as an instructive contrast, for here we *do* have 'pre-linguistic prototypes' (remembering Z 541) which provide a ready reference for its attribution to animals. Although it is a feeling hardly mentioned by Wittgenstein, it has had quite an airing in the literature, and is peculiarly amenable to his analysis. James Rachels (1976) cites a series of experiments carried out by psychologists at the North-western University Medical School (reported in 1964). The point was to test the extent to which rhesus monkeys would be prepared to set in motion a device which made food available to them if, concomitant with its operation, a fellow monkey were seen to suffer a severe electrical shock. Not surprisingly, given that we have already noted the instinctive tendency of many mammals to administer their own forms of relief even sometimes to human beings in distress, the experimenters concluded that 'a majority of rhesus monkeys will consistently suffer hunger rather than secure food at the expense of electroshock to a conspecific' (1976: 215). They tended to see it as 'an ethologically innate pattern that serves to preserve the species' (218).

Rachels rejects this. The lesson of the experiments is, he argues, 'that rhesus monkeys have a capacity for compassion, and by that I mean exactly the same moral virtue which we admire in humans' (215). He bases this conclusion not on the capability of animals for moral thinking, namely that such behaviour is good or right, but on the fact that, 'being compassionate only requires desiring that others do not suffer, and acting on that desire' (216). Now if the subjects had been adult human beings then this argument would have been unobjectionable; had we been in any doubt we could have checked for the presence of this desire by asking. But Rachels offers no argument whatsoever for the presence of simian desires in general, nor the specific one that others do not suffer, *independent of the experimental results*. He adds lamely that it is 'apparently among the desires' they have (216). But a moment's reflection will reveal the internal complexity of that belief were monkeys to possess it in a form that exhibited the moral virtue admired in human beings. Only a being able to master the concepts of 'self', 'others', and 'suffering', and to construct sentences involving them could begin to qualify. Yet it is certainly not unreasonable to talk of 'compassion' in the case of these monkeys, and even *a* sense of *belief*, manifested in what we see they do; a language-game similar in form to its human analogue (to mark the similarities) but differing in contextual content. And *what we see they do* was accurately reported by the researchers; the conclusion rejected by Rachels.

Anger and fear

The discussion of compassion will have paved the way for anger and fear. Both emotions have objects (or 'targets'), and betray characteristic, although certainly not invariable, behaviour patterns.

What is fear? What does 'being afraid' mean? If I wanted to define it at a *single* shewing – I should *play-act* fear.

Could I also represent hope in this way? Hardly. And what about belief?

(*PI* p.188)

The targets of an animal's fear or anger are usually clear enough and it is perfectly natural and necessary to speak of them. How else might we express the remarkable overt similarity to human reaction? Herring gulls with wings held 'akimbo' are poised to hurl themselves at an intruder. 'We say a dog is afraid his master will beat him; but not, he is afraid his master will beat him tomorrow. Why not?' (*PI* 650).

But the analogy with human fear is already beginning to break down. The discussion of the broadcast of *War of the Worlds* exemplified how *reasons* play an important role in our understanding of the directed feelings. People are argued out of their fear or anger if, to their satisfaction, it can be shown to have been groundless. A human being in fear or anger *means* something, and will typically give voice to this effect. If frightened they believe that what they are doing or feeling is a reaction to a perceived *threat* of some nature, and if made angry it will be under the impression of an unmerited slight, offence, or injury. (These targets are not intended to be exhaustive. Similar conditions will be true of remorse, guilt, hope, happiness, unhappiness, and even compassion. If a car driver can be convinced that an accident, in which a jay-walking pedestrian was killed, was wholly the victim's fault then it would be a *mistake* for them to talk about their continuing remorse or guilt-feelings, although in their confusion they might continue to do so.) But it is pointless to attempt to convince a dumb brute, cowering under the threatening lash, that its master is rehearsing his part in *A Midsummer Night's Dream*, or that he is not intending to hit it very hard. Only an outbreak of liberationist wishful thinking, linked to the availability of mysterious inner processes of thought, could tempt us to *identify* the quivering creature with a person cornered by a whip-wielding, and apparently aggressive, spouse. The clear implication is that contrasting language-games, related by the similarities of overt behaviour, are at work in talking of the respective fear and beliefs of the animal and human being. In the case of the animal the target or object of the emotion, being no longer amenable to reasons, now functions as a *cause* of the behaviour; much as a loud midnight crash will startle sleeping parents into leaping out of bed without the faintest idea of what they are doing, despite its being correctly describable by the zoologist as the first phase of a 'mutual survival' response.

Wittgenstein seems to be anticipating this sort of analysis in *Zettel* where the sense in which we might wish to talk of tail-wagging as meaning anything is compared, both to the open-mouthed attack of the crocodile, and also to a special interest that we might adopt in the mere predictive potential of human emotional behaviour (*Z* 521–3, above). He sees little mileage in such a use for *human* action, as we have already noted (although it would seem to me more precisely to mark off the sense in which we would say of the befuddled parents that they were fearful for their children – if one were needed), but he allows it more potential in the case of animals:

> There might be a concept of fear that had application only to beasts, and hence only through observation. – But you don't want to say that such a concept would have no use. The verb that would roughly correspond to the word 'to fear' would then have no first person and none of its forms would be an expression of fear.
>
> (*Z* 524)

What would tell in favour of such a hypothetical concept is that the use spelled out, albeit tantalisingly, by Wittgenstein does seem to pick out features of the attenuated language-game of fear and the other feelings that, I have argued, we use of animals. There would indeed be neither first person uses nor expressive ones, for the obvious reason that animals do not use language. But these points in support of such a coinage would be more than outweighed by its nuisance-value since it would undermine the whole point of talking about contrasting language-games of *fear*, or whatever, because the new term would fail to capture the similarities of the pre-linguistic prototypes of behaviour in human beings and the many animals to which we find it imperative to draw attention. Wittgenstein is right; such a word would not reflect what we need to say. Yet merely to weigh its possible merits is to foreshadow the complexities of the language-game that we *do* play.

Postscript

In Chapter 3 Regan poses the case of a deranged man, bereft of language, who exhibits all the characteristic behaviour of terror upon being confronted by a rubber snake. It is allegedly a counter-example against Frey which does provide 'sufficient reason to attribute beliefs' solely on the basis of behaviour (Regan 1983: 42). He argues that for an opponent to deny this would show 'that they do not understand the ordinary use of sentences of the form "He believes that p" ' (42). What is clearly at issue here is that if the man, being akin to an animal in his inability to speak, is capable of the fear of a normal human being, then animals will be also.

Now the thrust of Wittgenstein's remarks is that it is the whole task of philosophy to gain a 'synoptic view' of what a deceptively simple phrase like Regan's 'the ordinary use of sentences' conceals. 'Belief', in particular, is as multi-purpose as Medusa's hair. It is not a question of a particular attribution of belief being right or wrong but of understanding the use to which it is put in particular contexts; of appreciating which language-game is being played. An impartial bystander, viewing the incident cited by Regan, would unhesitatingly think the man to be afraid and perhaps, hoping to reassure him, call out that the threat was a childish hoax. But, upon realising that the victim was deranged and unable to understand, our bystander would almost certainly be hard-pressed to reassemble his reactions. Human imbeciles fill us with disquiet; as I suggested in the original discussion. Upon reflection, the attribution of fear and belief would undoubtedly stand but it now would be differently *grounded*; no longer in the social context of reasoning and commiseration, but upon the similarities of the imbecile's prototypical behaviour to that of the normal human being.

A *dog* that betrayed the same symptoms would present far fewer problems because animals are a commonplace and our judgements of them more routine. For Regan to insist that the imbecile's believing 'that there is something to be afraid of' serves as more than a harking back to what we would expect of someone *compos mentis*, is as obscurantist as Rachels' contention that the rhesus monkeys desire that others do not suffer.

'If a lion could talk . . .'

It is Wittgenstein's view that the behaviour of other people is, in normal circumstances, transparent to us: 'If I see someone writhing in pain with evident cause I do not think: all the same, his feelings are hidden from me' (*PI* p.223). Now the bystander in Regan's example, shocked by the recognition that not all is well with the frightened victim, will, it was suggested, be temporarily at a loss for words. Wittgenstein recognises this possibility in a more thoroughgoing form in several passages, one of which immediately follows the preceding quotation:

> We also say of some people that they are transparent to us. It is, however, important ... that one human being can be a complete enigma to another. We learn this when we come into a strange country with entirely strange traditions; and, what is more, even given a mastery of the country's language. We do not *understand* the people. . . . We cannot find our feet with them . . .

If a lion could talk, we could not understand him.

The bystander, as I developed the example, comes around to speaking of the imbecile's fear in a way that is differently grounded; there is a switch of language-games. But it does not come naturally to do this of human beings, indeed it would worry all of us but psychiatric nurses. Yet Wittgenstein's remarks remind us that it is a perfectly natural way of speaking of *animals*, their being omnipresent in our life and culture. It is a technique we master although the forms of our language make it difficult to *describe*. To this extent animals are also transparent to us but what is see is different; and this is reflected in what we say and do – we stroke a startled horse but do not even consider reasoning with it. Thus it comes naturally to the bystander to adopt an attitude towards the *dog* which had been somewhat bewildering in the case of an apparently adult human. The transparency of animals reveals the similarities of their *natural* responses and expressions to our own and it is on the basis of these that we employ closely related language-games. (The liberationists insist that this is enough to create an *identity*, to give animals human status. Many socio-biologists do the same but reverse the conclusion and transform humans into animals. Wittgenstein does this, but in a perfectly legitimate context: 'I want to regard man here as an animal; as a primitive being to which one grants instinct but not ratiocination. As a creature in a primitive state' (1969: 62).)

However, it is also evident that the lack of language, and all that that implies, is equally grounds for the respective language-games being related but also *vitally different*. Other ascriptions, such as those of hope, grief, and remorse, will be denied to animals entirely. But Wittgenstein does stress, and it must be emphasised, that our understanding of the language-games which demonstrate this transparency is hard won; they come naturally yet their true import is disguised by seductive verbal similarities and Cartesian fictions.

Our understanding of our fellow humans has its limits however; examples being Regan's unfortunate imbecile or the enigmas of Wittgenstein's 'strange country' (*PI* p.223, above). How do animals tie in to this contrast? The talking lion is supposed to hold the key but opinions are divided over what it unlocks. Churchill, for example, argues that it would speak to us of the common psychic legacy we share with the lower animals and that 'quite likely we would understand much, or even most, of what he said' (1989: 323). Perhaps! But I am inclined to the view that Wittgenstein should be taken at his word here: we *could not* understand the lion.

The remark operates at two levels. In the first place, much animal behaviour will *not* be transparent, as some *will* be. The wriggling of the fly or spider leaves us with various choices and no clear lead as to what to say. Churchill puts this well: 'I cannot construct the case in which I would confidently say "The fish are happy." I would feel far readier with puppies or calves' (1989: 320 fn.). The failure is not one of missing out on the inner world of the stickleback, but that its behaviour and its aquatic context only distantly evokes our own, whereas that of the mammals achieves a more secure footing. But secondly, and more significant, even when we wish to say that animal states *are* transparent to us, what we see is a primaeval *distortion* of what we see in other humans. Lacking language, animal behaviour does not have *meaning* for them as it can for us. Our own instinctive responses can be meditated upon and discussed. The case of the talking lion is one of extreme paradox. Were it to speak, it could only give voice to the prototypes of true understanding which, in the world of the lion, cannot be spoken of. But this must not be thought to undermine the intelligent and accurate observations that we make about lions or other primitive creatures.

Ted Hughes' hawk, who has roosted since the frontispiece and without introduction, is, I like to think, doing the talking for Wittgenstein's lion and speaks of the selfsame paradox. For it truly to talk, and for us to understand, would be to live the 'falsifying dream' of the liberationists.

6

WHAT ANIMALS ARE:
CONSCIOUSNESS,
PERCEPTION, AUTONOMY,
LANGUAGE

Wittgenstein and the scientists

Mary Midgley, it has already been noted, is critical of Wittgenstein.
He is, she contends, typical of those thinkers; she also includes Max
Black (1972) and Stuart Hampshire (1959: 97–100), who are not
disputing nor even interested in 'the very large literature of careful
discussion by zoologists and psychologists about the different kinds of
understanding and conceptual grasp which different sorts of animals
actually display' (1983: 57). She goes on to accuse him and the others
of, as it were, defining themselves into respectability: 'They are not
prepared to count as *concept* or *understanding* anything which does
not involve speech.'

This is a tempting criticism; typically half truth and half error.
Wittgenstein's discussion is certainly not peppered with references to
narrow-front migration, smoke-bathing, or Skinner boxes, (nor is that
of Regan, Singer, Frey, or Midgley herself, come to that), since his
concern is to clarify the implications of our everyday ways of
attributing psychological concepts like hope, fear, belief, understanding, and so on. Unless we are clear about these, in the case of human
beings, and then of the grounds for proceeding to apply them to
animals, we will be ill-prepared to assess the claim of the scientist or
other trained observer that a segment of observed animal behaviour *is*
thoughtful, or intentional, or hopeful, or self-conscious. When the
psychologist Donald Griffin describes the ability of great tits and
chickadees to obtain milk from bottles by 'pecking through their shiny
coverings with the conscious intention of obtaining food' (1984: 35),
it is obvious that were he not talking of a 'conscious intention', in the
normal human acceptation of the phrase, he would fail to arouse the
average reader's curiosity and sympathies. Earlier Griffin has be-
moaned the fact that 'throughout our educational system students

are taught that it is unscientific to ask what an animal thinks or feels' (1984: vii). It is *philosophy's* task to bring to light the roles of these terms, embedded in our language-games used of animals. Good science does not necessarily make for good philosophy.

The example is useful in underlining the error of Midgley's point about definition. We may certainly talk of animals, in the absence of speech, 'consciously intending' or being compassionate, both of which carry implications of understanding to some degree. The error is to confuse the identity of *terms* in the language-games used of animals and human beings, with an identity of implication. The differences are as significant as the similarities.

Consciousness

Now let us take Midgley at her word and ask what Griffin, as a representative scientist specialising in the field of animal thinking, has to tell us about possibly the most basic attribute of all animals, namely, consciousness. (We may then proceed, in the remainder of this chapter, to discuss some of the most important of the manifestations of this consciousness whilst tying in loose threads protruding from earlier discussions.)

Griffin opens confidently: 'Conscious mental experience, in men and in animals, remains a challenging unknown territory' (1984: vi). With Wittgenstein's approach in mind, this can only be a dispiriting beginning. For a start, it shows symptoms of the 'craving for generality' (*BB* 17–18): the lady regained consciousness, she sat up, she remembered her name – are these all landmarks of the same territory? More importantly, Griffin seems either to be confused or just wrong about consciousness. What is *unknown* about it? His comment suggests that it is almost as if, when someone woke up in the morning, they were suddenly possessed of something mysterious in becoming conscious, like a metaphysical virus. But the truth is that they just *wake up*. If I meet my young son from school, laughing with his friends and waving to me and the dog, who wags its tail and barks in return, should I be supposed not to know what I am talking about if I pronounce them both to be conscious? Whatever can Griffin be after? We soon discover:

> What is it like to be an animal? What do monkeys, dolphins, crows, sunfishes, bees, and ants think about? Or do nonhuman animals experience any thoughts and subjective feelings at all?

People have always been fascinated by the question of animal consciousness, because both pets and wild animals arouse our admiration and curiosity. They tempt us to put ourselves into their skins and imagine what their lives are like.

(Griffin 1984: 1)

This is crypto-Cartesianism. As John Cook pointed out in the preceding chapter, it mistakenly assimilates the concepts of capacities like understanding, thinking, remembering, and the other psychological verbs to those of *sensations* like pain, and thus turns them into specific yet insubstantial and wholly mysterious inner states, available only to private introspection, which correlate in some way with their behavioural signs. This is not the place to repeat Wittgenstein's rejection of such figments of linguistic bewitchment nor yet to deny that people and animals do have inner lives of pains, itches, tingles, thrills, and throbs. The basic point is that the language of conscious states has its primary ground in the interaction of humans, and of other beings that behave like them, and the question of the inferential access to inner worlds of 'subjective feelings' is not raised. Griffin is right to the extent that we do entertain fantasies of inhabiting other 'skins' (David Garnett's *Lady into Fox* (1932) is a good example of the literary genre, although Kafka's *Metamorphosis* (1961) is pre-eminent in casting the shadows of paradox involved in the attempt) but the failure to achieve this does not in any way put at risk our understanding of what others say of their own or others' *consciousness*. Nor in the case of animals will it undermine what we say of their consciousness, grounded as it is in their contiguity to the human paradigm. To describe both my son and the dog as conscious makes no assumptions about infantile nor canine 'subjective' worlds.[1]

Self-consciousness

My argument in this section, and in much of the chapter as a whole, will involve the exposure of a persistent confusion in the analysis of a whole series of allegedly revelatory examples of animal behaviour. The source of the confusion was located in Chapter 5 but it is elusive and uncompromising enough to need repeating. To attempt to understand human nature requires that we grasp the import of what we say. That we are able to speak to each other gives rise to the complexity of language-games that we are able to play, yet find it so difficult to *describe*. Language provides the context in which we can be said to understand each other. But language itself emerges from primitive forms; the 'pre-linguistic prototypes', to use Wittgenstein's phrase. Now animals share much of this pre-linguistic heritage with us, in varying degrees depending upon whether we are speaking of gibbons or goldfish, but (*pace* Washoe) stop short of speaking and the consequent metamporphosis of the prototypes that goes with it. Many of our typical reactions in the presence of animals acknowledge this disparity in the language-games and is further fortified by what we say of them. Yet it is sometimes easy to be dazzled by the well-intentioned enthusiasm of a Vicki Hearne, or by false philosophy, into misunderstanding or down-playing the differences, and because it comes naturally to us to say that both we and the dog are angry, or frightened, we conclude that what goes for the human must go for the animal, making certain allowances for sensuous and anatomical variations. This is the confusion that bedevils so much liberationist and even scientific thinking.

Regan is a patent offender. Having argued that animals can act intentionally (to which I will return in the section on autonomy), he thinks this to be 'possible only for those who are self-conscious' (1983: 75). This is consistent given that in the case of intention, and all other mental capacities, those of animals are viewed by him as ' "models" of human mental capacities' (75). Unfortunately, Regan has a grip on the wrong model.

Stephen Clark, on the other hand, is less doctrinaire. The congregating of woodlice, migrations of salmon, and nesting of wasps are adequately explained in terms of humidity reactions, chemical attraction, or fixed action patterns (1985: 44). He later cites more complex examples of bats bumping into things, and laboratory mice that are 'induced to leap into empty space with the conviction that there is a safe landing' (47). What he then writes almost gives the impression of avoiding the confusion which I diagnosed above: 'This is how self-consciousness arises, the capacity to locate oneself within physical and social space . . . to know where one is and whom one is dealing with and what is expected of one' (47). Clark could be implying that the doings of the bats and mice are the pre-verbal beginnings of self-consciousness, of which he provides a reasonable working definition. However, 'arises' is ambiguous and his later examples suggest, on the contrary, that a form of self-awareness has already *arisen* with the behaviour. But what *use* can such an attribution serve? The leaping of a dumb brute can hardly even sustain its conviction that there is a safe landing (although a reader would appreciate the attenuated implications) but the added weight of its needing 'to know where one is and whom one is dealing with and what is expected of one' is far too much. (Clark subtly assists the progress of self-consciousness into the debate by employing the misleading metaphor that many animals 'operate largely in terms of a learned map of the area' (47), to account for what they do. We know, of course, what he *means* – animals can find bones or their ways through mazes – but the cartography misleadingly evokes the human paradigm. Maps are consulted; but not by bats.)

The confusion has an interesting source which, again, in a distorted way, recalls Wittgenstein's 'prototypes'. Animals and human infants, Clark argues in *The Nature of the Beast* (1982), must 'have a pre-verbal concept of the beings that they are, distinct from others and from the environment, and having policies that are all their own. . . . Without such concepts I cannot see that human infants could acquire a language' (1982: 47). There are two related errors here. Firstly, Clark assumes that all substantives *name* such 'concepts': 'If I can learn a word for something, I must first have grasped that thing as something nameable, whether it be a tree, a cat, a word' (1982: 46). But Wittgenstein has been seen to argue convincingly that naming is a subsidiary use of language and that many substantives are not used for this purpose (the psychological participles like 'thinking' being the obvious example) and, furthermore, that naming itself is not a sort of primal act of speech acquisition but a clutch of language-games that need to be mastered like any others. For Clark to bracket the self with trees and cats as something nameable is to mistake its use. It is a relatively sophisticated concept emerging from the mastery of a series of interlocking language-games, such as naming, talking of hopes and aspirations, claiming property and equal shares, justifying one's actions, promising, and punishing. Its model is not unlike that of the language-game of *time*. Kenny makes the same point but slightly differently:

> A dog may well think that his master is at the door: but unless a dog masters a language it is hard to see how he can think *that he is thinking that* his master is at the door. There is nothing that the dog could do that could express the difference between the two thoughts: 'My master is at the door' and 'I am thinking that my master is at the door'.
>
> (Kenny 1975: 5)

This leads to Clark's second error. His 'pre-verbal' concept of the self could only be predicated of beings who already *had* some grasp of language. This is at the heart of Wittgenstein's criticism of St Augustine's account: it is 'as if the child could already *think*, only not yet speak' (*PI* 32); as if it were learning, not its native language, but a subsequent one.

Other commentators, unlike Clark, cite their favoured items of behavioural evidence for self-consciousness as if they were authoritative without further argument. Singer, it will be remembered, in claiming that the higher mammals were persons, provides the support of the chimpanzee's frequent use of the sign 'Me Washoe'. This is about as convincing as claiming that her signing 'clock' manifests her mastery of 'time'. Griffin gives many further examples: that pets and other tame creatures come when they are called by their names (this would commend itself to Hearne), and that numerous species of birds, mammals, and even some fish and insects, seem to recognise *individual* members of their own species.

Our predictable reply would be that Griffin's examples are no more than contributory prototypes of self-consciousness. Thus a 10-month-old baby who failed to respond to its name, or to betray signs of recognition towards its mother, twin sister, or even its rattle, might well give therapists cause for concern; which is not to say that the normal baby, who does succeed in reacting appropriately, is thereby yet *self*-conscious. Griffin replies to such scepticism rather lamely: 'Allowing that an animal can be aware of outside events but denying that it can be self-aware becomes somewhat ridiculous – can the animal be aware of other creatures but not of itself? (1984: 205). A thought to the quotation from Kenny (above) will show how comprehensively Griffin's comment misses the point. Self-awareness even in an absolutely minimal form, is not merely to recognise oneself, but to be aware of recognising oneself *as oneself*, with much of what that implies.

But G.G. Gallup's mirror experiments, from the mid–1970s, are a particular favourite of those prowling for overt evidence. Here is Griffin's account:

> Chimpanzees are first given an opportunity to familiarize themselves with mirrors and then, when they are under deep anasthesia, their foreheads or earlobes are marked with a conspicuous spot of rouge or similar material. Chimpanzees lacking experience with mirrors pay no attention to such marks, but those that are accustomed to . . . mirrors reach directly for

the new spot. This seems clear evidence that they recognise the mirror image as representing their own bodies.

(Griffin 1984: 74–5)

Now this is certainly intriguing evidence of the ability of some species to adapt to mirror images (problems gleefully exploited in Lewis Carroll's *Through the Looking Glass*), and it is curious that follow-up efforts showed monkeys and even gibbons failing the tests. It is however not at all obvious that the results yield the conclusion that Griffin draws, nor is it clear that even if they did we would have evidence for saying more than that the creatures recognise their *own* bodies. But for *self*-consciousness to get a foothold it would be necessary to establish that they were aware *of recognising themselves*; which is awareness of a different order. The added complication of seeing the image as a vehicle of 'representation' is also unwarranted. Are we being invited to invest chimpanzees with an incipient grasp of mimetic theory for good measure?

It is not fanciful to allow animals recognitional capacities. However, *self*-awareness has affinities with the fear or belief that something will take place on the day after tomorrow; it is, as Churchill puts it, 'a transaction that is made in language' (1989: 314).

Perception

The previous section depicted all sorts of situations in which it would be natural to describe animals or human babies as *recognising* something – names, parents, fellow-creatures, their own bodies (but not their 'self') – and it was concluded that there was nothing out of order in so doing. Now recognition involves the use of the senses. Only within the language-games of certain literary genres would it be legitimate to describe a tree, which opens its leaves to a shower, as recognising anything. But animals, to varying degrees, employ all the senses available to human beings, with perhaps a few extra ones, and often with a far greater range of sensitivity. Now the fantasy involved in inhabiting the bodies of animals, previously alluded to, and skilfully exploited by writers like Kafka, certainly extends to a curiosity over what animals might be said to see, hear, smell, or otherwise sense. What can we say of this?

Now this question will be answered in the wrong way if we forget the qualifications, forced upon us by the adoption of Wittgenstein's notion of language-games, which permeate the implications of such talk about dumb animals. Frey would solve the problem in the following manner: Recognition involves certain *beliefs*; specifically, that the object has been previously encountered, that we are not imagining it, and so on. But only a self-conscious user of language could be capable of this. So animals are incapable of recognition. Now Regan's response to this, exemplified in the imbecile's fear, would be to insist that since ordinary usage almost seems to demand that we describe that unfortunate as recognising a snake, and because this is only possible of someone who holds the necessary beliefs, then he *must* hold them somehow and somewhere. This, as we saw, will not do. Regan is right to the extent that to talk of recognition in such circumstances does have a purpose, as it would of a dog's staccato barks and tail-waving on hearing its master's voice, but he fails to realise that the same form of words now features in a related, but different, language-game. A far narrower range of beliefs are attributable to the dog, specifically those that hark back to what we could immediately read off from similar behaviour in the case of a human being; thus the dog believes his master is at the door but it would be a false move in the game also to ask if it believed that its master would be late the next day. Lacking language, such a belief is not even possible. However, the child who dances with delight upon hearing her father's key in the lock does *unmistakably* believe that he is at the door, in normal circumstances, but, without asking her, we will not know if she is aware of the next day's possible delay. Yet she *may* do; and it is certainly a legitimate move in this revised game to be curious enough about it to ask. Now given this analysis of the animal's 'thin' or attenuated concept of recognition, it will not be open to Frey to employ the strategy he uses against 'simple' desires, which bypass beliefs, by attempting to trap their advocate with the question whether or not the animal is aware that it has them (1980: 104–5, and Chapter 2, above). It will be aware of its master, in that it hears and smells him, and of its own exertions, in that it is awake, but it will *not* be aware that it *recognises* him, for this is of the order of tomorrow's delayed return – a linguistic belief of which dumb brutes are incapable.

In clarifying our confidence in another's consciousness, human or non-human, it was seen to be an error of Griffin's to pose the problem in terms of putting ourselves into another's 'skin' or to experience their 'subjective feelings' (1984: 1, above). The same will apply in deciding what we may legitimately say that animals, in the absence of language, see, hear, or smell. We must remind ourselves of the contexts in which the relevant terms are acquired. The distracted car driver who arrives at her destination without mishap *ipso facto* saw where she was going. Her inner life or 'subjective feelings' are irrelevant, although not non-existent (indeed her inattention might have been due to severe toothache). Furthermore, learning to perceive involves getting to *know*. The infant learns to talk of hearing its mother in the garden, smelling hamburgers cooking in the kitchen, or seeing the dog enjoying itself with a ball or being hurt by the cat. There is a mistaken tendency, nourished perhaps by too partial examples, to see perception as the passive reception of evidence from an external world from which we make inferences to its causes. Thus it might erroneously be said of the dog's leaping to catch the ball that what I *really* see are just its *movements*, upon the basis of which I make a leap of faith to its inner, privately introspective, enjoyment. But an example like this clearly reveals the artificiality of such an analysis of what we *mean* when we say we see, and we have already considered the grounds for rejecting such theories in accounting for capacities like remembering, and emotions such as grief or anger. (In the case of sentience the illusory difficulties rapidly multiply. Do we *really* see the movements of the dog, or, in the spirit of such theorising, should we limit our visual world to one of rapidly succeeding shapes and colours from which we hazard the inference that a leaping dog is in the vicinity?)

Perception, therefore, at least in the human domain, seems to involve being able to talk about what we see, hear, or smell, and thereby to entertain beliefs about its objects. This is not to imply that we need always be certain nor never make mistakes; but in cases of doubt we should nonetheless be ready with some description: I see something black and circular in the road, I hear creaks and rustlings downstairs. However, this might well be thought to overstate the case, and we must not ourselves draw too heavily upon selected examples. What do we say of our driver, who was so preoccupied with her molars, that she can recall nothing of her trip? Her passenger, let us say, observed that she braked suddenly to avoid some pigeons and then carefully negotiated some roadworks as well as stopping at several sets of traffic lights. Surely we do not wish to deny that she saw these hazards despite her being unable to tell us anything about what she saw. And should we say the same of the large dalmation sitting beside her, and also of her 6-month-old child strapped in the back seat? (We must suppose both to be located at vantage points.) Of the driver it would be reasonable to say that she *must* have seen them but she has forgotten about the pigeons and just didn't *notice* the lights and roadworks. (It is a mistake to assume that we must automatically notice everything we see.)

But what of the dog and the infant? G.J. Warnock, a distinguished post-war philosopher, offers a strange analysis of seeing which allows no place for judgement nor even the capability of it, as was the case with our driver, and which would include both the dog and the infant. He writes:

> Suppose that, when I saw Lloyd George, I made no mistake only through making no judgement whatever. . . . Suppose that I was an infant in arms. Even so . . . there is reason to say that I saw him, even though I then neither made, nor could have made any judgement at all, either right or wrong, about who or what it was that I saw.
>
> (Warnock 1955: 204)

But what *might* the reasons be for saying such a thing? Imagine the driver's passenger attempting to draw the baby's attention to the pigeons, the traffic lights, and the roadworks. It might, if it is able, focus its eyes upon the speaker, having heard the voice, but it will certainly not understand. Even if it began to howl or to wave its rattle, we would hardly claim that by so doing it was discriminating between the items mentioned and a myriad others; indeed it would be odd to talk of its discriminating at all. Not until it does begin to react to such objects in recognisable and predictably different ways can the baby be said to be capable of noticing the objects in question. A developing grasp of speech will facilitate the process. Given these considerations I think Warnock is wrong to claim that there are reasons for saying that the baby *saw* these things. But the case for the dalmation, depending on its age and alertness, might be stronger. It could well become agitated at the dispersal of the pigeons, turn its head towards the lights, and bark heatedly at the roadworkers. The kinship evoked of human adult reactions in such circumstances, remembering our previous analysis of recognition, would be reason enough to say that the dog noticed the workmen and didn't like what it saw; albeit a 'thin' attribution.

Warnock's example, and its supporting analysis, might well be grounds for arguing that any living creature whatsoever might see anything. His babe in arms would be no more responsive to Lloyd George's leonine appearance than would an accompanying parakeet in a cage and if both, having seen him, were then carried around the National Gallery, it would be equally valid to claim that they had seen

149

the works of art on display as well. Warnock's error is to have neglected the necessity, in any account of seeing, of the subject's *capability of noticing* what it can be said to perceive. We can generalise from the rights and wrongs of his account of seeing to the use of the other senses as well. That a subject *is* capable of noticing whatever is to be perceived can be broken down into two individually necessary and jointly sufficiently conditions:

1. They can *recognise* the object; be it their mother, a hamburger, a pet's enjoyment, traffic lights, or workmen. There is a temptation to construe this by saying that the subject therefore has the *concept* of a mother, hamburger, or whatever. This formulation would be acceptable if the analysis were to cover only perceiving by human beings. But if the perceptual powers of babies, higher mammals such as mature dogs, and of more primitive beings such as parakeets and fish is also covered, then to talk of concepts unduly evokes the possibility of a linguistic criterion. Kenny disagrees: 'Anthropomorphism comes in only if we attribute to [animals] concepts whose possession cannot be manifested by recognition and non-verbal reaction' (1975: 51). If however, as I have argued, the recognitional capacities of dumb creatures are parasitic upon the human paradigm, and to that extent attenuated, then to talk of concepts is to over-emphasise the similarities to human beings at the expense of the differences.

2. The object must be such that the subject's senses are acute enough to pick it out. Thus we could not claim that an adult must have seen a speck of dust at a range of more than a foot or so, whereas birds could be said to see a small insect at 400 metres.

What animals are capable of discriminating between has been subjected to rigorous experimental study for many decades. Walker, for example, reports on Pavlov's success in training one dog to salivate to middle C, whether played on a clarinet, tuning fork, or organ pipe, but to no other note varying by more than a semitone however played; whereas another animal reacted to any notes but only when reproduced by one particular instrument (1983: 246). Researchers studying the other senses document numerous similar results, and what occurs in laboratories will be outnumbered by those discriminations occurring naturally in the wild that nobody knows anything about. This might be thought to throw into disarray our grounds for specifying what animals see, hear, and otherwise sense. Surprisingly it does not; which is in no way to disparage the scientific value of such research. Similar experiments, of greater variety and equal sophistication, have long been used to test *human* perceptual abilities but cause scarcely a ripple over the apparatus of our everyday perceptual judgements. Their importance will undoubtedly be misjudged however if we persist in the error of thinking that perceptual judgements, or those about consciousness, involve the replication of another's inner experience, human or non-human. The judgements we make are surprisingly flexible. 'Did you see that shabby old character with the red nose?' I ask. 'That was no shabby old character', I am firmly corrected, 'it was the Archbishop – and his nose is just cold.' Here there is a variation in background belief and 'subjective feeling' perhaps, but which allows for either judgement being preferred, even were I totally unaware of what an Archbishop *was*. It will be the same in our judgements about animals. Of either of Pavlov's two dogs we might say, as they salivated to the sound in question, that they heard a clarinet, middle C, a note, a sound; and we would be correct in each case. The prototypical reactions of dogs, in such circumstances, and their similarity to those of humans, are the grounds for our confidence in the judgements. But as we descend the evolutionary scale, and the human paradigm is more distantly evoked in the diffusive movements of fish, birds, and insects, we will be uncertain *what* to say. As Wittgenstein observed: 'If however I doubt whether a spider feels pain, it is not because I don't know what to expect' (Z 564).

Frey argues that animals cannot have any perceptions at all since this involves making judgements, attaching predicates to subjects, of which, lacking language, they are incapable. To say that the cat perceives the ball is stuck requires that it has the belief that it is, and this involves its possessing the concepts 'ball' and 'stuck'. Obviously he does not deny the cat's whining and agitated leaping in the presence of the ball, nor does he refuse its possession of 'sensory data', but these will not show *what* the cat believes; namely, 'what categories of things it recognises'. He also contends that if one attempts to isolate the judgemental aspect and base the perceptual claim upon what remains, all we have is behaviour and the 'sensory data', which is not perception (1980: 118–20).

Our analysis should clearly indicate the several blind alleys which Frey here explores. Firstly, he misses the variety of forms in which perceptual words figure and which derive from the contexts in which they are acquired; being oblivious, it would seem, to the role of language-games. Thus perception, as he conceives it, is tied too closely to the human paradigm; those normal contexts in which we require that someone be able to tell us about what they see. This is not invariable however; the case of the distracted driver or that of my seeing an Archbishop in ignorance of such phenomena are both problematical. Animals, infants, and deviant adults are said to see, hear, smell and so on, in those special circumstances, where we feel impelled to mark the similarity of their behaviour to that of human beings situated likewise whilst allowing for the inability to describe what they perceive. Statements about beliefs play a far less obtrusive role in these games. So we say 'Of course the cat believes the ball is stuck – it is conscious, its eyes work, why else would it behave as it does?' but disallow that it might have the belief *that it believes* the ball is stuck', this being linguistic (Kenny 1975: 5). This would allow us to say that the cat believes the ball is stuck but does not *understand* that it is. We might well say the same of a very young infant. (The more detailed working of this language-game was explained earlier in this section when discussing an animal's recognitional capacities.) Secondly, we are now in a position to see how we can isolate uses of perceptual words from implications of possible judgement, for what remains is not just behaviour and 'sensory data', as Frey supposes, but pre-linguistic *prototypes* of the fully developed language-game. It is unfortunate that Frey gets caught up in talk of 'sensory data' for it tends to deflect attention towards the workings of 'inner' sense and away from the whole context of the appetitive or like behaviour of the animal or human being. Vision plays a necessary but not at all exclusive role in the attribution of the perceptual words and their belief corollaries.

Autonomy: ends and means

Jane Goodall's chimpanzee, Figan, and Bernard Rollin's police dog are the sorts of example particularly favoured by enthusiasts anxious to elevate the moral status of animals. They are allegedly instances of rational action; of using *means* to achieve *ends*. But it is vital, before we canonise the creatures, to note that acting for an end (requiring teleological explanation) is almost a defining feature of the living world as a whole. Naturalists shower us with intriguing accounts, both anecdotal and experimental, and their range tends to put in perspective the sense, if any, in which we might wish to claim that some were *consciously* purposive and others not. However, there is a useful terminology to hand in the distinction between purpose, which betrays intent, and function, which does not.

Chickens are pecked by their social superiors in order to maintain a rigid *status quo* within the flock. The kangaroo rat, like many desert rodents, conserves water by remaining underground by day to avoid the heat of the sun, emerging to feed only by night. J.H. Fabre, the famous French entomologist, describes how the mud-dauber wasp lays each of its eggs in separate mud cells which it has constructed, providing in each an advance supply of fresh food consisting of spiders paralysed by its sting. It then seals each cell with 'daubs' of more mud and leaves the offspring to hatch in fields of plenty. A small fish that strays near a sea anemone, one of the lowliest life forms, will be stung by a tentacle and held paralysed by it. The other tentacles then combine to force the prey into the creature's apology for a mouth (Burton and Burton 1977: 75–7). Cats have been known to laze, apparently half-asleep, for up to an hour beside a mouse hole, yet instantly to cut down the unwary prey that, even momentarily, shows itself.

All of these descriptions are shot through with implications of reasoning from means to ends; for *human beings* to perform similar actions would, under normal circumstances, be to act purposively, with conscious intent. But given the dumb actors portrayed, there seems to be a clear need to draw distinctions between, at one extreme, the cat and the chicken and, at the other, the sea anemone and the mud-dauber; despite the fact that for many readers, ethologists included, the wasp's habits will be the most intriguing of all. But the problem will not be where to draw the line but *how* to draw it. For *where* it has been drawn is everywhere; from the insistence of Thorndike, and the early behaviourists like Watson and Hull, that all is to be explained, including human behaviour, in terms of con-ditioned reflexes, to the open-handedness of well-meaning liberatio-nists like Rollin who argue that even worms and sea anemones should be given the benefit of the doubt since we cannot be *certain* that they do *not* feel pain and therefore have a consciousness (1981: 31). Again, pursuant upon the discussion of recognition and perception, the criterion I will adopt will be the closeness of the behaviour to the pre-linguistic prototypes of human behaviour.

Anthony Kenny's analysis of the differences between the voluntary behaviour of animals, a position acutely argued for by Aristotle, and that of human beings, gives us a useful start. It is beyond doubt, he argues, and most psychologists and ethologists would agree, 'that animals act for the sake of goals, and that they may be conscious of their goals, in the quite literal sense that they may see or smell what they are after' (1975: 19). (Kenny does not add that if we were talking of the perceptions of fish or bees, our judgements might lack the confidence of those made of cats or apes.) But, he continues, animals are limited in two fundamental ways:

1. Animal goals are very short term. Kenny calls them 'immediate goals' (1975: 19). They lack the remote aspirations of human beings for which, presumably, a linguistic grasp of categories involving at least the present and future would be necessary. But Kenny's notion of 'immediate goals' is not free of ambiguity. Clear examples of it would be the cat leaping for its ball, or a lion in pursuit of a zebra. But must a foraging hyena be conscious of the food it has not yet uncovered, or a homing salmon aware of its destination as it begins the laborious trip upstream to its natal stream to spawn; both exemplars of goal-seeking behaviour? There are two possibilities. On the one hand we could insist that the creatures *had* to be conscious of their goals; that the salmon, for example, smells its home stream. Or, on the other, it could be claimed that these were long-term objectives and that the animal was conscious only of intermediate ends; the hyena was following the promptings of its hunger. Scientific observations might contribute towards a decision but Kenny's notion need not carry this degree of precision because of the second, much more important, distinction.

2. Not only must we limit the scope of animal goals but we must also limit the *sense* of the claim that animals act for the sake of goals. Kenny here explicitly invokes St Thomas's distinction between perfect and imperfect knowledge (which was discussed in Chapter 1). The actions of animals are less 'full-bloodedly voluntary' than the intentional acts of human beings. Kenny explains:

> When a human being does X in order to do Y, the achieving of Y is his reason for doing X. When an animal does X in order to do Y, he does not do X *for a reason*, even though he is aiming at a goal in doing so. Why not? Because an animal, lacking a language, cannot *give a reason*. . . . It is only those beings who have the ability to give reasons who have the ability to act for reasons.
>
> (Kenny 1975: 20)

This is well put. Aquinas is right; and it is a credit to his genius to have put animals so neatly into a perspective consistent with Wittgenstein's analysis. Kenny sums up the position:

It is undeniable that animals intend *to do* things in the sense that it is often true of them that unless interfered with they will go on voluntarily to perform various actions. But, if Aquinas is right, they do not act intentionally, intending a goal which is the reason for their actions.

(Kenny 1975: 21)

This cuts the Gordian knot. It builds on the argument in the preceding section where it was argued that because the cat sees and tries to extricate the ball stuck in the tree, it *thereby* manifests only those minimal beliefs that we would attribute directly to a human being in similar circumstances. We would disallow any involving the mediation of language, including, of course, the belief *that* it believes. But, to repeat and stress, the minimal attributions involve different language-games since the claim that the child Mary believes the ball is stuck, or that she desires it, is made of a being who does use language and the judgement carries with it this enhanced contextual implication. In the case of dumb animals, infants, and sufficiently deprived adults, the grounds of the attribution will be the similarity of the pre-linguistic prototypes to the developed human paradigm.

We might even wish to speak of animal *intention*, but if we do so it will be in terms of its 'natural' expression: 'What is the natural expression of an intention? – Look at a cat when it stalks a bird; or a beast when it wants to escape' (*PI* 647). The cat will see a bird and pursue it, to that extent knowing what it wants; but it will not know *why* it is doing it, and to that extent *what* it is doing. There is no mystery here and any paradox is only apparent. The child Mary, in the hurly-burly of lacrosse, is simply chasing a ball. She provides us with numerous natural expressions of intention. But to attempt to *isolate* them, in practice, can be no more than an illustrative device since the language-game we use of human beings encapsulates the possibility that at any moment Mary can be summoned from such a state, or summon herself, to one of reflection about her reasons for adopting this or that tactic. The same would apply to the abstracted car driver. But for the animal there is no escape; it is condemned to the natural expressions in perpetuity, and the language-game we use of *it* is appropriately minimal. This will account for the fact that although it is the obvious lesson of Darwinism that species mutate, they cannot be said to be aware of this nor in any sense to change *themselves*. They are true primitives.

Kenny makes a similar point when arguing that we can talk of

155

animal wants only to the extent that they are restricted to their conscious needs. This will recall our discussion in Chapter 2, where Frey extended needs (understood as what are 'in the interests' of something) to plants and machines. But, as I argued there, the conscious appetitive behaviour of animals is more than enough to drive a significant wedge between the expression of their needs and the mere presence of those of plants and machines. Kenny does the same, and he relates animal wants to Aristotle's notion of *epithumia*, or sensual desire: 'It is *felt* desire, and it is desire for something *now*, desire which is more or less continuously felt until it is satisfied (like hunger, sleepiness, thirst)' (1975: 49). This, I think, is an illuminating way of pointing to the prototypical role of *sensations*, accompanying as they do (but not constituting) our developed language-games such as those of pain or memory. Frey's attempt to discredit these 'simple' desires will not work here; and for the same reasons that it was finally discredited earlier in this chapter. The animal will be aware of its prey in that it consciously perceives, pursues, and devours it, but it will be *un*aware that it is doing these things for the sake of satisfying its wants. So there will be no possibility of *self*-consciousness entering the equation, for which, as we have seen, a command of language is necessary.

Clearly the analysis that I have provided will have considerable implications for our understanding of the attribution to animals of free choice. The horse dragged to the water is compelled to approach it, but if it drinks it does so voluntarily. But *choices*, as philosophers since Aristotle have argued, involve some form of deliberation. A human being, situated as was the horse, would be expected to give reasons for its refusal to walk to the trough (I'm tired, not thirsty). But dumb animals are incapable of considering themselves in this light; which is not to imply that human beings always do, only that they can normally be expected to if required. Animal choices, by contrast, admit only of causal explanations. The horse's response to being dragged to water takes the form of a typical pre-linguistic prototype of human choice. Similar considerations apply to the comparison of human and non-human preferences.

Preferences bring us to Regan who is rightfully critical of the counter-intuitive implications of Frey's blanket denials of beliefs, desires, perceptions, emotions, and so on to animals and is at great pains to stress their similarities of behaviour to that of human beings. Unfortunately he pays little attention to the *differences* and the effect these have upon the implications of what we ascribe to animals whilst using the same forms of words. Regan *mentions* the fact, of course, but in common with all the liberationists, only to downplay its importance. Thus, he tends to argue in a fairly straightforward way from the similarity of behaviour in human beings and animals to a mutual possession of the same 'concepts'. Following the criticism of Frey, Regan moves to establish a particular belief, the 'preference-belief', which he will use to prolific effect of his dog Fido's love of bones.

> On the basis of his behaviour, therefore, we have reason to maintain that Fido believes that bones are related to his desires or preferences in the following way: Bones satisfy certain desires he has and are to be chosen to satisfy those desires.
>
> (Regan 1983: 59)

On the previous page Regan has conceded that since dogs lack language, 'Fido of course cannot tell us, or reasonably be expected to tell us, whether he has this belief.' But has it he certainly does, and 'if there is some one belief that is essential for possessing our concept of a bone, the preference-belief has at least as strong a claim to that title as any other belief. . . . We have rational grounds to attribute a grasp of our concept of a bone to Fido' (63). Regan has achieved his declared aim of crediting animals 'with beliefs in a full-blooded way' (52), intending an identity with the complexity of *human* possession. But he never explains how such a belief about bones could *possibly* be held by a dog since it has such obvious linguistic implications particularly as grounds for possession of the *human* concept. Nor does he consider that animal behaviour might provide us with prototypes of human understanding on the basis of which we might consider something akin to different language-games, reflecting both the similarities *and* the differences implicit in the respective cases. The preference-belief is then seen to generate, simply by invoking the human precedent, a whole series of other attributes with which 'we begin to approach a fair rendering of the mental life of these creatures' (81): perception, memory, desire, belief, self-consciousness, intention, a sense of the future, emotions, and the capacity to experience pleasure and pain. The insensitive, high-handed, and cavalier nature of Regan's methods are plain to see.

Language possibilities

Investigating animals is big business, both commercially and academically. This is hardly surprising. Given their importance there are self-interested reasons for finding out all we can about them. Now the many attempts to teach the rudiments of a human language to primates, or more recently to porpoises and dolphins, are fascinating and probably equally useful in extending the boundaries of our knowledge of their recognitional limits. But the results are often seized upon in an ill-digested way by popular writers, occasionally the scientists themselves, as confirming that the animals have the linguistic competence and cognitive awareness of human beings. This can even be scientifically counter-productive as the psychologist, Stephen Walker, warns:

> Because claims for the conversation-like attributes of chimpanzee gesturing have been exaggerated, it is sometimes suggested that, on the contrary, their gestures have no meaning at all. It is perfectly possible, however, that something useful may be learned from experiments which fall short of demonstrating human levels of linguistic competence in apes, and I believe this is true of the projects designed to teach chimpanzees sign-language.
>
> (Walker 1983: 354-5)

The most basic error, which I attempted to pinpoint in discussing the sense in which the cries, hoots, and gestures of animals are 'primitive forms' of language in Chapter 5, is to confuse the predictive value of the effects of such behaviour with the conscious *intent* of a speaker to communicate in some way. Only if this latter requirement is met can we begin to talk of linguistic competence. If this be thought to be disingenuously restrictive, an attempt to *define away* the opposition, then consider the alternative. Much human behaviour imparts information to a sensitive observer of which its instigator may be quite unaware – blushing, rapid eye movements, hesitant speech, or 'nervous' titters. But none of this has any more to do with language than a new-born baby's screeching or a plant's wilting from lack of water, except in the unlikely event (possible only in the human case) of an attempt to deceive. But this, being a deliberative move to impart *false* information, would be a reversion to the linguistic. The 'primitive forms' of language are its pre-linguistic *prototypes*, as I emphasised in Chapter 5, and not primitive language. Much of Vicki Hearne's othewise sensitive attempt to depict the complexity of canine discrimination, of which we have little or no inkling, is undermined by this mistake.[2] That in certain threatening situations they are able to react, almost instantaneously, to the characteristic scent of an aggressor is hardly surprising. A cobra doesn't hang about either. Many species would not have survived without the weapon of the pre-emptive strike. But to describe this as an uncanny ability to read someone's intentions, as Hearne does, is optimistic to say the least (1987: 56). And even Griffin (1984: 196) is unenthusiastic about K. Pryor's not dissimilar attempts to communicate with porpoises.

But the explicitly linguistic experiments with primates continue to intrigue the non-specialist above all. Given the bodily likeness of the great apes to ourselves, and what we are told of the similarities of brain-size and structure, sensory apparatus, pregnancy span, and early cognitive competence, this is as it should be. The research has gone through four phases:

1. Attempts, mostly pre-1950, to teach the apes to imitate human speech. Gua and Vicki were the most well-known subjects.
2. The very productive switch in techniques to the use of Ameslan, initiated by Allen and Beatrice Gardner at the University of Nevada with Washoe in the mid-1960s. Maurice Temerlin's Lucy and Herb Terrace's Nim Chimsky (after Noam Chomsky) were other luminaries.
3. The work of David Premack, begun slightly later at the University of Pennsylvania, employing a magnetic slate on which coloured metal-backed plastic tokens, bearing abstract symbols, can be arranged. Premack's prize pupil was a wild-born chimpanzee, Sarah.
4. Duane Rumbaugh's training of Lana, and other chimpanzees notably Austin and Sherman, to use a computer keyboard made up of small rectangular screens upon which visual, iconic-like, symbols of lines, circles, and dots can be displayed. This was originally contemporaneous with the experiments of Premack and began at the Yerkes Regional Primate Research Centre of Emory University in Georgia.

It is particularly unfortunate that the earliest work came to nothing. W.N. and L.A. Kellogg adopted the then revolutionary idea of rearing an infant chimpanzee in their own home in the 1920s but the experiment with Gua was abandoned after a year because no signs of vocalisation resembling human speech were observed. Another family of psychologists embarked upon a similar project in the late 1940s. K.J. and C. Hayes, after six years of laborious training, had succeeded in getting Vicki to utter only four grunt-like sounds vaguely resembling Mama, Poppa, cup, and up. Other attempts had been no more successful in the interim. Apes in the wild are not observed to vocalise that much and those in zoos, although prepared to imitate human social habits, never copy their speech. Yet Vicki was certainly bright and, for example, enjoyed playing with photographs, putting those of other chimps in one pile and, allegedly, that of herself together with those of Dr and Mrs Hayes in another (Jenkins 1976: 86). What is regrettable is that the more successful methods to follow, including Ameslan, had to abandon speech; yet many theorists, linguisticians and philosophers in particular, insist upon its primacy: 'Language is speech and the linguistic competence underlying speech. Writing is no more than a secondary, graphic representation of language' (quoted by Lyons 1970: 18).

Ameslan is gestural and very different from the British 'deaf and dumb' language which is a finger alphabet not unlike its aural equivalent, the morse code. As Walker points out, it smacks of question-begging to translate animal gestures directly into words; but there is no alternative. Thus 'pen' is the first finger of one hand drawn across the palm of the other, a beckoning with the whole hand or finger ends is 'gimme', slapping the thigh is 'dog', and an index finger drawn over the back of the hand is 'tickle' (Walker 1983: 355). After four years of training, in a homely laboratory atmosphere where scientists working in shifts conversed (or 'signed') to Washoe and to each other exclusively in Ameslan, she had mastered the use and recognition of 132 signs together with the ability often to pair two of them (but rarely more than two) in significant combinations and under appropriate circumstances. 'Sorry dirty', 'more food', 'come hurry hurry', were typical. The claims were made not simply on the say-so of the individual trainers, although these were influential, but after the intricate analysis of extensive videotapes; techniques particularly associated with F.G. Patterson and Herb Terrace. This can provide reasonable evidence that, at the simplest level, one-to-one correlations exist between signs and objects or simple needs. The ape will slap its thigh when it sees a dog or sign 'gimme food' when it can be supposed to be hungry; or reverse the process, if the trainer signs, by producing the appropriate object.

It has been far more difficult however, despite the film technology, to assess the extent to which the gestures are used naturally yet significantly in the more taxing contexts of play and what some researchers call 'free living'. It is hardly encouraging that Terrace himself, whose book *Nim* (1980) is regarded as a classic in the field, after an exhaustive analysis of filmic evidence concluded that only a very small proportion of Nim's gestures, in both training and free living, could reasonably be thought to have been initiated by the animal; the vast majority were repetitions of what humans had just signed or, to a lesser extent, merely random. More pertinent perhaps, since it casts light upon the vexed question of syntax (the rule-governed combination of several words into a meaningful whole) was Terrace's conclusion that Nim and similar Ameslan apes, despite appearances, were unable to improve upon the meaning of two-sign utterances since longer sets were merely repetitious or random. Griffin, to exemplify this, reports a signing sequence by Patterson's Koko: 'Please milk please me like drink apple bottle', and one from Nim, 'Give orange me eat orange give me eat orange give me you' (1984: 200). Recent researchers, such as H.L. Miles (1983), claim to have had more luck but even then, giving them the benefit of every doubt, 'there remains a large gap between the signing of these trained apes and the speech of children who have vocabularies of approximately the same size' (Griffin 1984: 199).

Washoe, in 1970, moved to the University of Oklahoma with Roger Fouts, a research assistant of the Gardners. Fouts then began work with Lucy, at that time 5 years old, who had been raised since birth as one of the family of a psychotherapist, Maury Temerlin, and his wife. Lucy is a departure in that she appears to react to small segments of spoken English, to which she responds with her own Ameslan, in which her ability became roughly equal to Washoe's. This would appear to have more promising implications for 'free living' observations but most of Fouts' research on Lucy seems to have been directed towards syntax formation; without conspicuous success (Walker 1983: 357). The only source we have is Maury Temerlin's own account of her upbringing, *Lucy: Growing up Human* (1976). It is fiercely partisan, often embarrassing to read, and its anecdotal methods put even Darwin's in *The Descent of Man* to shame. (Peter Jenkins (1976), who visited both Washoe and Lucy in 1973, reports that Fouts was cautious about Lucy's abilities at this time and Jenkins himself seems to have been more impressed with Washoe.)

Premack's plastic tokens which Sarah, his only real success, was required to arrange in series on the magnetised slate, were designed to discover the extent to which she could make judgements about the qualities of objects; for example, 'the apple is red and round'. She began by being trained, using rewards to reinforce correct responses, to distinguish 'Sarah apple cut' from 'Sarah apple wash' and to act appropriately. She progressed to the use of prepositions like 'on' and 'under', then to comparisons like 'same' and 'different', and finally to manipulate tokens about tokens (i.e., self-referentially, in terms of their colour, shape, and size). The apparently impressive result was that Sarah made distinctions of the following sort: 'yellow question banana' would be replaced with 'yellow colour banana', or 'round question apple' with 'round shape apple'.

Terrace (1980) and others, including Walker, are unanimously critical of Premack's methods. Firstly, the translation of very simple movements with tokens into verbal terms, with all the implications of linguistic competence, is highly dubious: 'There is no evidence that the involvement of tokens in such things as grammar and semantic categorisation approaches the way that words are involved with these things in man' (Walker 1983: 364). The same criticism can, with perhaps less force, be directed at the translation of the Ameslan gestures. Secondly, and most serious, are allegations of 'Clever Hans' errors; named after the German horse early in the century that gave correct answers to arithmetical problems shown it on a blackboard (by tapping with its hoof) until it was unmasked as reacting to unwitting symptoms of tension in its trainer which caused it to stop at the right moment. Certainly Premack's findings are under this cloud since Sarah's performance suffered considerably when in the presence of a trainer who did not know the answers that she was supposed to give, and it would seem natural to expect that the more broadbrush methods of the gestural teaching would be equally suspect. But, given the interpersonal nature of the Ameslan work, it is difficult to devise accurate tests to detect inadvertent undue influence.

Duane Rumbaugh's use of computer keyboards with which two chimpanzees can be in touch with each other in the absence of trainers is, in part, an attempt to bypass these difficulties. The research team succeeded in getting their prize pair of chimps, Austin and Sherman, to flash images at each other and to respond appropriately by fetching the object signified for the other or to return empty-handed if it were not there. They performed even more complex tasks, but not more revelatory ones. They certainly do not justify Geoffrey Cowley's absurdly optimistic claim in *Newsweek* that, 'They have since dispelled any doubt that apes can really understand signs' (Cowley 1988: 54). In particular, the conviction still remains that what we have in all these experiments is a series of adaptive responses, induced by training, to obtain the numerous rewards on offer throughout the training. Furthermore, Rumbaugh's programme does not obviate the use of trainers to interest the animals in the keyboards and to guide their reactions. The possibilities of observing the communicative interaction of more than one ape is certainly something of a methodological breakthrough but it is a far cry from the use of language, observable in very young children, in which the exchange of information rapidly becomes an end in itself, rather than a means of problem solving, admittedly of a high order, which we know to exist in animals anyway.

We can now see how misleading it was for Singer to claim that Washoe, 'now understands about 350 different signs, and is able to use correctly about 150 of them. . . . She also uses signs expressing future intentions' (1979: 94). What in fact these experiments provide, in the absence of vocal speech, are a series of artificial analogues which can, with interest, be compared to the early learning efforts of perhaps a 2-year-old infant. They certainly go beyond the pre-linguistic pro-totypes of language, and demonstrate the capability of certain individual apes to outpace other species. The efforts with pigeons and parrots bear only shadowy comparison. To this extent, the fascination of the experiments is justified. But the overwhelming fact that emerges from the decades of dedicated work, using ever more sophisticated technology, is that the creature skills develop no further. At a comparable stage our infants are learning to talk. The apes are exhibiting previously unknown resources of problem solving, and the experiments will doubtless continue. But it is not language nor, it would seem, will it ever be. The evidence points to an evolutionary dead-end. Let a scientist sum it up:

> Human language is unique to humans, and although some of the distinctive features of human speech, such as the mimicking of sounds, may be observed in other species, the resemblance between, for instance, the trained gesturing of a chimpanzee and communication via sign language among the human deaf is in some senses no greater than the resemblance between the speech of a parrot and that of its owner.
>
> (Walker 1983: 378)

The status of animals: primitive beings

My contention is that our understanding of what animals really are has not been portrayed with rightful subtlety. In particular, the role of language in the equation has been grossly underestimated. The implications of its absence in animals permeate to the very heart of our everyday talk about them. The liberationists exemplify the varied confusions that abound when these are ignored.

Clark, for example, allows that animals are spared our miseries about money or job prospects, and goes on: 'It does not follow, however, from their lack of these distresses that calves cannot be acutely distressed at the absence of their mothers, nor that chickens are not distressed when unable to stretch their wings.' He expands upon this: 'It does not follow from their alleged unawareness of the possibility of death that they do not fear death, and flee it as the greatest of evils' (1977: 40). Clark simply refuses to allow that such behaviour by a creature lacking language transforms the *content* of what they can properly be said to fear or be distressed at. If I am right then to say 'The chicken is distressed by its close confinement' is a dual acknowledgement of sympathy at the presence of behavioural prototypes similar to those of distressed people, and a strong veterinary hint of a possible cure; but no more. Were the chicken a 5-year-old child cramped in a tiny cupboard, our judgement would carry implications of a different order, for the child would be capable of knowing, under normal circumstances, *that* she was distressed and *why*. Clark's introduction of death is even less convincing and here, I think, we might even object to the use of the same form of words for animals and human beings. That the calf is afraid of *death*, let alone its fleeing it as the greatest of evils, seems misleadingly to ascribe to it a self-conscious grasp of death and evil, possible only of beings capable of language. Yet if we deny the creature this understanding, which even Clark himself seems to acknowledge, yet insist with him that it nonetheless fears death, then it is in the distinctly paradoxical position of fearing something of which it could not, in *any* sense, be aware.

Midgley is similarly dismissive of Wittgenstein's remarks about hope and fear (*PI* p.174, quoted above pp.131–2). Like Clark, her argument is an all-or-nothing affair: either animals hope and fear or they do not. There is no sense of the various nuances involved in the attributions, nor that some might be inconceivable without language. That feral cats may arrive every Wednesday to be fed is obviously, she seems to think, evidence that they have a 'count of days' and anticipate hopefully what is to come:

> Consider migrations, pregnancies, seasons, brief harvests and
> the constant need to anticipate the movements of prey or

predators. Many animals move continually. . . . They have to be able to think how long this or that will last, or when it will recur. . . . Within this framework, the feat of believing that someone will come the day after tomorrow does not seem at all out of the way.

(Midgley 1983: 58)

There is no suggestion that we are to take this other than literally. Yet it seems inconceivable to be able to do so without investing every creature from worms and viruses, which follow very precise cycles of action, to the higher mammals, with the sagacity and foresight of seasoned desert nomads or intrepid Viking explorers. This is anthropomorphism.

How much more appealing, intriguing, and clear of hopeful mysticism, is the Burtons' account of the doings of honey bees, the best known of the social insects and a sub-species frequently favoured for human comparison:

A colony of honeybees is a miracle of organization. The individual bees appear very purposeful in carrying out their manifold tasks. . . . The overall control of the nest's activities comes from pheromones secreted by the queen. . . . Together they are called 'queen substance'. The queen spreads them over her body and they are licked off by the workers, who pass them to the rest of the colony by trophallaxis. Queen substance prevents the workers from rearing new queens. . . . Another pheromone is secreted by guard bees to alert other guards when danger threatens and they distribute a unique 'colony odour' to help guide returning foragers.

(Burton and Burton 1977: 223)

Food-sharing, or trophallaxis, allied with the power of pheromones to trigger patterns of action, is the regulatory bond which gives the colony its aura of the miraculous and an account in these terms is wholly sufficient.[3] To feel the need to smuggle in supplementary tales of time-keeping and conscious good husbandry, inconceivable in the absence of language, seems almost to belittle the primitive nature of these little creatures upon whom such tasks are imposed.

This then is the status of animals. They are *primitive* beings, to recall the psychic hierarchy of Aristotle and Aquinas and the *scientific* legacy of Darwin, spanning the continuum between plants and human beings. They exhibit the pre-linguistic sensations of pain and the

165

ancestral tokens of human attributes such as deliberative intent, rational planning, choice, desire, fear, anger, and some beliefs, where our guiding criteria are the close similarity of their behavioural patterns, in like circumstances, to our own. Only in an evolutionary context are these tokens the *beginnings*, let us say, of planning or choice. Their anger or fear antedates even that of the young infant who is in the *process* of integrating its pre-verbal behaviour with ill-formed vocal utterances (although we might well wish to stretch a point and allow the inclusion of the Ameslan apes, particularly Lucy, up to, but not beyond, this point). What we observe, however we dignify it, is the *pre*-linguistic prototype and it will include the gestural and vocal 'primitive forms' of language observed in the vast majority of higher species. Clearly animals, unlike plants, are conscious; but *self*-consciousness, like hope, ambition, remorse, and envy, come only with the capability of speech. (Clearly the categorisation cannot be exhaustive. The diversity of the language-games in which the terms are employed rules out mathematical precision.)

It is as primitive creatures that we must assess the claims to proper treatment made on behalf of animals. Its significance will be far-reaching, and this should be hardly surprising since similar considerations already dictate our legal and moral procedures for dealing with those human beings who, for whatever reasons, fail to measure up to normal competence.

7

AGAINST LIBERATION: THE ETHICAL DIMENSION

Common sense and moral theory

We are all theorists in a variety of ways. We argue out the whys and wherefores of putting our aged relatives in geriatric homes, taking early retirement, buying a pet for the children, or taking them to the circus. Many of our decisions will have enduring practical implications of what could be called a *moral* sort. In two of my cited cases what we do might have moral relevance for animal welfare; although the label 'moral' would probably be disputed if our uncertainty over the pet or circus were solely on grounds of cost or distance of travel.

But such theorising, however 'moral', does not make us *moral theorists*. (Here, as we have previously noted, we should beware of confusing the methods of philosophy, and also those of the 'humanities' generally, with those of the natural sciences where the aim *is* to explain the behaviour of apparently diverse phenomena in terms of general laws; the more general, the more fruitful.) Rollin is prey to this confusion. Our initial attitude to a moral question, he argues, is a response to moral intuitions, or, as he put it less felicitously, 'gut feelings' (1981: 4–6). Where these are 'virtually universal' there is no problem. Animal welfare, however, presents us with situations where 'our intuitions are mixed and inchoate and inconsistent' (5). We are concerned, he suggests, about our own dog but not our neighbour's, or are in favour of killing ten Siberian tigers as long as they are not the *last* ten.

Rollin is also severe on the sophistry of the late medieval Catholic Church in sanctioning the trial and often excommunication of countless creatures (and the then, if feasible, hanging, flaying, burying alive, burning, or otherwise executing them) whilst denying that they were free agents. The favoured species, if that is the right adjective, tended to be locusts, pigs, and cattle, but Edward P. Evans, in his marvellous book, *The Criminal Prosecution and Capital Punishment of Animals*, published in 1906, lists numerous others, including eels, weevils, dolphins, and turtle-doves, that were prosecuted over the period AD 824–1906. (Rollin, however, is mistaken about this. The proceedings seem bizarre but the Church was not inconsistent. Evans makes clear, in discussing a refutation of the Cartesian view of animal nature by a Jesuit, Père Bougeant (1739), that it was the received ecclesiastical view that Satan's allies, the myriad horde of fallen devils due for torment at the Day of Judgement, occupied themselves in the meantime by taking over the bodies of new-born babies and those of any other creatures.[1] Thus, prior to baptism, infants were exorcised. Animals were demoniacs and possessed souls, albeit not to be seen in the best company, but were unequivocally free agents (Evans 1987: 66–7).)

Rollin continues predictably. The intuitions about animals send 'mixed messages' but are unfortunately just starting points: 'So we must turn to theoretical accounts in the hope of finding some stable conceptual framework for tethering our intuitions or for cultivating new ones' (1981: 6). But Rollin overplays the card of inconsistency, as the historical evidence has shown, and consequently sells intuitions short. There is no inconsistency in my and my neighbour's holding that we each should look after our *own* dog (or sleep with our own wife, come to that). The proposition about the tigers also makes good sense; that specimens are the last remaining, be they tigers, books, or bottles of port, affects the propriety of their disposal. The intuitions survive unscathed.

Admittedly, moral theories have a distinguished lineage and a rhetorical advantage can be gained by invoking them, or, indeed, inventing them, particularly if we include, as we should, the world's religious dogmas. To have the Almighty on one's side, or one of his lieutenants (even Tom Regan) has its uses. Theories, however, operate in mysterious ways. They are not, as Rollin seems to imply, distillations of our intuitions which we then dispense in new applications. The reverse tends to happen. We can adapt our theories, or cast around for fresh ones, to suit our intuitions.

Singer's utilitarianism, for example, has already been seen to be eminently manipulable. He argues, justifiably, that the theory can support all animals being equal; but Regan, with equal justification, is suspicious of its potential redeployment in meat-eating circles and research defence organisations (1983: 200–31).[2] So Regan, anxious for an alternative theoretical platform from which to put into orbit his conviction that the immediate and absolute prohibition of all exploitation of animals is imperative, proposes his theory of 'inherent value' to serve the purpose. But the laxity with which he argues for its deployment, as we saw in Chapter 3, gives inherent value a defiantly marshmallow consistency. Thus this in its turn can be spread as thickly or as thinly as one's intuitions require and therefore used in defence of competing practical positions, most notably in the debates over abortion or the environment.

Darwin's theories have been used to support the view that *homo sapiens* is the pre-eminent of species, and have fuelled beliefs in the morality of the survival of the fittest, whilst also lending support to positions, reminiscent of Albert Schweitzer's, which emphasise universal kinship and the duty to care for the lowly and enfeebled.[3] The world's great religions are even more notorious for simultaneously looking in different directions. A relevant sidelight on their propensity to beget splinter groups, all claiming allegiance to the true spirit of their faith, is the current attempt to establish an authoritative position for vegetarianism, and animal rights generally, within Judaism. Rabbinical writers, whether orthodox or reform, uphold a tradition of not causing distress to living creatures whilst supporting the eating of meat and the role of the schochet or ritual slaughterer in its preparation. But enthusiasts like Sidney Gendin (1989: 25–32) and Roberta Kalechofsky (1989: 168–9) claim to have found a chink in the armour of the Torah with the aid of the writings of Rav Kuk, Israel's first Chief Rabbi.

Mary Midgley is alone amongst prominent liberationists in refusing to truckle to moral theories that, as she sees it, unduly promote one aspect of the problem (consequences for the utilitarians, the value of life for Regan) at the expense of others equally important:

> It follows that the contemporary search for 'a moral theory', meaning a single legitimate form for all justifications, is misguided. I find it particularly disturbing that this red herring has become so prominent in current discussions about animals, because there is difficulty enough in getting proper attention for the matter without wasting it on these academic artifacts.
>
> (Midgley 1986: 196)

She prefers to engage her readers at the coal-face, as it were; that of the formation of moral intuitions, or the making of decisions. I quite agree with this approach although (I add hastily) with little of what Midgley has to offer it. But she is unwise, I think, given her pragmatism, to ignore the *rhetorical* value of such theories and systems of belief.

The nature of choosing

If, as I have argued in the previous section, moral or ethical theories do not provide formulae that replace the need for intuitions, but, on the contrary, are used in the service of new ones, it is these intuitions that we must focus on. How do we come by them? (The term 'intuition' has an unhappy history by implying, as it does, a mysterious source of knowledge. Rollin talks of it as 'feelings', and so avoids this, yet his examples rather suggest *choices* for this course of action rather than that.)

Choices (the term I shall use) can be impulsive and even instinctive. Rollin emphasises this aspect of them. Yet even when they are, we feel the need to justify them; which is where Rollin resorts to moral theory. In addition, of course, choices can result from lengthy weighing of odds. Here is a simple example of the complexity at issue. I am driving along a narrow main road, used by fast-moving traffic, with my children in the back seat. A car some distance ahead strikes a large dog but does not stop, leaving the creature walking-wounded but in obvious distress. My children, seeing what occurred, cry out. I glance in the rear-view mirror to see other cars close behind; slowing down but then speeding up again. I do not stop. Now is there much point in talking of *intuitions* here, moral or otherwise? My driving on was not a blind impulse, for I had reasons to stop with which I would have justified myself had I done so, but I discounted them in favour of other reasons for continuing. I made a *choice*. Yet if I reflect upon what happened, in what some might call an existential manner, or attempt what physicists might call a 'thought experiment' to reconstruct my situation, I can see myself as having been assailed by various impulses: to assist the dog and stop the car, to comfort the children, to drive on lest I and they were to be injured in an accident, to avoid the horror of confronting a demented animal.

My point, in this rough-and-ready example, is to isolate certain basic impulses which appear not to be dependent upon others. The urge to stop the car will not qualify, but that which served as the reason for stopping, namely to assist a distressed animal, well might. In like manner, the impulses to escape danger to myself or the children, or evade the animal's agonies also appear to be basic. Evidence of this is that if we attempt to justify them no obvious answer is forthcoming. It is useful to recall Wittgenstein in this connection: 'It is a help here to remember that it is a primitive reaction to tend, to treat, the part that hurts when someone else is in pain; and not merely when oneself is' (Z 540). Thus to the question 'Why do you feel affection for your children?' or 'Why are you inclined to assist animals (or fellow citizens) in pain?', it would sound lame and otiose to reply that it is because your children are kind and decent, or that you assist others in the hope that they will assist you, or that you do both to contribute to the greatest happiness of the greatest number of creatures. The answers should be in terms of what people do naturally. They are not reasons for the impulses but *causes* that hark back to the primitive responses that we share with many animals; yet qualified by noting that we, unlike dumb brutes, can reflect upon our impulses and resist them if we so decide, as happened in my example. In this context they are the ground of our *reasons* for acting.

My contention is, that as animals ourselves, we inherit genetically a whole network of such reactions within which our language-games are integrated and to some extent grounded. Thus a parent's moral duty to protect his or her children is grounded in instinctive feelings proper to our species. Parents that lack such feelings, and there are many, even if they do their duty 'for duty's sake' are nonetheless thought to be morally deficient. But parental feelings are only one piece of the jigsaw. The nuances of relationship, by which naturalists describe the societal life of animals, their instinctive protection of eggs and off-spring, the mating displays and individual protection of territories, and, in particular, the varying treatment meted out to strangers, from tolerance to outright aggression, all find their analogues in human interaction. (Remembering, yet again, that the depiction of dumb brutes in these terms requires a language-game specific to creatures that lack self-consciousness.)

The pressures of the moral arena

The child, as it gains a progressive mastery of language, grows gradually into an awareness of what it is capable. As language is integrated with its pre-linguistic impulses a genuinely human life begins to beckon. The baby's embrace of its mother, originally a mere impulse of survival and dependence, is transformed into a manifestation of love. The now conscious impulses, two or three of which dominated my example in the previous section, proliferate by this

171

means. More sophisticated inclinations emerge to compete with the basic ones, or with each other. Thus my impulse to assist the injured animal may be overridden by my reminding myself that I am on my way to get married and am already late. We are entering what some analysts call the arena of moral debate. It is important to appreciate its complexity for we might then be less likely to generalise its demands, or the way we decide between them, on the basis of the (by now familiar) too narrow diet of examples. Some problem-solving will take the form of a deliberative weighing of consequences, although quite often we choose the least likely-looking solution or toss a coin, but equally frequently we have little or no time for debate. Furthermore the sense in which we describe certain dilemmas, impulses, intuitions, or decisions as *moral* ones is notoriously imprecise.

The complexity we are faced with here is one of everyday messiness. The longer one debates a trivial matter such as whether it is right to put up with the notorious rudeness of the only fishmonger in town or to fight back, the deeper one is enmeshed in an ever-expanding web of implication. Yet we *do* have rough-and-ready scales of value; certain impulses regularly win out over others and, if the toss is there to be argued over, we will claim that this is how it *ought* to be. Driving instructors will tell us that if a cat or dog strays into our path, and we are unable to stop or otherwise avoid it in an orderly fashion, then we should run it down. Only a psychopath would include children in the instruction. So children take precedence over animals and other human beings generally do also. But the pressures mount. One works to feed, and slaves to entertain, one's *own* children, and sometimes their friends, feeling no such obligations towards those next door. It is thought neither whimsical nor absurdly divisive to spend money on one's friends but not on strangers; to attempt to do so, other than in special social circumstances, will be to make a fool of oneself. Many people furthermore (much to the irritation of utilitarians, it must be said) will think it right and proper to give tea and cake to the healthy beggar at their own gate but think little of those starving overseas; they are someone else's business, it is argued. It is tempting and indeed justifiable for the purposes of straightforward situations such as these, to tabulate a diminishing order of obligation: immediate family, relations, friends and colleagues, fellow countrymen, one's racial group, people at large, animals, and the natural world.

An objector will immediately point to the lack of stability of this simple, some will say simple-minded, hierarchy. The need to assist a stranger, even a foreign one, even a strange foreign animal, badly injured outside one's home will bring the children's party to a halt. Some people hate their relations and spend all their time gardening, and it is certainly the bone of much contention that racial and colour affinities, together with religious ones such as Judaism or Islam, cut across and militate against national allegiances. A.M. MacIver (1948) captured the slippery nature of all this particularly neatly in a short article, 'Ethics and the beetle', which despite its age still retains a cult following:

> Fellow members of a society are those, whoever they may be, who are *regarded* in the society as fellow members by the others. I myself feel that the cat and the dog who live in the same house with me are fellow members of my family circle, closer related to me socially than the human neighbour next door whom I know only by sight and name, and infinitely closer than some odd Brazilian or Melanesian, with whom my only connection is that we are fellow men.
>
> (MacIver 1948: 66–7)

All that MacIver shows here, and I think that it is all he intends, is that in certain circumstances, including those where domestic creatures are happily housed, one can argue for the promotion of animals in the hierarchy. But they become only honorary family, lacking the status of MacIver's wife and children; unlike them the animals will quickly be 'put down' when old or in distress. The position of animals *as a whole*, in the original table, remains as it was. The objector is forgetting its point; it is both provisional and one to be *argued over*. The misanthropic gardener elevates his roses and relegates his relations and if challenged, as well he might be, would give us possibly good reasons for so doing. Reasons are required; to have none would be weird. But to revert to normal and to prefer one's relations to the garden would not seem to require obvious explanation. So again the hierarchy retains its integrity. Where the objection does dent it, however, is in the ambiguity of key terms like 'fellow countrymen', something that MacIver points to. Would a Melanesian who happened to be one's cousin five times removed be a relation or a foreigner?

But the objection is salutary. The intuitive ordering will be in a state of perpetual disruption because of the pressures which give rise to varying likes and dislikes. The obsessive gardener hates his relations because two of them have criminal records. A foreigner who is stunningly attractive will readily upset the apple-cart of our preconceptions, as will a friend whom we discover has been slandering us behind our back. All sorts of influences are brought to bear upon us every time we turn on the radio or open a newspaper. Religious emotion is particularly potent. Sober citizens have been known to read about Mother Teresa, or other such charismatic figures, and be seized by the need to promote the well-being of the Calcutta poor above all else. Some have even left their families to do so. There are some observers who think this to be admirable; but there are others who believe that in such cases the basic obligations that should keep such enthusiasts at home have been obscured by pretension and sentimentality. Neither convert nor critic is obviously wrong.

Religion is not, of course, just practice but theory as well. We have already discussed theory's peculiar role in moral decision making. Yet it can sometimes be influential although, more often than not, it is the personal advocacy which brings about the conversion. A reader of Singer, let us suppose, is taken with the idea of ethics as taking the universal point of view and progresses to the principle of the equal consideration of interests, attracted perhaps by its sense of having rekindled the spirit of the Second Commandment in secular guise. But others will contend, with no lack of passion and sincerity, that if the principle of equal consideration is taken seriously and always to predominate, then it will seriously distort those natural impulses of affection and solidarity which dictate so many moral choices. The issue of 'moral distance' focuses on this. It is easy to argue, invoking self-righteous precedents, that the lady who hurries to assist the injured animal or pedestrian in the street or who feeds the beggar on her doorstep, but who fails to get excited about suffering in general and shows a disinclination to contribute to Oxfam, is really *not* a good Samaritan; that she is morally short-sighted in letting 'distance' be a factor, and that she should be equally concerned for suffering whenever and wherever. The slighted Samaritan can, of course, reply on her own behalf that she *does* care about suffering in general but that she cares much *more* about its manifestations that she can do something about and that involve her personally. This does not *settle* a continuing debate but it does not need to. This, I think, is what Bernard Williams has in mind in the following passage from *Ethics and the Limits of Philosophy*:

> Some moralists say that if we regard immediacy or physical nearness as relevant, we must be failing in rationality or

imagination; we are irrational if we do not recognize that those starving elsewhere have as big a claim on us as those starving here. These moralists are wrong, at least in trying to base their challenge simply on the structure of obligations. Of course this point does not dispose of the challenge itself.

(Williams 1985: 186)

It is enough to mount a convincing argument, in this instance by someone who is prepared to get dirty hands for her convictions; which is not to say that she must convince everyone. But it *is* an argument for the quite different model of moral obligation which I have suggested in this section.

Moral choice and legal obligation

Some readers, particularly those convinced that if only we thought long enough, or prayed hard enough, we would discover reassuring tethering posts to which to secure our moral choices, will view with some disquiet the position reached so far. This could be exacerbated by considering the possibility, not as remote as it might seem, that either party to the above dispute between the convert to utilitarianism and the Samaritan might in fact be convinced by the other's argument and take up a different moral stance. This is not to claim that there would be a change in their basic natural impulses (to assist animals or fellow beings, to protect children, prefer friends, and so on). The change would be nonetheless profound for it would involve a revaluation of the *priorities* given to these claims for attention. In fact such transformations are rare precisely because, if more than lip-service is to be paid to them, the practical implications are considerable; which is not to deny that lip-service, in the form of campaigning and complaining, has its uses. But what *is* true, I suggest, short of the occasional religious conversion or metamorphosis of lifestyle, is that the variety of circumstances make our decisions often unpredictable, but not thereby whimsical, to the extent that we often surprise ourselves. The nearest we can get to a guarantee of success in our moral choices is the cogency of the arguments that we bring to bear in their support coupled with the recognition that what we are almost invariably doing, as MacIver points out and thinkers like Sartre have laboured to establish, is continually deciding between possible alternatives.

There is at hand a convenient way out of the present morass. An earlier example posed the case of man whose feelings for his garden far exceeded those for his relations whom he disliked because their brushes with crime offended the respect in which he held the law. If religious example, and to a lesser extent philosophical theory, can influence our moral decisions, then that an action is legal or illegal will probably have even greater significance; less so for an old lag, more so for a judge. But the connection between moral choice and the 'law of the land' is far more intimate that this apparently casual connection suggests:

> The concepts of a right and a liberty (as opposed to freedom generally) probably originated however, in systems of juridical law, and it is in legal systems that they have their most subtle and interesting applications and most thorough and detailed elaborations.
>
> (Feinberg 1973: 55-6)

And what goes for a right and a liberty is also true of the other cornerstones of moral language: duty, obligation, right, wrong. The polemics of legal or parliamentary advocacy are close, formal analogues of much ethical debate; and the fines and other sanctions have their moral counterparts. The legal application of these central ideas will provide the model against which to compare the deviations, if any, of the moral equivalents.

The law: stability and animals

Individual moral decision although capable of exemplification has, because of its circumstantial and often impulsive nature, been shown to be impossible to pin down for classification. But the system of laws in place at any one time in a democracy worthy of the name has a permanence about it; partly due to the formality and bureaucracy of the institutions which sustain it, but, more importantly, because of the hydra-headed nature of the social processes which it facilitates. If income tax, the armed services, or even the Royal Family had to be revolutionised, it would be achieved by degrees with countless checks and balances. In addition, the everyday activities of the courts, in handing down precedents, and the workings of legislative assemblies like the US Congress and British Parliament, ensure constant modification and renewal at, as it were, the edges. But what remains at any one time provides a crystallised record of the society's received wisdom transmuted to some extent, of course, by the political intrusions of the democratic process and Christian tradition. (Christian belief was the forming influence of the law of equity which, in part, has to do with those legal 'persons' unable to help themselves.)

Now if we consult this record, and remember the success, in giving it its modern form, of a gallery of reformers of roughly utilitarian hue from Tom Paine, Bentham, J.S. Mill, and Tolstoy, to Bernard Shaw, Sidney and Beatrice Webb, and Evelyn Strachey, we might wonder why its provisions for animals do not embody more closely the ideals of that theory. Yet public opinion, as it is reflected in British law, has steadfastly refused to enlarge upon the spirit of the pioneer legislation of the early 1820s and 1830s, updated fifty years later, which introduced the protection of animals against *cruelty*.[4] The most recent legislation, the Animals (Scientific Procedures) Act 1986, as its title implies, is not a liberationist document. In my view this is as it ought to be. That animals should be treated humanely, and with this proviso, that they may be killed, experimented upon, hunted, raced, or petted is both the legal, and a perfectly defensible, position to hold. It is no accident that it seems to confirm the position of animals near the foot of our thumbnail hierarchy or 'order of obligation', discussed in previous sections. Furthermore the ordering, in general, is supported by legal requirements in numerous other areas. A parent is legally bound to feed, clothe, house, not to mistreat, and to see to the education of his *own* children, but not those of his neighbour; although those next door are legally protected against anyone's abuse or assault. It can be an offence, however, not to assist strangers, injured or in acute danger, where an obvious remedy is at hand such as pulling someone from wreckage or issuing a warning. But there is no legal obligation to assist people in general nor the world at large. The laws of citizenship provide a complete portfolio of legal entitlements which frequently elevate the members of a particular nation into a favoured species and the envy of a less fortunate world at large. In a less flamboyant way, numberless provisions of state law, county councils, and local authorities, regulate and make possible the wealth, power, and by most people's lights, the reasonable and necessary exclusivity, of clubs, societies, schools, and universities which foster fraternal and even class loyalties.

Reformers and those with axes to grind will argue that much of this is all wrong despite its being the case. But my argument has been that it is not difficult to defend something roughly resembling the *status quo* rather than being bludgeoned into a guilty conscience by accepting that one is a covert elitist or racist. The animal liberationists certainly think that the 'cruelty–kindness view', as Regan calls it (1983: 195–200), is speciesist since it ignores the extent to which animal awareness is akin to that of human beings. But if this is a mistake and animals are properly to be understood as primitive beings, at least as different from us as they are similar, then their modest entitlement to humane treatment, accorded them by common sense and enshrined in the law, might well be vindicated.

Rawls revisited: moral agents and moral patients

In Chapter 1, when discussing the extent to which Singer's principle of equal consideration of interests captured the sense of equality shared by Einstein and an Ethiopian tribeswoman, the status of Einstein's *tree* was mooted. The tree was arguably out of place in any equation involving human beings, however disparate, because it lacks their 'moral personality'. However, Singer objected to the importation of moral personality by contractualists like John Rawls on two main grounds and we are now in a position to supplement my provisional replies to his argument. In the first place, Singer countered, it would be difficult to locate the minimal qualification for the sense of justice and, furthermore, once established, it could well be to the detriment of equality since it might imply that we could have 'grades of moral status, with rights and duties corresponding to the degree of refinement of one's sense of justice' (1979: 16–17). My reply was, in essence, to accept what Singer found repugnant as, on the contrary, plausible features of what I have since called the 'moral arena'.

The contractualist position is supported by the Wittgensteinian model of language-learning. The vocabulary of moral and legal confrontation (duty, obligation, rights, and so on) is acquired in social contexts involving the recognition of 'give and take'. The infant Elizabeth will learn that being promised a sweet for behaving herself will result in more than the mere probability of its arrival; the penny will have dropped when she realises that a promise *entitles* her to the reward – it is her *due*, to which she has a *right*. She has mastered the language of contract. Furthermore, the young lady will learn the more vexatious lesson that she can *forfeit* her entitlements, in circumstances of which others will say were well deserved. A naughty child will, in this respect, suffer from either a diminution of moral status or, if the fault becomes a seasoned trait, a bad reputation. This is involved in becoming aware of oneself as a self-conscious moral *agent*. It is a gradual process of which there will be intermediate phases and it is hardly surprising that in such instances we will be uncertain whether or not to admit that the infant has made the grade. The opening shot of Singer's objection seems hardly to be in earnest. (Another implication of this way of looking at the origin of moral talk is that the child will learn her primary duties in familial contacts with her parents, close friends, relations, and the family pets. The horizons are gradually extended to include playgroup supervisors and classmates. Strangers, whom Elizabeth will have been warned to avoid, will be a late addition. This shows a developing scale of value, not dissimilar to the adult's hierarchy, although in the child's case there will special reasons, fortified by fairy stories, for promoting animals.)

The second objection of Singer's, more akin to our concerns, is that babies come below any conceivable threshold of moral personality, together with certain permanently retarded or brain-damaged humans. On contractualist grounds, he argues, they would seem to be bereft of equality. Animals too are incapable of moral personality. The three groups, together with the additions of which Rollin reminded us (the aged, the addicted, and the compulsive), are usually described as moral *patients*. Yet this can be confusing since many of the qualifiers, including the retarded, will have degrees of moral personality, which, for Rawls, is decisive enough to entitle them to direct justice. But even to those that have none, he argues, we still 'have a natural duty not to be cruel' (1972: 114). Yet he later seems to qualify this, in the case of animals: 'It does seem that we are not required to give strict justice anyway to creatures lacking this capacity' (512). So what is now the status of his later insistence that, 'Certainly it is wrong to be cruel to animals and the destruction of a whole species can be a great evil' (512)? Regan argues, at careful and considerable length, that Rawls is inconsistent here; that his duty to animals is in reality an *in*direct one owed not to animals as such but only to self-interested individuals who have purposes that include animals (1983: 163–74).

A great deal of ink has been spilled over the nature of indirect duties, to which I will return in the next section. It is sufficient at this point to remind ourselves of Bernard Rollin's argument, in defence of Rawls, that the interests of infants, imbeciles, and animals, will be included in the scope of those of the moral agent with moral personality. The potentiality of young children must be a concern of any community that looks to the future. The tribeswoman will doubtless have deep feelings for her children and be ambitious for their success in life, and affection and admiration for animals has had a place in all societies, even in that of Ancient Rome. It was pointed out, in Chapter 1, that such a defence will have conservative implications since it puts the moral patients at the mercy of those interests, whatever they might be, that prevail amongst moral agents in a society. Senescent Eskimos, for example, might be thought to have had a raw deal if the stories of the banishment from the familial hearth of those unfit to hunt and fish are to be believed. But no theory of moral belief ought to rule out such practices if tradition or special circumstances are generally thought to justify them. Now my argument in the present chapter, which grounds certain duties in our natural responses to each other, and in those towards infants and animals as well (instinctive responses that provide the initial springboard for language itself) lends support to Rollin's development of contractualism. That this may or may not be implicitly Rawls' own view is only of academic interest.

To round off this section we must return to Singer. The criterion of moral personality, to which he objected, was introduced to settle the status of Einstein's tree. Singer's own argument was that trees, lacking as they are in any capacity for suffering, cannot have interests. But with the hindsight of Frey's distinction (also Regan's) between *having* an interest and something's being *in* one's interest, this route is denied Singer because water, sunlight, and even perhaps preservation, in tune with the tree's needs, can rightly be said to be in its interests. It will thus earn a toehold in the moral company of animals; something that Singer could not accept. The postscript to this is that such a conclusion would follow from the revised contractualism and, I suggest, is in the mainstream of our moral thinking. The abiding and mounting preoccupation with preserving the natural world frequently, and quite rightly, takes precedence over the ravages and institutional vandalism of our fellow human beings. Our natural impulses towards mountains, waves, forests, and flowers may be less overt than those attaching to animals and other people but they are sustained by a fascination all their own.

Indirect duties

Henry Salt, writing at the end of the nineteenth century when laws protecting animals were firmly in place, complained that,

It is scarcely possible, in the face of this legislation, to maintain that 'rights' are a privilege with which none but human beings can be invested; for if *some* animals are already included within the pale of protection, why should not more and more be so included in the future?

(1922: 5)

The philosopher D.G. Ritchie, writing in 1894, pointed to the difficulties in drawing such simple parallels. Animals cannot be parties to a lawsuit, or be said to be guilty, they cannot be subject to the duties that attach to rights. And he offers a telling counter-example: 'Because a work of art or some ancient monument is protected by law from injury, do we speak of the "rights" of pictures or stones?' (1976: 182). He continues:

Thus we may be said to have duties of *kindness towards* the animals; but it is incorrect to represent these as strictly *duties towards* the animals themselves, as if they had rights against us. If the animals had in any proper sense rights, we should no more be entitled to put them to death without a fair trial . . . than to torture them for our amusement.

(Ritchie 1976: 184)

He adds that any killing of animals should be painless, and their use in experiments restricted as far as possible to 'the less highly organised' creatures. But these are only *indirect* duties of kindness since our direct duty is not to animals but to our fellow human beings whose objections to cruelty constitute genuine rights against us. In like manner, our duty to desist from damaging pictures or monuments (Ritchie conveniently aids his case by talking of 'injury') is grounded in society's desire to preserve its cultural heritage.

In a much-maligned passage from his *Lectures on Ethics*, transcribed during the late 1770s, Immanuel Kant puts the issue more baldly yet laces his account with intriguing illustrations:

Animals are not self-conscious and are there merely as means to an end. That end is man. . . . Animal nature has analogies to human nature, and by doing our duties to animals in respect of manifestations of human nature, we indirectly do our duty towards humanity. Thus, if a dog has served his master long and faithfully, his service, on the analogy of human service, deserves reward, and when the dog has grown too old to serve, his master ought to keep him until he dies. If then any acts of animals are analogous to human acts and spring from the same principles we have duties towards the animals because thus we cultivate the corresponding duties towards human beings. If a man shoots his dog because the animal is no longer capable of service, he does not fail in his duty to the dog, for the dog cannot judge, but his act is inhuman and damages in himself that humanity which it is his duty to show towards mankind. . . . The more we come in contact with animals and observe their behaviour, the more we love them, for we see how great is their care for their young.

(Kant 1963: 239–40)

Kant then goes on to describe how Leibniz (1646–1716), the great polymath, carried out field observations of caterpillars and similar creatures, being careful afterwards to return them to a suitable leaf out of harm's way, 'so that it should not come to harm through any act of his. He would have been sorry – a natural feeling for a humane man – to destroy such a creature for no reason' (1963: 240).

The liberationists are united in their opposition to these defences of animals. The resort of Ritchie and Kant to direct duties to human society which, as it were, underpin the lesser ones to animals is thought to undermine the seriousness with which we regard offences against animals. Part of the problem is, of course, that Kant's claim that animals lack self-consciousness, implicit also in Ritchie, finds no favour with contemporary enthusiasts; on the contrary, as we have had reason to note on several occasions, the liberationists depict creatures with so many human attributes that it is almost surprising to find them denied full moral agency. Clark puts the case against Ritchie:

Either those laws, from Martin's Act of 1822 to modern legislation against gin-traps . . . recognize that animals can be wronged or else are laws of manners, dealing with the vice or virtue of the state's citizens. Either the evil they seek to prevent is the suffering of animals . . . or it is the moral corruption of human beings.

(Clark 1977: 12)

(Readers should note the exclusivity of the choice presented here; something to which I shall return.) Kant, in particular, comes in for very rough treatment. Arthur Schopenhauer (1788–1860) accuses him of holding that animals are mere *things*: 'Thus only for practice are we to have sympathy for animals' (Regan and Singer 1976: 125). Regan relents to the extent of regarding this as an 'exaggeration' but concludes that, 'indirect duty views are committed to regarding how we treat moral patients as of no direct moral significance' (1983: 186). Only Midgley attempts to do Kant justice; although even she cannot resist a nod in the direction of the practice-ground. She uses the example of a shepherd who works off his malevolence towards the human race by ill-treating his dogs. But, she argues, 'Kant, himself a humane man, does not want to issue this general licence for redirected aggression. He therefore posits a set of shadowy near-duties to discourage it. But such a status can hardly work' (1983: 52).

In defence of indirect duties

Why is Midgley reluctant to admit to the existence of shadowy near-duties? Her answer is that 'The whole point of a duty is that it is bounden or binding' (1983: 52). A moment's reflection will show how restrictive this is. Kant talks of animals providing 'analogies' of human action and, in like manner, many everyday measures have a claim upon us only because they are analogous to more exemplary duties. If I am following someone who drops their wallet then it would be idle to deny that I have a duty to pick it up and return it. But what if they drop litter? Should I return it and risk a quarrel? Or cravenly deposit it in a bin? Or merely kick it aside? If a slate falls on their head I would, in normal circumstances, be obliged to assist. But if it were pigeon droppings then it would be a moot point as to whether merely to murmur condolences and hurry on or to set to work with a clean handkerchief. However, the fact that such quasi-duties are a commonplace does not, of itself, advance the cause of animals.

I remarked that Kant's argument was intriguingly illustrated. Indeed, his examples repay study since they seem to run counter to traditional interpretations which concentrate upon his theoretical comments. Let us return to Midgley's malevolent shepherd. Further suppose that he had tried Kant's remedy of being kind to his dogs, only to discover that it served merely to fan the flames of his misanthropy. Now Kant does argue that animals exist 'merely as means to an end' which involves man. But if, as Schopenhauer (1965: 95-6, 175-82) and Regan (1983: 182) believe, Kant held that therefore animals were mere *things*, like sticks and stones, then why would he not condone the shepherd's return to the beating and tormenting of his dogs in order to assuage his ill-humour? Midgley is right. Kant would condemn such goings on because they would be *inhumane*. But what price humaneness, that great virtue of the

Enlightenment, if animals were mere things? Being kind to them would be the worst sort of sentimentality, or, as Ritchie delightfully puts it, 'a mere hypocritical formula to gratify pug-loving sentimentalists, who prate about a nature they will not take the trouble to understand' (1976: 183). Had Kant believed this he would have been quick to point it out; but he does not. Indeed it would have undermined every one of his examples. Leibniz would have been little more than an impressionable fool in Kant's eyes had the caterpillar that he treated with such consideration been a mere *thing*. Yet the sorrow of Leibnitz, were he to have needlessly destroyed it, is described as 'a natural feeling for a humane man'. And a few lines later we read: 'A master who turns out his ass or his dog because the animal can no longer earn its keep manifests a small mind' (1963: 240).

Two competing strands of emphasis run through this passage which it is misleading of Kant to have entangled. The first, emphasised in the traditional readings of, say, Schopenhauer and Regan, is that kindness to animals is only of value as a psychological *cause* of human fellow-feeling. On this view, understandably, animals would be of no more worth in themselves than drugs or edifying books that produced the same effect. They would indeed be *things*. (It should be mentioned that the use of certain creatures in the treatment of mentally disturbed patients bears witness to their therapeutic effectiveness. So Kant would not be wrong to press this claim). However, were this the extent of his case then, for reasons which we have seen, his examples would be curiously ill-chosen. Their plausibility requires that the disinclination to be cruel to animals is a *mark* of true humanity; part of its *content*, rather than merely a possible cause of it. Thus the cruel master of the ass or dog has a 'small mind'; he is deficient in humanity. The sorrow of a Leibniz, confronting the caterpillar, is natural 'for a humane man'. The inclinations to treat animals kindly are grounded in the analogies to be observed in human behaviour. They are, as I have argued earlier in this chapter, instinctive responses to the pre-linguistic prototypical behaviour of animals. This makes it much more plausible to condemn the malevolent shepherd, on Kant's behalf, for he is employing means which are themselves inhumane, albeit for a humane end.

This interpretation seems to leave Kant's theoretical position intact. Moral patients that lack self-consciousness (babies, the severely retarded, and animals) remain 'merely as a means to an end'. But what now rescues them, for Kant, from the lowly state of sticks and stones are the natural and tender impulses of humane people towards them. These would probably be intensified in the case of those patients of our own species, particularly babies. The ends to which they might properly be put would be severely limited by these considerations. They exist 'merely as a means' which is only to say that, lacking language and self-consciousness, they are unable to plan and debate projects of their own as do moral agents. In this sense, Kant argues, 'the dog cannot judge', which does not mean that it is fair game for any purpose we might devise. This brings us finally to the vexed sentence which sounds so anthropocentric: 'That end is man.' This, again, is no declaration of open season; it points merely to the obvious fact that moral agents must necessarily set the agenda. Only rational beings can weigh up the merits of competing claims for attention, be they those of moral patients or other moral agents. It is up to moral agents to decide how moral patients should be treated; since animals, infants, and imbeciles lack self-consciousness.

This way of looking at Kant will help to defuse Clark's criticism of Ritchie. The two competing themes in his account which, much to the confusion of some of his critics, Kant fails clearly to demarcate, both contain valid claims; so I have argued. This suggests as much as a triple purpose in Kant's analysis of our concern for animals. In the first place, prompted by our natural humane feelings, we wish to minimise their suffering. Secondly, there is a need to further the general humanity which such behaviour augments. A third possible concern is that both may conflict with some human end, perhaps the need to control a population of deer or to eat meat, in which we take an interest. Legislation is similarly motivated. The legal protection of Ritchie's ancient monument will have at least a dual purpose; the prevention of future damage to the structure, and the recognition of an addition to our heritage. Clark's example of laws prohibiting gin-traps and similar cruel contraptions are no different. They encapsulate the democratically arrived-at beliefs both that it is wrong for animals to suffer in such ways, and also that legislation will lead to an amelioration in the behaviour of farmers and poachers. As I hinted parenthetically following the quotation from Clark, it seems perverse for him to insist that we must choose one at the expense of the other. Furthermore, although Ritchie argues that 'cruelty to animals is rightly supposed to be an offence against *humanitarian* feeling' (1976: 183), I see no reason for concluding that by so saying he is denying that animals can be wronged, particularly given the wide measure of protection he accords them. The general public could hardly be described by Ritchie as viewing cruelty to domestic pets with 'horror' were it not that its sympathies were outraged by perceived wrongs.

The varieties of legal subject

The not always well-focussed objections of the liberationists to talk of indirect duties reflects an intense dislike of what they see as the arrogance of thinkers like Kant and Ritchie. The implication, they fear, is that when the chips are down it is only rational human beings that really matter.

In the preceding section I gave ample evidence that the fear is unjustified. Kant is in favour of consideration towards animals, not just because of the salutary effects upon human beings but because cruelty calls forth the sympathy of humane people. Ritchie is equally punctilious in their regard. But, it will be objected, these theorists actually regard the status of moral patients as akin to that of slaves, and we would expect also to be reminded that contemporary opinion in the civilised world, despite pockets of resistance, is still largely in agreement with this view. Now there are grounds for this disquiet despite its being misplaced. Slavery was not exactly an enviable affair, its memory haunts much of our literature and is aggravated by the recent Colonial past of many nations. It was an envenomed back-cloth to the movement for civil rights, particularly in the United States. Feminism has an equally enlivening history.[5] Given that Singer and his supporters deliberately cast the manifesto for animal liberation in the image of these two charismatic originals, to benefit from their impetus, it is no surprise that complaints about second-class citizenry, or unequal rights justifiably voiced on behalf of blacks and women, surface in the other arena of cats, dogs, apes, and dolphins.

But the analogies which are used to justify the transition are dubious at best. Normal slaves, blacks, and women are, despite their generic and individual differences, caught within the extremes of Einstein and the Ethiopian tribeswoman. They are moral agents, able to entertain and argue for their place in the world and the entitlements that go with it; in short, they are rational beings. It is not arrogance to deny this of animals. Even the enthusiasm of a Maury Temerlin (1976) does not tempt him to attribute this level of sophistication to Ameslan Lucy; in part, for the obvious reason, that she would then be at risk to what is on the other side of this coin – moral guilt.[6] Moral patients are, for the most part, innocents. Clearly writers like Kant and Ritchie are impressed by this fact. In this section I want to clarify what follows from it; specifically, to what extent the entitlement to something is affected by the nature of the beneficiary.

Here is a simple illustration of what is at issue. A lady dies having willed money separately to her husband and the family Dalmation. If the will has been properly drawn up, the dog's legacy will be administered by an independent trustee. Now if the executors of the will delay paying out then the husband can claim that he has a legal *right* to his money. Now what of the Dalmation? Certainly its trustee can claim the money, as of right, to be used for what is in the dog's interest. But does the *dog* have a legal right, against that of the trustee perhaps, that the funds henceforth be used in its interests? Yes, if by this we mean that a third party could urge this on the dog's behalf and that sanctions of the law might well ensue. But the dog knows nothing of rights and entitlements. Does that matter? Yes, again. For the original testator might, as frequently happens, have left trust funds to be administered in the upkeep of someone's grave. With no less force than on the dog's behalf might the third-party claim that the law should intervene to see the job is done, but there would be no inclination to talk of the right of the grave to be maintained. But if talk of a *right* were insisted upon it would be seen as no more than as a flourish of personification to emphasise that the trustee had legal *obligations* towards the grave. The talk of rights in the three cases seems to carry diminishing implications. The husband has rights in a paradigm sense. The grave, on the contrary, has them in the minimal sense of its being merely an emphatic statement of someone's duties towards it. The dog, as might be expected, looks in both directions – towards the grave, whose total incapacity to understand rights it shares, yet also towards the human being with whom it has appetitive instincts in common. (This is close to Ritchie's position, but not identical since he neglects this last point and puts the dog too hastily in the grave.) If it has rights they are at best analogical ones. As Bernard Williams writes:

> There are good reasons for not inflicting pain on animals, but no particular point is made, except rhetorically, by grounding this in *rights*. Rights are a distinctive kind of ethical reason, and they are best explained in terms of assuring expectations . . . a consideration that does not apply to other animals.
>
> (Williams 1985: 216n.)

H.J. McCloskey, whose writings in this area have been influential, misses this analogical nuance, whilst otherwise arguing towards a similar conclusion in his article 'The right to life' (1975):

> The idea of a chooser, a decider, who has a full capacity for rational decision and choice, seems to be central to our idea of a holder of rights. . . . Rights are thought of as things which are possessed, enjoyed, exercised, yielded up, foregone, etc.
>
> (McCloskey 1975: 414)

The last sentence is particularly to the point since it stresses the complicated role of rights talk in everyday human transactions. Rights can be earned (to a salary at the end of the month or to a place on the Board), they can be purchased (by paying an entrance fee), they can be entered into in all sorts of ways (white has the right to move first in chess). Most of these possibilities exclude animals but where they do not (we might, for example, feel it appropriate to praise the sheepdog by saying that it has earned the right to a good meal) the attribution is clearly analogical since it is based upon such a slim comparison with human capacity. The most important point of departure, however, is that rights, whether moral or legal, can involve correlative *duties*. Citizens' rights can be forfeit if we fall foul of the law. My right to the first move at chess carries with it the duty to continue with the game, and so on. Animals obey orders, the guard-dog does its duty, but as we saw in Chapter 5, such attributions involve a language-game only reminiscent of the human paradigm. In more extreme manner we might wish to register our displeasure at the felling of a row of fine trees for a road-widening project by saying that they had the right to be left in peace. McCloskey is right, up to a point, in claiming that in cases such as these we have changed the concept: 'What we are ascribing and according are not rights in the ordinary sense of rights' (1975: 416). But the idea of a continuum of language-games employing the same word, whose contexts recall more or less distantly the analogous human original, seems more adequately to capture the spirit of what we need to say in such circumstances.

Moral rights as legal rights

The preceding section returned to a theme that originated earlier in the chapter. Legal models were invoked, certain entitlements under a will, to illuminate a moral notion. There are close analogies between the two spheres. But, of course, they are far from identical. In the first place, our everyday lives are governed by clusters of obligations, many of them in conflict, which are not the law's concern. The previous examples used to rehabilitate Kant's 'shadowy near-duties' against Midgley's criticism are mere tips of the moral iceberg. The rules of dress, and etiquette generally, sustain a great industry whose fashions seem to preoccupy some people's whole lives. To breach them can be a grave moral fault. The same implications attach to the playing of games or the membership of clubs and so on, although what is of even more interest are the 'unwritten' rules which underwrite the more formal, quasi-legal, ones. Without unwritten rules civilised life would be impossible. Indeed we are rarely aware of them *as* rules, until they are broken, since they are typical of the settings in which we received our moral training. Many were originally instinctive and, *to that limited extent*, occur naturally in animals: we normally make way for others in the street, keep promises or apologise, treat people politely and respect the sense of another's property. These are all constituent pressures of the moral arena.

Morality is frequently invoked to influence legislators. This is a commonplace that does not need arguing for. In 1911 the Parliament Act was passed permitting members of the British parliament to be paid for the first time. The argument was that some candidates, particularly from the emergent Labour Party, were not of independent means and would be otherwise unable to serve if they were elected (the first Labour MPs had appeared in 1906). This is a good argument as it stands but one can well imagine that it would have been pressed in terms of these hopefuls having a *right* to be paid if they succeeded. Prior to the legislation this right could only be a moral one; once enacted it would have legal standing as well. In like manner the suffrage of women prior to 1918 was a claimed moral right.[7] Now although the law may be extremely complex it also aims for clarity in its pronouncements or it would fail to work. One either is or is not legally entitled to an American passport, or to benefit from a will; difficulties, if any, crop up in satisfying the qualification. Where genuine ambiguities of scope arise (is a skateboarder a pedestrian or a driver?) then the aim is to reintroduce clarity by judicial precedent. There are reasonably explicit 'rules of recognition'. Laws, whilst they are in force, are in this sense inalienable. If one qualifies, there is the right to a passport; if the relevant Parole Board decides in favour then the prisoner is entitled to be released.

The moral arena also contains more motley claimants. Do I have a *right* to pursue the person who drops litter, using its return as an excuse for expressing my anger? In this case, even if one reinforces the claim by supposing that littering is illegal, the answer must be No. The most that can be said is that a good case can be made out for so doing; law-abiding spectators would probably be sympathetic, depending upon the outcome. The use of 'right', in such circumstances, seems to be a clear case of special pleading that my decision is justified by some unambiguous legality. Since I know that it is *not*, then my use of it is a bit of *rhetoric*. It would have been more honest to say that I thought the litterbug needed a lesson. A young girl at a picnic, let us suppose, has some peanuts taken from her plate by a foraging squirrel and indignantly throws stones at it. Her elder sister rebukes her: 'It's only providing for its family; it has a right to them.' Here the rhetoric is obvious, backed up as it is by the personification of instinctive animal behaviour into that of a desperate mother driven to crime. Had another *child* taken the nuts without permission then parents would probably treat the moral rights of ownership seriously since there are close legal analogies; in this case with stealing. In like manner, it seems natural to claim the moral right that promises will be kept, and for apologies to be due if they are not; or the right to polite treatment, since they trade upon the legal parallels with contract, and assault and slander.

I am not arguing that moral rights get their sole authority from contiguous laws, although they can, but rather that the existence of such laws, having been passed in a deliberative and ultimately democratic manner and being constantly under test by the legislature, is *evidence* that these types of transaction are important enough for the maintenance of civilised life as to require such formal recognition. This seems close to what Williams says, in the above quotation, that rights are to be understood as 'assuring expectations' of which animals are incapable (which is not to deny that *we* might have such expectations concerning the treatment of animals):

> People must rely as far as possible on not being killed or used as a resource, and on having some space and objects and relations with other people they can count as their own. . . . Considerations that are given deliberative priority in order to secure reliability constitute obligations; corresponding to those obligations are rights, possessed by people who benefit from the obligations.

> (Williams 1985: 185)

Moral rights in dispute

Now what remains to be settled is the status of those claims for moral rights that do not enjoy the reflected sanction of the law (examples of which I have already slighted as rhetoric), and those, perhaps more all-absorbing ones, that are thought meritorious enough by some to *become* laws. Two obvious, and ultimately successful, candidates were cited above; the first being the alleged right of those elected to Parliament to be paid for their services, and the second the claim that women had a moral right to vote. Both proposals provoked a considerable amount of opposition at the time; the drama of the bitter, tragic, and prolonged struggle of the suffragettes, in particular, will endure as part of our cultural heritage. Arguments against the first measure were also pushed with vigour. They really mattered in a society remote from our own where the prestige of many professions, including the polite ranks of clergy and the armed services, catered to the motivations only of duty, vocation, or ambition. This was fair comment at the time; some of it doubtless justified. The reasons for resisting women's suffrage were equally entrenched in traditional prejudice, as we would judge it with hindsight, but they were nonetheless sincerely felt for all that.

The point to stress is that rights which we now tend to regard as unquestionable were bones of serious contention in the past, and, like present-day calls for the return of capital punishment, might well have remained so. The reverse also is the case. What the Victorians and Edwardians accepted, and the law enshrined, as natural privileges due to birth, social connection, and education, are fiercely contested these days. Now the rights to vote and to receive reasonable payment for one's work are representative of a special category of alleged rights. They are examples of what are variously called 'natural', 'inherent', 'inalienable', or 'human' rights.

Animals possess legal rights; although, as we have seen, the notion is more restrictive than that of human entitlement. Laws in most countries protect them against cruelty and other forms of abuse. But liberationists like Regan and Clive Hollands (1985), as we saw in earlier chapters, scorn this as requiring no more than kindness towards animals (Hollands, for example, dismissed it as 'a Victorian concept') and demand a great deal more. Their language frequently evokes the domain of human rights, no more so than in the 'Declaration against speciesism', which concluded Chapter 1, where we have a transliteration of the US Declaration of 1776. If, as seems to be the case, animals are alleged to posses rights with all the charisma attaching to these more fundamental notions, we need to clear the air by examining the extent to which human beings do.

Natural rights

The law, I have argued, is relatively fixed. It will fail to perform its function of maintaining a stable society if people's expectations cannot be reasonably guaranteed for some time to come. But its provisions are not sacred. Even in cases where a written constitution exists, such as in France or the United States, the introduction of interpretational devices can soften the letter of the law (witness the continuing debate in America between 'strict constructionists' and the rest). The US citizen's historic right to bear arms, for example, is thought by most of them to be both outdated and counter-productive, yet it was taken by the founding fathers to be 'self-evident', inherently the due of human beings. Were they wrong? Are its contemporary critics at fault? Or is natural rights a confused notion?

I suggest that it *is* a confused notion. The only plausible way historically to guarantee the authority of such rights has been to see them as the issue of a divine law-giver. In this guise they embody fundamental truths which are permanent throughout time and space. This is the theory of Natural Law. In ways that are seldom very clear, although in which inevitably revelation plays a part, the terrestrial instruments of the Divine (the Biblical prophets, the rabbis, Mohammed and the Koran, Christ and the Bible) derive from these natural laws not only the more temporal and local moral paraphenalia but also, in collaboration with jurists, dictate the content of the civil law. Both the French and American Declarations make explicit reference to their theological inspiration.

Theories, however, as we have already seen, are notoriously prone to being wielded in support of often contradictory ways of behaving and believing. The natural law doctrine of a core of unassailable and self-evident moral truths rapidly gets squashed by the mountain of successive interpretations which devitalise even the simple phrases of something like the Ten Commandments. It was this impatience with the manipulative potential inherent in talk of natural rights, and the possibility of its being used to delay or reverse urgently needed measures to ameliorate the lot of the common man, which was Bentham's reason for dismissing it all as rubbish. In a famous passage in his *Anarchical Fallacies - An Examination of the Declaration of Rights* (1795) we read,

192

That there are no such things as natural rights . . . no such things as natural rights opposed to, in contradistinction to, legal: that the expression is merely figurative . . . Reasons for wishing there were such things as rights, are not rights; – a reason for wishing that a certain right were established, is not that right – want is not supply – hunger is not bread . . .

Natural rights is simple nonsense: natural and imprescriptible rights, rhetorical nonsense, – nonsense upon stilts. But this rhetorical nonsense ends in the old strain of mischievous nonsense: for immediately a list of these pretended natural rights is given . . . there is not, it seems, any one of which any government *can*, upon any occasion whatever, abrogate the smallest particle.

(Bentham 1962: II. 500–1)

This gave rise to so-called legal positivism. Any talk of rights other than those enshrined in the (positive) law is dangerous because it can be used by fanatics or the self-serving to subvert that law. The mere fact that people are convinced that freedom, for example, is a good thing, even that God desires it for us, does not make it more than wishful thinking. Rights without the backbone of legal sanction, Bentham contends, is just talk. The only principle that should guide legislators, and it is a moral principle stemming from the revolutionary ferment on both sides of the Atlantic, is to advance the general welfare. (Note that its pre-legal status would deny even this as a *right*.)

Since the Second World War, however, the climate of opinion has reversed itself. It is again fashionable to talk, this time of *human* rights, with the same inalienable and even self-evident character of the earlier natural rights or the rights of Man. The United Nations 1948 Declaration lists no fewer than thirty main Articles with numerous dependent entitlements. It represents a summation of the received humanism of the latter half of the century, including the main provisions of its eighteenth-century predecessors (life, liberty, security, and the pursuit of happiness) and with gestures towards more partial demands for Trades Union membership, paid holidays, and freedom to travel, yet without any obvious grounding in a religious deity. Most of its requirements are incurably vague and therefore fair game for the most wilful of interpretors, others, such as the right of unrestricted travel or for paid holidays (tell that to a Sudanese peasant), are totally impractical. It is difficult to view the talk of 'rights' here other than in the light of Bentham's scepticism. The provisions are well-intentioned hopes, for which arguments may be forthcoming, but with which many will disagree. Its sole authority is that of the United Nations Organisation itself. The charge of rhetoric sticks. The language of rights evokes the context of legal entitlement backed up by civil enforcement. In some cases, those where laws have been *enacted*, this will be justified, but for those that remain mere hopes it is no more than a persuasive figure of speech.

Regan (1983: 268) quotes the philosopher Richard Hare who in his article 'Justice and equality' denounces those obsessed with asking about their rights; they will,

> being human, nearly always answer that they have those rights, whatever they are, which will promote a distribution of goods which is in the interest of their own social group. The rhetoric of rights, which is engendered by this question, is a recipe for class war, and civil war. In pursuit of these rights, people will, because they have convinced themselves that justice demands it, inflict almost any harms on the rest of society and on themselves.
>
> (Hare 1978: 130)

This is strong stuff, true only in a minority of instances, but Hare's point is that the potential for stupidity and even tragedy is always present when people mislead themselves and others into thinking that if they want something strongly enough then they are *entitled* to it.

Some contemporary defenders of human rights, and with them animal rights, such as Bernard Rollin, use in their support the arguments of Ronald Dworkin in his influential book *Taking Rights Seriously* (1977). Dworkin's starting point is that the content of a particular law is almost invariably open to the interpretation of judges. Hard cases test the 'rules of recognition' and, in the absence of explicit guidance, impossible for every contingency, judgements are made on the basis of prevailing feelings about 'justice or fairness or some other dimension of morality' (1977: 22). For example, in an important case where a murderer claimed an inheritance, having been named in the will of his victim, judges invoked the moral opinion that someone ought not to profit by their crime (23). This referral to morality, Dworkin argues, is endemic to all law. The concentration of the legal positivists upon the use of utilitarian considerations to guide legislators, judging everything in terms of the common good, can

194

result in individual injustices, and human rights are necessary to protect the individual against these.

In attempting to elaborate upon this and to answer the question, 'How do we establish *other* rights, or define the content of the rights which *are* enumerated?', Rollin shows how little Dworkin's argument serves to deflect the Benthamite scepticism. 'The answer is simple', Rollin comments, and quotes Dworkin's argument that the American Bill of Rights 'must be understood as an appeal to moral concepts rather than laying down particular conceptions', taking this (rightly) to mean that 'one must use *moral arguments*; one must present moral reasons and discussion'(1981: 75). Surely we need to invert Rollin's naivety here: the answer is therefore anything *but* simple. To ground the many provisions of, let us say, the UN Declaration of 1948 in the mere possibility of their being defended by moral argument is to consign them to a very combative arena indeed, the vagaries of which we have explored in this chapter and are precisely those exploited by Hare in his gloomy quotation. It will certainly not provide the stability necessary for rights which are supposed to be inalienable and imprescriptable, let alone self-evident.

What might perhaps be rescued however, to which Dworkin gives us a clue, is the sense of a cluster of very basic rules, the observation of which seems necessary for the understanding of rational existence as we know it. These are the 'unwritten rules' of civilised life discussed in the preceding section: the keeping of promises, treating others politely, respecting their property. The sense in which they are *natural* is that such ways of behaving are grounded in instinctive reactions, and their prototypes are observed in some animals. They provide the basic impulses which prompt decisions and, as we have already seen, serve for us as important *reasons* for action. But their versatility and the unpredictability of the individual moral dilemma, including, in particular, the implications of competing reasons which may be brought to bear, make it impossible to specify the *courses* of action in support of which these reasons will necessarily lend themselves. The closest to an available touchstone will be those rights which, at any one time, have survived the rigours of debate and enjoy the protection of a legal system. This is not an acid test, far less a self-evident one, but, as I have tried to show, contenders that profess to be are sure to fail.

How animals should be treated

If, as I have argued, it is normal and typical of human beings to have basic impulses to assist other creatures in distress, to find them appealing to view, and in some cases to enjoy their close proximity (infants reach out naturally towards a puppy but get agitated by wasps or beetles), it does not follow that we know how to treat them. At the simplest level we may be in doubt, for example, whether to approach an injured bird for fear of exacerbating its plight, or be uncertain whether the bitch giving birth needs assistance. In such cases we consult the veterinary experts. But there are, of course, problems of a different order which also test the reliability of our initial impulses. Is the donkey pulling a loaded cart, the sheep on its way to the slaughterhouse, or the dilapidated parrot on a perch, happy or being treated cruelly? If our inclinations are to intervene, should we do so or resist them as sentimental? Here the expert will be less authoritative. Even if we are assured that the creatures in question are not in any pain, some people will prolong the argument either by insisting that they *must* be in some sort of distress, or by claiming that even if they are not overtly suffering, what is happening to them is cruel and unwarranted exploitation.

Now how we answer these questions will depend crucially upon what we think animals to be. If we claim, as Regan does, that animals enjoy a whole range of cognitive abilities *in the same sense in which we ascribe these to human beings*, then what follows is that 'human and animal welfare do not differ in kind' (1983: 116). Consider the following example. Cases frequently come to light in which submissive children have been treated literally like household slaves, often into late middle-age, by domineering parents. That they made no complaint and knew no better would never justify such treatment. Critics would stress the extent to which the children's freedom to map out their lives for themselves, to make genuine preferences on the basis of a range of possibilities denied them, had been stifled. Doubtless they would also point to the misery, frustration, and sense of a life wasted, that this belated recognition would inspire in the children themselves. Such mental distress is only possible for beings capable of comparing one chapter of their lives with another. The possibility of reason-giving, of being capable of the awareness *that* one's life was one way, *that* it is now different, and *that* futility is the result, involves, as I have contended at length, the possibility of language. Only for such beings is ignorance *not* bliss.

Yet Regan argues for animal welfare on the same model, making the explicit comparison with human beings:

> It is . . . no defense of consigning either humans or animals to environments that ignore their biological, social, or psychological interests . . . to claim that these individuals do not know what they are missing and so cannot be any worse off for not having it.
>
> (Regan 1983: 117)

So the implication is that in such instances animals also would be worse off. But how? There are two possibilities. Overt suffering might be the result; but Regan immediately rules this out (as one also would in the case of my example). Such environments are harmful to the interests of 'humans or animals . . . whether they cause suffering or not' (117). The alternative is that the dog, like the children, has the *capability* of becoming aware of the misery of its present existence, although it may never in *fact* do so. But, in the absence of language, this is impossible. Regan persists in smuggling in such propensities. That Fido eats from the bowl of meat rather than from that containing eggplant is 'grounds for saying that the dog prefers his normal food' (85). As a special language-game, pointing only to the pre-linguistic prototype of human action, this would be acceptable. But this comes down to saying no more than that the dog eats the meat not the eggplant. But Regan wants more; specifically, he wants the *human* context of 'prefer'. Of the animal's need for water, he points out, 'like us, and in this respect unlike flowers, they *prefer* to have these needs satisfied' (89). But the human context involves the capacity to weigh the merits of the case, to give *reasons* for one's choice or to dismiss them. This involves language.

The alternative to Regan's typically liberationist view of animals, which I have argued for in this book and summed up in the concluding section of Chapter 6, is that animals are *primitive* creatures. Judging their welfare now becomes in many ways a much easier matter since we do not have the intervention of mysterious interests which, on Regan's model, they must be supposed to have yet will be unable to give voice to since they do not speak. No. Our true guide should be their perceived needs, their 'simple' appetitive desires devoid of the human implications that 'desire' carries with it of being self-conscious. The welfare of human beings, even the comparatively straightforward needs of health, food, and sex, are assessed largely in terms of the individual's view of their own life. But the needs of animals, what we see to be 'in their interest', cannot be guided by their own views of themselves for (lacking language) they cannot have any. We can only look to the practices within which *we* treat animals, be it as pets, racing animals, food, experimental subjects, or denizens of the wild, tempered by our natural disinclination to cause them needless suffering, or treat them with disrespect. These practices dictate the criteria for our judging what constitutes needless suffering. The *needless* suffering of race-horses, for example, is assessed differently from that of laboratory animals. (We will return to these practical issues in the next chapter.)

The argument in the preceding paragraph is tantamount to accepting the interpretation put upon Kant's dictum, earlier in this chapter, that animals are means to an end: 'That end is man.' That they are not 'ends in themselves', to continue with Kantian terminology, simply marks the contrast with human beings whose desires and needs operate within the context of the pattern they impose upon their own lives. Yet this will not rule out our taking seriously the 'preferences' of animals themselves (using the term in the sense of the attenuated language-game proper to them). But the value of so doing will still be measured against *our* purposes for them. Farm animals that eat cow parsley with apparent avidity will, if they lose weight, be properly prevented from so doing. If their appetites return following the deprivation then it would be pointless of anyone to argue, after the manner of Regan, that by barring them from eating what they prefer the farmer is harming their interests. Only if they showed signs of overt suffering, such as palpitations or symptoms of unusual aggression, ought the farmer feel constrained to act. Thus, for animals in the absence of suffering, ignorance *is* bliss.

Flights of fancy: the exaggerations of welfare

If animals, particularly mature birds and the higher mammals, are taken as possessing more or less the full range of human capacities, with the exception perhaps of moral agency, and if the only dissimilarity is that the capacities are manifested in more limited ways, then there will be an almost irresistible temptation to give them moral status approaching that of recently discovered Stone Age tribes such as the Dani of Irian Jaya. Now if we can give a sense to a residue of basic rules which qualify as human rights, as I have argued, then a respect for life would certainly be one of them. And if the Dani are being systematically wiped out, as Edward Whitley alleges, then such rights are being shamelessly violated (1989: 18). Rollin's parallel is predictable:

> What of animals' rights to life? The point seems clear. If one takes the position that human right to life is absolute, then one must show a morally relevant difference between human and animal life that justifies denying that an animal's right to life is absolute, and I believe we have shown that such a difference is not readily found.
>
> (Rollin 1981: 48)

(In fairness to Rollin he does allow that such rights may be breached, but only for life-or-death reasons. Our 'mere gustatory predilection for meat', in his eyes, certainly does not qualify.)

Now there is a huge gulf between the liberationist picture of mammals having the moral status of honorary *human* beings, albeit primitive ones, with rights in tandem, and the view which I have advanced that mammals are primitive *beings*. Fish, beetles, protozoans, and trees, will be successively more primitive beings. If the Dani are being killed simply to make space for settlers from Java then it is appalling, and for reasons previously advanced on behalf of the Ethiopian tribeswoman. But if animals are primitive beings then none of this applies to them. An animal does indeed strive instinctively to keep alive, much as it will forage for food (plants in unconscious and less mobile ways do also), but, lacking language, it is unduly anthropomorphic to describe this as hoping or aspiring to live to a ripe old age; except perhaps as a joke. It would be even more fanciful to claim that the animal has plans. If, furthermore, animals lack self-consciousness, as I have argued in Chapter 6, then no sense can be given (a far stronger claim than that we do not know) to the contention that they are aware of the prospect of death and terrified at its implications. (I will return to this point in Chapter 8.)

This must not be seen as condoning the random killing of animals; far from it. In the first place, elaborating upon arguments in previous sections, our instinctive impulses to avoid cruelty will normally extend to their needlessly being killed. (That some people lack these impulses is normally grounds for criticism; we call them sadists, cruel, or, if it is by way of business, then merely hardened.) Secondly, what is or is not needless killing will again be determined by the role of the animals in the practices in which *we* employ them. The wardens in a National Park, or game reserve, will cull only those deer necessary to match the herd to the available food supply. Unless and until the killing of animals for food becomes illegal then farmers will rear and select those creatures that need to be killed to meet the demand.

Rollin's confusion stems from his assumption that because animals have needs we may conclude that they have interests, which, like those of human beings, are owing to the possessor. This is not so. We pay attention only to what is 'in the interests' of an animal, since it is incapable of the awareness *that* it has an interest. And what *is* 'in the interests' of animals is mediated by human practices that involve them. Rollin quotes some biblical examples of regulations which, as he quaintly puts it, 'bespeak an eloquent awareness of the status of animals as ends in themselves' (52). This would be mildly surprising given that the primary emphasis of both the Old and New Testaments is of man's 'dominion over the fish of the sea, and over the fowl of the air, and over the cattle, and over all the earth' (*Gen.* 1 v. 26). Two of his examples are the prohibitions against plowing 'with an ox and an ass together' (*Deut.* 22 v. 10), and against muzzling the ox 'when he treadeth out *the corn* ' (*Deut.* 25 v. 4). But these are just as convincingly seen as injunctions which any sensible farmer, keen to use his animals most efficiently, would employ. Needlessly to hamper working animals bespeaks more eloquently of bad husbandry.

This brings us to another group of alleged animal rights which relate to its functioning as a biological organism. Rollin writes: 'An animal has a right to the kind of life that its nature dictates. . . . This nature is defined by the functions and aims (not necessarily conscious aims) of the creature in question' (52-3). It is in this spirit that Rollin interpreted the biblical examples. The patriarchs of that distant agrarian culture are supposed to have been motivated by the rights of farm animals to do what comes naturally to them. But other examples will better illustrate what Rollin has in mind:

> A captive giraffe has a right to a cage in which it can stand straight up . . . Or a bird surely has a right to fly, and keeping a bird captive in a small cage that prevents this is immoral in much the same way as is not allowing a person to express himself verbally . . .
>
> (Rollin 1981: 53)

Most reasonable people would side with the rhetoric of 'rights' here, particularly of the giraffe's plight were it unnaturally cramped. The analogies with human incarceration are uncomfortably close. But the ground of the complaint would not be that the giraffe's right to self-determination was being thwarted, as we would say of a human being in a cage, but the general distaste at the conviction that the animal must be suffering severe discomfort.

Now what of the bird's right to fly? This example is far less clear cut. If the bird were dashing itself against the bars, feathers flying, then the similarities to human suffering would arouse impulses to assist, even to release it, like the giraffe. But what if the bird were quiescent? To say, in the abstract, that birds have a right to fly seems to me rather foolish if it be taken as saying more than that most birds fly naturally. But it does not follow from this, as Rollin seems to suppose, that we *ought* to allow them to do so in the absence of clear signs of distress. We have only to think of numberless caged birds the world over who are better fed, more healthy, and longer lived than their fellows in the wild, yet apparently contented despite their inability to do little more than flap their wings. The temptation is to anthropomorphise their plight, to compare them with human beings in similar situations (as Rollin does explicitly) who would almost certainly be distressed at the opportunities that they were foregoing and make protest. Yet if, like John Cromartie in David Garnett's novella *A Man in the Zoo*, such a person did not object to being caged up (Cromartie enjoyed it) then we would raise no objection to its continuing, however unenviable we might think it to be (Garnett 1932). Why not adopt the same approach to the bird who shows no distress and, lacking self-consciousness, is incapable of considering its position one way or the other?

Animals and imbeciles

It is impossible to discuss in any depth the merits of treating animals in one way rather than another without making comparisons with human infants and imbeciles. It goes without saying that almost invariably the instances of animal behaviour that we find ourselves discussing involve adult creatures. Yet the capabilities of mature mammals and birds to fend for themselves, to care for their offspring, and to interact with their own and other species, far surpass those of the 12-month-old baby or the anencephalic with whom they are so frequently bracketed. These abilities promote animals in our affections or, to put it more academically, are moral points in their favour. Yet most babies rapidly and without effort cross the language barrier, emerging slowly into self-consciousness and incipient moral agency, a barrier which for animals is insurmountable. Babies also become human adults; the significance of which will be reserved for the next section. Imbeciles may well have *been* adult persons, if their disability were due to accident or disease.

These variations may well affect our decisions about the treatment proper to subjects in the respective categories. Yet it is dangerous to be doctrinaire about precise significance. Moral theorists, and not just liberationists, get very excited about marking out the differences between cases which are 'morally relevant' and those which are not. (Utilitarians like Singer, for example, put exaggerated emphasis upon the capacity for suffering, whilst Regan, as we have seen, takes refuge in the theology of 'inherent value'.) But the realities of decision making, as I have tried to show earlier in this chapter, are not so readily pinned down. It would surely be over-hasty to argue that a mother, for example, who clearly preferred her showjumpers, or even her collection of books, to her children, was necessarily in the wrong; she might nonetheless treat her offspring very well. Even so, our feelings about the mistreatment of the permanently retarded tend to be particularly strong. It is a category, as we have seen, which encompasses a range of disabilities from Down's syndrome (whose victims may even learn to read or write) to microcephaly (where the manifestations of life are no more than those of a vegetable) and these differences are usually of account. That a hospital lets babies with minimal brains and no conscious potential die would occasion less hostility, and many might even approve, than if mongoloids were dealt a similar fate. Yet if it were known that microcephalic babies (perhaps older infants as well – would it make a difference?) were regularly sold to research laboratories, then there would undoubtedly be an outcry. The liberationists are alive to the implications of these sentiments for the cause of animals. Stephen Clark in his article 'Animal wrongs' puts their case as well as it can be put:

> We know that we ought to care for the subnormal precisely because they are subnormal: they are weak, defenceless, at our mercy. They can be hurt, injured, frustrated. We *ought* to consider their wishes and feelings, not because we will be hurt if we don't, but because *they* will be hurt. And the same goes for those creatures like them who are of our kind though not of our species . . . If the one is wrong (as it surely is), so is the other, for they are, in moral terms, the very same act.
>
> (Clark 1978: 149)

This argument invites us to ignore the relevance of any distinctions which we may draw between subnormal human beings and other animals. If we accept it, as many people seem to with enthusiasm, then we would have to include the rats, mice, dogs, cats, and numerous other creatures used in the laboratory, in our outcry over the revelations about the sale of microcephalic infants. The argument will have done its work. Yet it will strike others as suspicious, if well meaning, sleight-of-hand. Three difficulties present themselves:

1. It ignores the obvious discriminations which we make between similar treatment of different species *within* the animal kingdom. The casual shooting of a chimpanzee or a horse is surely regarded as more reprehensible than routinely stepping on a beetle or laying a trap for mice. All are equally weak, defenceless, and at our mercy but there is no question here of 'the very same act'. It is not just that beetles and mice are pests (we might have said the same of ladybirds and the pursuit of wildfowl), but rather that the relative similarity of the larger mammals to ourselves materially affects our thinking and is reflected in our instinctive responses.

2. Clark does not help his case by talking of the human 'subnormal' for it is a class, as we have seen, that manifests a wide range of distinctly human abilities. Our care for the teenage mongoloid, for example, is powerfully influenced by its own plans and aspirations, and this will obtain to a diminishing extent with the more severely retarded. In many cases the possibility of being used in painful research would be a prospect that they could grasp and would not relish.[8] That none of this is within the competence of animals would seem to influence a preference for them as laboratory subjects. In such cases the similar treatment of human subnormals and lower animals would be far removed from 'the very same act'.

3. Clark's argument might appear to be on firmer ground had he restricted the human comparison to total imbeciles (anencephalics and the like) where the complete lack of linguistic ability, and even of its behavioural prototypes in many cases, would prevent any appeal to exclusively human propensities. That we do not treat animals with at least the same respect that we treat such unfortunate human creatures is seen by the liberationists as 'speciesism' in its purest form based as it is only upon the anatomical difference. There are four cumulative replies to this charge. First of all one can deflect it by denying that some forms of species solidarity are mere bias. If *homo sapiens* is unequivocally demarcated from the rest of the animal kingdom by the

language barrier then it would seem reasonable to accord something like honorary status to those existing in its image, as it were, but otherwise enfeebled through age or retardation. Certainly the spirit of the *legal* provisions for such unfortunates is onerous in its detail and wide in application, extending even to strict regulations covering the proper treatment of human *corpses*. Even household pets, as MacIver reminded us, can be accorded similar if less formal privileges. This urge for special consideration, in the second place, is reinforced by our normal instinctive responses to assist those in distress which tend to operate even more peremptorily within species than across them. Thirdly, human imbeciles will usually have relations or medical custodians deeply concerned for their welfare whose wishes have a right to be heard. Again only pets (and some zoo creatures) bear comparison. Finally, it is possible to reverse the flow of the argument and consider whether the attention paid to what some will regard as mere wrecks of humanity, quite apart from the treatment of human corpses, is not exaggeratedly sentimental. Perhaps, after all, anencephalics *should* be considered for suitable research, although I personally would not subscribe to such a view.[9] This reversal of the argument will clearly not assist the cause of animals.

The comparison with human imbeciles can serve to show animals in a more creditable light. They are, as we have frequently observed, capable of feats of sentience and locomotion that surpass anything of which we are capable. The rather weary drawing of parallels between animals and instances of human retardation diverts attention from their true source of value to us. Animals may be primitive beings but they are not thereby defective ones. In this sense, animals (and we might add primitive peoples and even the environment) are *sui generis*; they are perfect of their kind. I can make the point more contentiously. The vast amount of medical research devoted to the early detection and treatment of foetal abnormalities is witness to the fact that society would prefer that there were no retarded babies born. This does not imply that existing defectives should be done away with, nor that we should condemn the decision of a couple, whose foetus is at risk, that to have a retarded baby would be preferable to having none at all. Nor is it to deny that defective dependants will often, and quite understandably, attract far fiercer loyalties by that very fact. The point is that normally such parents would prefer that their babies were *not* defective and would welcome a non-controversial cure were it to become available. Actively to wish to give birth to a retarded baby, or to insist that one remain so when it might be otherwise, would be perverse and eccentric. In this sense the world would be a better place without mental retardation, madness, and senile dementia. But if someone were to claim that it would be a better world without birds and bears, trees and rivers, and the Dani people, then we would have to assume that they were either joking, lying, or crazy.

To highlight the *sui generis* nature of animals is not liberationist. It serves only to put their comparison with human imbeciles in proper perspective. It is a substantial prop but supports no more than the traditional safeguards for the protection of species and against cruelty and abuse.

Infants and potentiality

In the preceding section we saw the obvious advantages for the liberationists in urging that animals be included in the respect and sympathy normally accorded to human sub-normals. But the inclusive nature of this category required that comparisons be limited to the most severe cases; those lacking any semblance of human capability. Now normal pre-linguistic human infants, for a relatively brief period of their development, share none of the conscious hopes, plans, and desires for a continuing life, of the mongoloid child. To this extent the baby is comparable to the total imbecile; or, if we include its sentience, limited locomotion, and prototypical behaviour, it is not unlike a cat or gibbon. Yet society tends to lavish care and protection upon normal babies far surpassing that accorded anencephalics or even cases of Down's syndrome and mongolism where letting die ('passive euthanasia') is frequently defended. Now if the liberationist can persuade us that this passionate regard for normal young babies is based upon an unjustifiable prejudice in favour merely of our own species, and that apart from this, animals are no different, then consistency should require that both groups ought to be accorded the same treatment.

The obvious objection to this ploy is that whereas babies, soon to be crossing the language barrier without let or hindrance, have the *potential* to develop into normal autonomous persons, even the highest animals do not. It is on this account that we talk of the baby's right to life, much as we would of a normal adult. (We cannot, of course employ this argument on behalf of anencephalics, although mongoloids could benefit from a variant of it.) It is, however, vulnerable to a well-known reply. Singer, for example, although he is here questioning the alleged rights of the human *foetus*, admits that it must have a potential that

> surpasses that of a cow or pig; but it does not follow that the foetus has a stronger claim to life. In general, a potential X does not have all the rights of an X. Prince Charles is a potential King of England, but he does not now have the rights of a king. Why should a potential person have the rights of a person?
>
> (Singer 1979: 120)

This is a good argument for it should warn us that there are degrees of potential not all of which are automatic claims to fame. (This realisation seems completely to disarm McCloskey (1975: 415), for example.) This is well illustrated in Singer's own context of the abortion debate. The one-day-old normal baby is a potential person with a right to life that very few would deny it. But so is the 6-month-old foetus. In its case, although just viable, opinions over its right to life are fiercely contested. Now what of the zygote, the newly fertilised egg? It too, in a sense, is a potential person but it would seem the act of a fanatic to insist that it has a right to life. And what of the sperm? It also, with the right degree of cooperation, may become President of the United States. The principle seems to be that the closer the potential person approaches its realisation and the fewer the remaining hurdles to surmount, the more attributes of the *actual* person seem proper to it. But precision is lacking; the debate over the foetus at six months contrasts with the unanimity over the zygote and new-born baby.

Let us now turn to Prince Charles. Note how Singer muddies the water in his case. The general principle (line 3) uses the world 'all', the implication being that a potential X has *some* of the rights of an X. This is true of anyone a mere heartbeat from the monarchy. Prince Charles has many of the powers of a king, particularly in the Queen's absence, and to a diminishing extent so do the other princes, princesses and minor royalty, at further removes from the throne. Someone is doubtless fiftieth in line, and still a potential monarch, but with no supermarkets to open or ships to name, the rights have run out and the potential succession will be little more than a talking point. But Singer omits the 'all' in the two concluding sentences of the quotation which gives the misleading impression that Prince Charles has *none* of the rights of a king.

What can we say of the infant? We are aware of its potential. All being well, it will slowly qualify to make decisions upon progressively more major matters. It will gain the rights to an education, and eventually to marry, vote, and buy alcohol. But it does not *now* have these rights although it is highly desirable (for us) that its future progress towards them be facilitated. What is therefore owing to it, what is 'in its interest' are our custodial duties of care and protection. These are the only rights of persons (we can certainly call them rights since they are protected by law) that it is necessary and makes sense to attribute to the infant now. Animals bear no comparison, lacking this potential; the care and protection due them is no less peremptory but it is dramatically limited in scope by their 'primitive' status.

So, against Clark, it must be argued that it is misleading to claim that because animals, imbeciles, and normal infants are all weak, defenceless, and at our mercy, to treat any of them in the same way (say by killing them for food or using them in research) is 'in moral terms, the very same act' (Clark 1978: 149). A great deal hangs upon the species difference, the human capacity of the less subnormal, and the potentiality of normal infants. Furthermore, the possibility of reversing the flow of the argument on behalf of imbeciles, mooted in the preceding section, and to wonder if our regard for them is not in part sentimentality, will not work for normal infants. The reversibility depended upon the permanence of severe retardation whereas infants are not defective and their human potential is a fact.

If the direct comparison with human beings, defective or otherwise, is not to be the touchstone of our treatment of animals; if they are, as I have argued, *sui generis* primitive beings, then what may we do with them? What is permissible? It is to such practical questions that we turn in the final chapter.

8

CHAPTERS OF DISCONTENT: EATING, EXPERIMENTING, ZOOS, BLOODSPORTS

INTRODUCTION

Bernard Williams touches upon several themes emerging from the last chapter which will directly affect the practical conclusions of this one:[1]

> A concern for nonhuman animals is indeed a proper part of human life, but we can acquire it, cultivate it, and teach it only in terms of our understanding of our selves. Human beings both have that understanding and are the objects of it, and this is one of the basic respects in which our ethical relations to each other must always be different from our relations to other animals. Before one gets to the question of how animals should be treated, there is the fundamental point that this is the only question there can be: how they should be treated. The choice can only be whether animals benefit from our practices or are harmed by them. This is why speciesism is falsely modelled on racism and sexism, which really are prejudices. To suppose that there is an ineliminable white or male understanding of the world, and to think that the only choice is whether blacks or women should benefit from 'our' (white, male) practices or be harmed by them: this is already to be prejudiced. But in the case of human relations to animals, the analogues to such thoughts are simply correct.
>
> (Williams 1985: 118–19)

The message here is straightforward. If we are required to make a decision which has consequences for other people, and if we wish to treat them properly, then it is vital that we take into account their own views on the matter. Simply to decide upon the basis of what *we* think is best for them can be a form of prejudice.

Many contemporary abuses bear witness to this. The alleged displacement of the Dani in Irian Jaya is one. The deplorable and apparently continuing goings-on of the American fundamentalist New Tribes Mission in the Gran Chaco wilderness of Paraguay, if the reports of Norman Lewis are even half true, is another (1989: 20–4). To round up clans of Ayoreo Indians with the dubious intent of rescuing them for Christianity, massacring those resistent to 'taming', imprisoning the remainder and allowing them to sink into ill-health and torpor, seems monstrous. Even if the treatment were kindly it would still be prejudiced. If we were convinced that conversion would be in the Ayoreo's interests, it nonetheless should be entered into willingly.

With animals it is different. The *best* that can be hoped for, on their behalf, is that human beings are kindly disposed towards them. The most primitive people, as we have seen, have a clear sense of what is owed to them in social and quasi-commercial transactions. For others knowingly to ride roughshod over these expectations is where the concept of 'exploitation' begins to get a foothold. But animals can have no expectations in this sense since they lack moral personality – a sense of rightful give and take. The entitlements that animals assuredly have, embodied in prolific legislation, are those that human beings have given them. They are based upon our ways of treating animals, whether it be killing them painlessly or protecting an endangered species or preserving a natural habitat. The same, of course, goes for human infants or incompetents (and for trees as well). In all of these cases special considerations, which I have elaborated, serve to limit what is thought to be appropriate treatment; but in none of them do we consult the recipient's point of view, for there is no such view to be had. Even when we defer to a creature's apparent preference (for a particular type of food, let us say) the decision will be dictated by *our* desire to keep it fit and healthy.

Abuses and abolition

If Norman Lewis, a reputable journalist, is to be believed, then the Ayoreo Indians have been shamelessly abused by the New Tribes Mission with, it seems, the open support of Paraguay's ruler. Less is known of the Dani's fate, but let us suppose that Whitley's worst fears are justified (1989: 18). What, if the means were available, should be done? In the absence of a convincing case for the defence, we would undoubtedly require that the Indonesian authorities be seen to have cleaned up their act and that the New Tribes Mission be put out of business in South America and perhaps worldwide. But would it not be dangerously confused to call for an end to all missionary activities or every government resettlement programme, even in Indonesia and South America? A practice may be abused without its necessarily being a bad one. We would not wish to outlaw parenthood on the grounds that some children are abused, even murdered, in the home.

Most of the calls for the abolition of our routines involving animals, particularly those appearing in the Press or the propaganda material issued by organisations like Animal Aid or the League Against Cruel Sports, ignore this basic logical point. So-called 'horror stories' (gory illustrations depicting the de-beaking of turkeys, dogs being hanged, huntsmen exulting over the corpse of a fox, or reports of a senile researcher who failed properly to anaesthetise his animal subjects) may well be effective copy and have an impact upon gullible readers but are of limited argumentative worth. A genuine case for abolition, if it is so based, needs to establish both that the alleged abuses are as stated and that they are endemic to the practice; thus *unavoidable*.

KILLING FOR FOOD

The number of animals killed to satisfy our taste for meat dwarfs those used in the other main areas of controversy, those of experimentation and hunting. Richard Askwith (1988: 22) gives the British Home Office figures for 1986, which are a typical comparison for the UK. Just over 3 million experiments were performed upon animals, mostly rats and mice. Richard Ryder's figures for 1987 are slightly higher at 3.6 million (1989: 242).[2] UK Government statistics for 1988 and 1989 show a steady decline in the use of research animals since 1977 (Highfield 1990). But around *400 million* animals are eaten annually in the UK. The irony, of course, is that since a considerable proportion of these were bred for the purpose, a large number of animals would not otherwise have lived were they not destined to die prematurely. (Askwith also mentions 'some 100 million birds and small rodents' estimated to have fallen prey to domestic cats, although surely such a statistic could hardly be arrived at with any confidence.)

What these figures will not have taken account of is, for example, the 54,000 kilos of frogs legs imported in 1986 mainly from Bangladesh and Indonesia. Frog-catching gangs ensure that this is a thriving trade in these countries although it is conducted in hideously unhygenic conditions and there are adverse ecological implications due to the increase in malerial and other waterborne pests. Partly for these reasons, and partly due to pressure from western organisations like Compassion in World Farming, the Indian government has recently banned the slaughter of frogs for this purpose.

A related example, which provides a useful introduction to a more detailed look at the complaints levelled at our own practices, frequently surfaces in the national Press. Campaigns are being waged against the Republic of Korea where laws forbidding the eating of cats and dogs, the latter a traditional source of medicinal potency, are openly flouted in the ubiquitous 'boshintang' (dog-meat soup) houses. 'Gae sogu', a dog-meat wine, is also popular. Yet the so-called 'International Alert' issued by the World Society for the Protection of Animals, which highlights the charges, is curiously ill-focussed. Its petition refers to the 'inherent cruelty' of dog eating (the use of 'inherent' seeming to imply that abuse is inevitable) but the support-ing literature does little to substantiate this. The dogs are raised mainly on breeding farms and are described as 'generally well kept in outdoor pens with adequate room'. The traditional method of slaughter by slow strangulation might well seem revolting but that is admitted to be a 'waning practice'. Its replacement by 'a sharp blow on the back of the neck or a blow from a mallet to the forehead' is relatively humane if administered skilfully. The transport to market is certainly slipshod but the dogs illustrated look in good condition and, indeed, would not sell if they were dilapidated since the animals are generally sold live. If there *are* abuses then they are clearly avoidable, and this, as we have seen, provides inadequate grounds for abolishing the (in Korea's case admittedly illegal) practice of dog eating.

Vegetarianism as a test case

Clark, Regan, and Linzey are, for different reasons, in favour of the total abolition of everything associated with meat eating. Linzey, of whom I have said little, bases his case upon strong 'theos' rights for animals emanating from the God of Christianity being on the side of, or '*for*' his creation (1989: 40–4). It is an insecure notion which runs into troubles that Linzey himself raises (43–4): the Old Testament seems to point to something approaching a psychic hierarchy, and Christ ate fish and conceivably meat as well. But the most serious hurdle is the fact of a creation in which animals kill each other. Linzey rather lamely consigns this to the problem of evil. Yet Clark sees it as a perfectly natural phenomenon and not to be condemned nor

211

interfered with (1977: 166–7). Linzey's theology is typically manipulable into something approaching Clark's position. If God created primitive living things like plants for animals to eat (do plants have *theos* rights?), then why should He not have created more complex but still primitive beings which kill each other and may be eaten by man who has been set in dominion over all else?

The liberationists, with the possible exception of Rollin, do seem to regard the use of animals for food as the cardinal vice, although it is run close by the fuss over furs and field sports. Perhaps it is due to the disproportionate numbers killed for food, or possibly that becoming vegetarian is an unmistakable gesture that it is within anyone's competence to make. From it follows a series of hardline implications for the other practical issues. The only other dissenter is Mary Midgley who, with good sense, questions the pride of place given to an unambiguous vegetarianism (1983: 25–7): 'What the animals need most urgently is probably a campaign for treating them better before they are eaten', and she augments this by advocating a gradual move towards the consumption of less meat (27). She needs to have added the caution that much depends upon the reasons why people are vegetarians. My brother just dislikes the taste of meat and is faintly surprised that other people do not. But he is not critical of meat eaters. (He is, I suspect, in a minority among vegetarians.) But if there were a sea change, and they became the majority that meat eaters are at present, and if this were fueled by the arguments of Regan or Singer, then surely it would be reasonable to expect a knock-on effect in the other contentious areas.

Considerations of utility: human welfare

In *Animal Liberation* and all his subsequent writings on the topic, Singer employs his animal-enhanced equality principle to argue that the consequences for all concerned would on balance be best served by almost total vegetarianism. (The 'almost' allows for exceptional circumstances where, let us say, killing is the only way to obtain food (1979: 55, 105).) What are the interests put in the scales? Firstly, there are considerations of *human* well-being. The evidence that it is inefficient to use meat for food is well documented. If the grains, soy beans and fishmeal, which are used in the feeding of food animals in the developed world, were consumed directly by human beings then there would be something like a ninefold gain in the nutritional spin-off. In other words, 90 per cent of the nutrients are lost in the transformation of the grains into meat. It is worth noting that the beneficiaries would not be the members of the developed world: 'If we stopped feeding animals on grains, soybeans and fishmeal the amount of food saved would – if distributed to those who need it – be more than enough to end hunger throughout the world' (1979: 160).

Now the ending of all hunger would undoubtedly benefit many in underdeveloped countries in the short term; although the demographic and political implications might be slightly chilling if one ponders upon international stability in the next century. But what of the claimed benefits for the health of developed nations? The only fact upon which dieticians seem agreed is that in general we eat too much meat and too few vegetables, which distorts the balance of fat in our bodies. Research suggests that the incidence of cancer, cardiovascular complaints and other degenerative diseases, quite apart from the general ill-health resulting from obesity and lack of exercise, diminishes if our intake of meat, and other sources of fat, is lowered. For instance, in Japan the diet, still mainly fish and rice, contains considerably less fat than that of Europe, North America and Australasia. The Japanese also enjoy a lower incidence of cancer. But as Carl Simonton, the radiation oncologist prominent in the holistic health movement, and others point out, this does not isolate diet as the sole or even the main cause and it is likely that cultural factors, for which Japan is unique among industrialised nations, may be more significant (Simonton *et al.* 1986: 38–40).

Population studies have shown that the susceptibility of institutionalised catatonic schizophrenics to cancer is very low. (Catatonics typically do not speak or appear to listen or take necessary initiatives; they cut themselves off from human contact.) But the incidence of cancer among paranoid schizophrenics in the same or similar instiitions eating the same or similar American diet is higher than that of the normal population (Simonton *et al.* 1986: 38–40). These and similar studies suggest that the stress put upon diet, in the case of cancer and related conditions, might be misplaced. Furthermore, meat as a known but not unique source of calories, protein, and vitamins of the A and B groups, is almost invariably included in balanced diet sheets. Only proselytes urge that we should all desist from it entirely; and there are exceptions among even them. I am not claiming that meat is indispensible for good health; it is only necessary to show that a diet to which it contributes can be no less healthy than one from which it is excluded.

Utility and western society

But let us, for argument's sake, concede the nutritional point. Whatever weight this would add to the utilitarian scales, would need to be colossal to offset the social and economic ills which might well follow. Frey in *Rights, Killing and Suffering* (1983) paints a detailed picture of the possible downfall of whole economies the minutiae of which, although hinting strongly at overkill, are nonetheless plausible enought to be disturbing (197–203). I will mention only three areas of potential catastrophe. In the first place, a huge number of industries would be undermined, bringing the misery of unemployment to employees and their families where alternative jobs were not available. Many localities in Europe are dominated by livestock and poultry farming and vaster areas such as the states of Iowa, South Dakota and Texas are deeply involved. Argentina, Australia and New Zealand would have a considerable proportion of their national economies wiped out. Secondly, our social lives would need readjustment. If it is difficult to change habits like smoking or drinking, despite the best of intentions, then the switch to nut steaks and vegetable lasagne might be just as painful, and for those forced to it because of the unavailability of meat it would also be deeply resented. Most traditional French, Italian, British, American and even Oriental restaurants would cease to exist in their present forms. Thirdly, the idea of the European countryside, valuable to many as a source of beauty, history, and national pride would also be transformed. Sheep would not safely graze nor would spring lambs nor calves; the average farmer could hardly be expected to stock them for old times' sake. Clark is beady-eyed in his dismissal of what he seems to regard as sentimentality:

> We are entitled to ask why it matters, if it is true, that there should be no such poor slaves to be seen. Because we get aesthetic pleasure from the scene, and are therefore entitled to instigate whatever distress be necessary to achieve our satisfaction?
>
> (Clark 1977: 65)

His alternatives are predictably bleak: 'Much of what is now sheep country could profitably be reforested with nut-trees' (1977: 60). Rural Britain would more and more resemble parts of the American mid-west. Life would be strange indeed.

Singer's attempt to duck these difficulties by arguing that social changes of this magnitude would need to be phased in slowly will not survive scrutiny. The problems would re-emerge in other forms. What, for example, would be the time-scale envisaged? Thirty years? Would impatient abolitionists like Regan be prepared to wait that long? If Frey is an exponent of gloom and doom, then Regan is a master of myopia on this issue and shows an unbecoming lack of sensitivity which suggests that his answer would be No. In the first place, he argues, farming is a risky business (he compares it to 'road racing') and if the demand for his products dries up then it is just bad luck on the farmer and his dependants. In the wider context Regan contends that, 'though the (economic) heavens fall' there is no case for protecting society 'if the protection in question involves violating the rights of others [viz. farm animals]' (1983: 346–7).

The dark side of farming

Most vegetarians are so, I suspect, primarily because they object to the death and what they see as the suffering to which animals are consigned by meat eating. The suffering involved which receives most publicity takes place in intensive or factory farms, although it is not confined to them. These are a practical necessity[3] and it would be quite impossible to meet the present demand for meat and dairy products, except in certain rural areas, from the products of traditional farms that were the order of the day in Europe and North America up until the Second World War:

> Now, virtually all of our poultry products and about half of our milk and red meat come from animals mass-produced in huge factory-like systems. In some of the more intensively managed 'confinement' operations, animals are crowded in pens and cages stacked up like so many shipping crates. . . . There are no pastures, no streams, no seasons, not even day and night. Health and productivity come not from frolics . . . but from syringes and additive laced feed. . . . The typical cage in today's egg factory holds four or five hens on a 12- by 18-inch floor area.
>
> (Mason 1985: 89, 91)

Jim Mason is writing of Britain in the early 1980s. The percentages for the rest of modernised Europe, with the exception of Switzerland, are slightly higher and for North America they are higher still. Patrick Sutherland estimates that of 170 million farm animals in

Britain 'about two thirds never walk on or eat grass' (1989: 62).

Horror stories abound, originally fuelled by the publication of Ruth Harrison's *Animal Machines* (1964), a book which in Britain directly influenced the setting up of the first parliamentary inquiry into the new methods of animal husbandry under the chairmanship of F.W.R. Brambell. (It reported in 1965; nothing was acted upon for about six years and even then very little was implemented.) Close confinement encourages aggression and distorts instinctive behaviour patterns. The result is often cannibalism, especially in chickens and turkeys, which are debeaked and often have their toes cut by the same hot-knife machine as a preventative. Pigs also are prone to the habit. With these it is often initiated by acute tail-biting which gets out of hand 'and then the attacking pig or pigs continue to eat further into the back. If the situation is not attended to, the pig will die and be eaten' (quoted by Mason 1985: 95). The factories are rife with diseases needing attention and routine dosing of the animals with vitamins and drugs takes place, often to the point of dependency.

Singer, like Ruth Harrison, gives prominence to the methods employed in the production of veal that were pioneered in Holland. By now, due in part to media coverage, these are fairly well known. The calves, when only a few days old, are tethered by the neck in a stall about 60 cms wide and 150 cms long, until they are too large to turn. It has a slatted wooden floor and is often without bedding lest it be eaten. The calves remain 'crated' until taken out for slaughter between three and four months later during which time they are fed a milk-derivative liquid diet 'enhanced' in the usual ways with vitamins, medication, and sometimes growth-promoters. The feed needs to be as iron-free as possible in order that the eventual meat will be the light colour preferred by consumers. Because the animal is denied the natural iron in what would be its natural food it develops anaemia. As Singer puts it, 'pale pink flesh is in fact anaemic flesh' (Regan and Singer 1976: 32). This is not the end of its troubles. The instincts to suck and later to eat roughage are often vented on the wood of its stall. Stomach ulcers and other digestive disorders are rife and there is a high mortality rate amongst veal calves despite their brief lifetime.

Defects of utilitarian abolition

Now Singer thinks it is undeniable that what we have here is a catalogue of inequality. Unless we are confident that the meat we eat was produced without suffering, the equality principle 'implies that it was wrong to sacrifice important interests of the animal in order to satisfy less important interests of our own' (1979: 57). However, this conclusion is not without its difficulties.

1. Even if *all* meat and dairy products were produced by intensive husbandry and the alleged abuses were rife it would nonetheless be perfectly fair to argue that the possible catastrophic consequences of widespread vegetarianism for human beings, which have been pointed out, would more than outweigh the continued suffering of the animals. Clark not only dissents but is hopeful enough to scorn utilitarian considerations about humane husbandry and so forth:

> This at least cannot be true, that it is proper to be the cause of avoidable ill . . . this at least is dogma. And if this minimal principle be accepted, there is no other honest course than the immediate rejection of all flesh-foods and most bio-medical research.
>
> (Clark 1977: Preface)

2. Not all meat and dairy products are produced intensively and Singer seems to allow that if we are confident that ours came from animals humanely bred and slaughtered then we are doing nothing wrong in eating it. Admittedly he has some reservations even about free-range farming such as the need for castration, transportation and slaughtering techniques but, as Francis and Norman point out (1978: 516), since Singer himself thinks that much of this suffering could be eliminated, it is simply a matter of working to bring these improvements about. Someone concerned at the suffering might well think it more appropriate to work for reformation rather than abolition.

3. Although it is undoubtedly the case that farm animals *do* suffer from many of the horrors of intensive husbandry (it cannot be pleasant for a pig to be eaten alive) there are serious questions to be asked about the extent and nature of the alleged suffering. Dr Livingstone's paralysis of feeling when seized by the lion is worth recalling. An observer would have been convinced that Livingstone was in hideous pain but this was not so. Injuries in war and disasters provide numerous anecdotes of the anaesthetic effects of shock; a doctor in the aftermath of London's Clapham rail crash of 1988 reported having treated several victims lying or sitting by the track in a state of bewilderment and oblivious of serious wounds; in one case an ankle was completely severed other than for a few shreds of flesh. In most of the accounts of animal abuse, be they in factory farm or

primate laboratory, even the more sensitive monkeys are portrayed in similar ways: comatose, agitated, even neurotic, often with serious injuries, but not necessarily *in pain*. This is so even of accounts by activists anxious to maximise the horror (Pacheco and Francione 1985: 136–7, Barnes 1985: 160). We owe it to clarity to disentangle the varieties of suffering possible in a given situation.

Here is another example of the need for vigilance when assessing usually well-intentioned accounts of distress. Singer, in his depiction of the hapless veal calf, protests that, 'Obviously the calves sorely miss their mothers. They also miss something to suck on' (Regan and Singer 1976: 31). The previously-mentioned use of the wood of their stalls as a substitute is adequate grounds for the second complaint. But to describe their state as one of *missing their mothers* sounds suspiciously like hyperbole designed to wring illicit sympathy from the reader. (We noted the same imputation by Clark (1977: 40) in the concluding section of Chapter 6.) Are we meant to take it seriously? Premature babies are routinely taken from their mothers on the maternity ward into intensive care, or sterile areas, often for long periods and although their mothers might miss them, it would be thought sentimental to claim the opposite. What *is* true is that the absence of, say, its mother's milk may affect the baby's medical condition and, to this extent, it misses the milk (although unable to be aware of the fact) but not its mother. The baby can certainly suffer complications if deprived of mother's milk and it might well be claimed that talk of its missing its mother is a special language-game pointing only to the source of the deprivation, but Singer is certainly not using the phrase with this in mind. His use is anthropomorphic. The calf is supposed to miss its mother as it might be said of a 4-year-old child. But this requires the *self*-awareness of a developing language-user: a grasp of the significance of its mother, her absence and hoped-for return, and so on. This is something that not even a Washoe or Lucy, far less a baby calf, begins to approach.

Slaughtering

Similar arguments to those just put forward can be used to defuse the claim, frequently made by liberationists, that animals awaiting slaughter are aware of their fate. Harriet Schleifer is a vigorous employer of selected horror stories: 'Thousands of animals are assembled in a single location, close to a building that all of them must enter to die. They cannot remain unaware of their fate, and intense fear is the natural and inevitable result' (1985: 71). This is designed to evoke chilling reminders of men, women, and children huddled in ghastly expectation; dying in pogroms and concentration camps. But the analogy is misplaced. Animals must, and can only, remain unaware of their fate since to be even possibly otherwise would involve an understanding of dying, and its implications for one's desire to continue living. (I likewise criticised Clark in Chapter 6.) Schleifer is confusing the agitation, or even prostration, which occurs in badly run holding-yards as a result of heat, noise, overcrowding, or lack of water, with the uniquely human fear of death.

This is not to condone the abuses of transit animals. They are rightly illegal. If the strict regulations in most western countries governing the transportation, temporary holding, and eventual killing of farm animals, were more effectively policed, and often inadequately staffed inspectorates brought up to required strength, then mistreatment could be all but abolished. (In Britain, for example, only a few of the larger slaughterhouses, mainly in urban areas like Birmingham, have a permanent staff of qualified veterinarians to check procedures.)

Abattoirs are forbidding places. Visits are not encouraged and, if permitted, are best not preceded by a heavy lunch. But far too much can be made of this. The world is full of unlovely places and we should even be grateful that people are prepared to do important work in uncongenial surroundings like prisons, operating theatres, field hospitals, soap factories, coal-mines, and sewage farms. Slaughtermen in the UK need to be licensed (although the requirements are often easily met and there are no statutory national standards) and those that I have observed take a grim pride in doing the job with efficiency. (Doubtless there will be the odd sadist in their midst but this is predictable of any group of more than thirty people.)

A contentious issue within the trade, relevant to our enquiry, was the growing problem of ritual slaughter required by orthodox Muslims and Jews which must be undertaken by special religious functionaries like the Jewish *schochet*. Despite being generally unlicensed these tend to work alongside the regular staff usually in the larger urban abattoirs. Traditional methods require that the animal bleed to death after having its throat cut; an agonising and unsavoury procedure lasting between one and two minutes. This, however, can be avoided by 'pre-stunning' before blood-letting; a compromise which ensures that the animals die insentient. Yet for some time the imposition of this compromise was resisted and resented as seeming to undermine the spirit of the ritual methods. But times seem to have changed and pre-stunning now meets only token resistence, if any at all. Indeed recent reports on the Muslim-owned United Food Corporation, centred in County Mayo and one of the world's largest meat suppliers, suggest that the Islamic ritual, which governs all its slaughter, can be interpreted as requiring only that the killing be performed by the appropriate Muslim using normal abattoir equipment (Murdoch 1990: 28).

Conclusion

It is certainly possible to defend vegetarianism. Apart from merely disliking the taste of meat, like that of anything else, one might also decide that the cruelty involved in some intensive farming, although not endemic to it, is unacceptable even in the short term. Others might be persuaded by the current furore over the possible spread of spongiform encephalopathy (BSE) to nonruminants such as poultry and pigs, and decide to give up all meat (contrary to the majority of expert opinion). But it is equally justifiable to eat meat whilst being concerned about current abuses in its production and preparation, none of which, given time and energy, are thought by bodies like the RSPCA, to be irremovable. Intensive farming is, after all, in its infancy and the campaigns against it, both in Britain and the USA, have resulted already in remedial legislation on such issues as debeaking, overcrowding, cage sizes, and the use of steroids and other growth promoters.

But attempts to convince us that the eating of meat and fish is an evil invasion of the inalienable rights of animals and that it should cease forthwith are a sham. They can only succeed with the help either of opportunistic flights of fancy such as inherent value or *theos* rights, or by otherwise obscuring the differences between creatures like ourselves, who use language, and those that do not. The result of so doing is the sad and mischievous error of seeing little or no moral difference between the painless killing of chickens and that of unwanted children.

EXPERIMENTATION

All of the practical issues raised in this chapter have their expert domain. The possible spread of BSE from ruminants to other food animals, even to pets and human beings, is a typical case in point. The propriety of using animals in scientific education and research is, however, dominated by esoteric debate to the extent that the average reader is easily overawed into thinking that there is no room for non-specialist opinion which is other than rattle-brained (of which there is no lack). Obviously for the average electrician, stockbroker, or humanities-trained academic to be laying down the law on the value of a human blood substitute from cows or the spread of BSE would, as things stand, be foolish. Yet it would be quite proper, and indeed is necessary, for non-scientists to have views about whether or not to buy meat for the coming weekend. Furthermore, let us suppose that it becomes established, to the satisfaction of most experts, that there is a definite if slight possibility of the spread of BSE to human beings, similar decisions will remain to be made. (People drive cars despite knowing that thousands die in them each year.)

Things are no different in the field of animal experimentation. Firstly, the researchers dispute amongst themselves over the value of experiments where animals *need* to be used. Colin Blakemore's much publicised work on the eyes of monkeys and kittens is an example. There is also dissension over the value of many proposed alternatives to the use of animals. Secondly, although the majority of the research community favours the use of animal subjects, within the existing legal safeguards, it contains respected figures who are well-known in the animal rights movement. Donald Broom, Professor of Animal Welfare at Cambridge, and Gill Langley, scientific adviser to the Dr Hawden Trust, are two of the better-known in the UK. (Langley is also a member of Animal Aid, an organisation with a radical image opposed to the use of animals in any research, who was unfortunate enough to be beaten up in 1987 by a member of an even more extreme splinter-group.) Martin Stephens and Andrew Rowan are two of many such sympathisers in the USA; Rowan's *Of Mice, Models and Men* (1984) being particularly highly regarded. Finally, and most significantly, the public would be seriously worried, whatever the prevailing view in the laboratory, if it were to think that little of moral significance separated the killing of animals from that of certain groups of human beings such as babies or imbeciles. This is only marginally a scientific matter, over which the research community is largely silent or divergent. It is a philosophical problem, a fact recognised by scientists themselves on both sides of the argument. Gill Langley acknowledges the 'support of eminent philosophers such as Peter Singer and Tom Regan' (1988: 6), whilst the then Director of

Intramural Research at the US National Institute of Mental Health, Frederick Goodwin, a vigorous critic of the rights movement, sees the need to undercut their assumptions. He writes:

> The stakes are enormous. The animal rights movement threatens the very core of what the Public Health Service is all about. . . . A pro-active stance should include a vigorous focus on the fundamental philosophical underpinnings of the animal rights movement, namely the moral equivalence between human beings and animals.

Goodwin's letter was given a predictably rough ride by the liberationist press. The usually respectable *FRAME News*, the newsletter of the Fund for the Replacement of Animals in Medical Experiments, published it in full (1988: 1–2), and Langley in the Dr Hawden Trust's *Alternative News* analysed with some alarm the signs of a fight back on the part of the American medical establishment after many years of tactical passivity known as the 'bunker strategy' (1988: 6–7). The more aggressive attitude of researchers, after enduring a decade or more of letter-bombs, threats, disruption and other forms of intimidation, seems to have spread to Britain (Askwith 1988). Yet, as I write, the attacks by extremists with sophisticated explosives upon scientists, whom their more moderate critics agree are decent people, continue. The Animals in Medicine Research Information Centre (AMRIC) was founded in 1985 to speak out on behalf of such workers, yet the climate remains an unhappy one, thriving on propaganda, half-truths, and plain ignorance, as well as violence. Askwith quotes Marjorie Johnson, the Press spokesman of AMRIC:

> Many scientists would like to influence public opinion by speaking out about their work, but they know that to do so would put them in danger. There is no question that any scientist who 'goes public' today will find his life transformed for the worse.
>
> (Askwith 1988: 18)

Pain, suffering, distress, and anxiety

It is difficult to discuss the abusive treatment of animals, or indeed of human beings, without using one or more of these terms. We have already, on several occasions, drawn attention to the variegated ways in which people suffer pain (by worrying about its implications, for example) which are inapplicable to animals. Are animals therefore incapable of suffering? A lot might seem to hang upon this question since the term is highly emotive – suffering is an unpleasant experience, to be avoided at all costs. But need it be? A moment's reflection upon, let us say, Frey's analysis of the concept of 'interests', will show that it need not be an *experience* at all. Plants can suffer from too much sun or too little water, or a watch from rough handling. This must not be dismissed as mere metaphor since it could also be true of the reader, for whom a health check might reveal their having suffered from a range of complaints in blissful ignorance. An animal obviously can also suffer in this way, although like plants and watches and *un*like the reader, the fact can never be brought to the creature's attention.

The other concepts betray similar logical peculiarities. A flower or tree might well be said to show signs of distress much as an athlete might unwittingly show symptoms of it, although it would be inappropriate to describe a watch in that way. The same seems to be true of anxiety. Animals again can easily be accommodated at this level but it will not follow from this that they will be capable of the conscious distress or anxiety of a parent at an injury to their child, or of the hamstrung athlete warned by the doctor that they must give up running.

Writers almost invariably insist upon ignoring, conflating, or otherwise confusing these implications. Part cause is undoubtedly what some see as the need for straightforward yet all-inclusive *definitions*; the lack of which can often be used by politicians and official bodies as a strategic delaying tactic.[4] Any attempt to define 'suffering', for example, is bound to fall between the two stools of being unhelpfully imprecise (such as 'a diminution in wellbeing') or too precisely exclusive ('an unpleasant emotional response'). Another problem, and one discussed at length by Wittgenstein in BB and PI, is that definitions of the lexicographical sort have only limited relevance. To attempt to encapsulate 'pain' or 'red', in the sense in which these are sensations or experiences, within a form of words, is no more illuminating than trying verbally to capture the stink of durian (a tropical fruit with a foul odour yet hypnotic taste). Here the emphasis must be upon the contexts in which the word or phrase is acquired. The initiations are encouraged by sniffing the fruit or by being shown a colour sample of red. This is ostensive definition. The child is introduced to pain in the contexts of burning its finger or comforting the dog injured in an accident. In this sense the committee chairman who attempts to hide behind the lack of a definition of pain will, to be consistent, need to be sceptical of the noisy contortions of a cow or sheep crushed by a tractor. Rowan, like Ryder, is a prolific definer of the wrong sort. He first of all distinguishes human suffering from that of animals but then defines the latter as 'the unpleasant emotional response to more than minimal pain and distress' (1989: 97). This is hopeless. Not only does it ignore the sense in which suffering can be unwitting but it also begs the question in favour of saying, when specific symptoms like struggling or urination occur in animals, that these are properly to be seen as 'emotional responses' (which covertly elicits our sympathy for the *conscious* distress of the stricken human parent rather than the *symptoms* of it observed in the struggling, yet unaware, athlete).

The Wittgensteinian model puts these concepts in proper perspective. They have their primary application in the human sphere but are employed, with diminishing implication, in language-games involving other creatures to the extent that similarities with human behaviour exist. This extends even to plants and, to recall Descartes, complex machines. Being human there can be for us no other benchmark with which to operate. Rose and Adams, in Langley's collection, wrongly see this as some form of limitation: 'Possibly the greatest difficulty that we have in furthering our understanding of pain and suffering in other animals is the limitation of the human model' (1989: 63). Similar confusions seem to account for Marian Dawkins' difficulty in pinning down objective criteria of animal suffering beyond obvious *pain* reactions like tail or limb-biting (1980: 110–11).

Much of the technical literature on the subject seems to confuse the two sets of questions distinguished in this section. There are primarily those about animal welfare; what makes creatures *healthy* ones given what we strive for in our treatment of them as pets, as a food source, in zoos, or conserved in the wild. These do seem to admit of answers in terms of the working criteria of veterinarians, farm and abattoir inspectors and zoo managers. But other concerns seem to centre around whether animals might properly be said to be 'happy' or 'free from worry', not in the sense of being healthy and free from pain but rather with the human paradigm in mind. Certainly we do wish sometimes to say this of animals and, strictly by analogy and with the appropriate language-game in mind, justifiably do so. But it seems only marginal to our treatment of them and, not surprisingly, highly informal.

Replaceable and rare subjects

We have already noted the over 3 million animals used annually in the 1980s in UK research laboratories; the total having dropped from 5.6 million to 1970. (Not all of these will have been killed. The Animals (Scientific Procedures) Act requires only that a 'protected animal' must be killed if, at the conclusion of a series of 'regulated procedures' it 'is suffering or likely to suffer adverse effects' (section 15), although it *may* be killed nonetheless.) Although the total numbers used in the USA are vastly higher, Rollin (1981: 91) gives a figure of around 100 million for 1980 but this had reportedly declined by about 10 per cent by 1988, the percentage breakdowns are remarkably similar. Rats and mice account for 75–80 per cent, 0.5 per cent are dogs, 0.2 per cent cats, and the remaining 20 per cent mainly comprises smaller rodents and other vertebrates like fish and birds. In percentage terms the number of larger mammals, including primates, is very low.

The sheer numbers of creatures involved, particularly rats and mice, demands that where practicable they are bred for the purpose. Other methodological requirements such as those of standardisation and the preference for certain species on account of their docility, ease of handling, and intelligence (such as beagles and the albino form of the wild brown rat) are best met by regulated breeding. Indeed the 1986 UK Act specifies that all mammals, with the exception of birds and farm animals, are 'to be obtained only from designated breeding or supplying establishments' (Schedule 2). The irony, remarked upon in connection with the supply of food animals, repeats itself here since the vast majority of these creatures will enjoy a well fed, decently housed, and sometimes even pampered existence, prior to a painless death. The Act explicitly allows for release 'into the wild, to a farm or for use as a pet', where circumstances permit (Personal Licence: Standard Conditions, 9). Inevitably, however, pain will sometimes need to be inflicted, and in the absence of anaesthetic, which must be set against this point. Richard Ryder, for example, lists fifty sample procedures from both sides of the Atlantic (1976: 38–46), some of them highly disturbing. But, again, we must beware the limits of anecdotal evidence; several of Ryder's examples are from the 1930s and 1940s (and one from as long ago as 1909) and would breach today's legal standards. We are not told of the use or otherwise of anaesthetics, nor of any benefits flowing from such research.

The rearing of vast numbers of animals that will never live out their natural span, and that are killed for human purposes, will only seem immoral if (yet again) there is a confused identification with similar programmes were they to involve human beings. Killing an animal harms it, of course; so does cutting down a tree. But if there is no question of the animal's being aware of this harm in prospect, and if it is coupled with a painless death, then the question merely reverts to one of our own justification for the practice. Do *we* have a need to eat meat or to conduct experiments upon animals?

Different issues, although of a similar order, surround the demand for laboratory subjects captured from the wild. This highlights the predicament of chimpanzees, the ape closest to *homo sapiens* and consequently much sought after by researchers. But chimpanzees do not breed well in captivity, partly because of a long pregnancy and childhood, and trapping them in the wild is expensive and wasteful enough to put them at risk of extinction. Yet they are the only animal known in whose bloodstream the AIDS virus survives for any length of time. The implications of these facts should be obvious and the status of chimpanzees as a threatened species is a powerful consideration in favour of banning their use in the laboratory, if only as a remedial measure, despite the pressures of the AIDS lobby.

Vivisection in education

Dissection has traditionally been a means of acquiring a knowledge of anatomy. Pupils in the UK and USA, taking even very elementary courses in biology and zoology, were taught the skill. But pressure from the rights movement has influenced even the British Veterinary Association. Its widely available policy leaflet now acknowledges that, 'it is clear that a very large part of school biology need not involve dissection' whilst warning that students intending careers in the subject (and in associated areas like dentistry, or human or veterinary science) will be required to dissect at college or university level. Yet, in the UK, even this is no longer true. A mainly student organisation, Euroniche, with active committees in West Germany, Norway, Britain, Spain, Ireland, Denmark, and the Netherlands, is mobilising its members through its newsletter to question the use of dissecting techniques or even of animal tissue in university biology courses throughout Europe and Scandinavia.

However, there are at least two separate complaints, with differing implications, which need to be distinguished. Applicants in the UK have the least to object to. Dissection here takes place on cadavers or using tissue taken from them. There can be no question of cruelty or abuse. Only a total abolitionist, like Clark, Linzey, or Regan, opposed to *any* killing of animals for human purposes (other perhaps than in self-defence), could have serious objections to it. Indeed it is possible to circumvent the argument that the cadavers needed for educational purposes involve substantial extra killing since tissue is regularly collected from abattoirs or from research laboratories where the animals have been used in licensed procedures. (Deeply anaesthetised animals, once finished with, are also frequently used for intramural practice purposes, in such institutions, prior to humane killing.) It is a worthwhile conjecture that many, particularly the young, set their faces against these forms of dissection as a morally enhanced form of squeamishness. This is understandable up to a point. I personally find it repulsive to handle dead creatures or to 'gut' them for cooking, but it is not an attitude to commend in professionals like surgeons, veterinarians, nurses, forensic and medical scientists, service and police personnel, even mortuary attendants, undertakers, and butchers, who will regularly need to perform far more unsavoury tasks with equanimity.

However, of genuine concern is the potential cruelty resulting from 'survival' or 'recovery' surgery used in the training of some veterinarians in the USA and probably other parts of the world as well. (Euroniche (1989) alleges that it has recently been used on pigs in Utrecht.) The animals in question are anaesthetised, of course, but are then allowed to recover and may then be subjected to repeated surgery. Rollin condemns it outright, and most instances of it would fall foul of the UK 1986 Act (sections 14 and 15):

> In Great Britain, veterinarians are trained without ever laying hands on an animal, save for therapeutic purposes. In the United States, it is considered necessary that prospective veterinarians and medical students do a good deal of practice work with animals in order to develop technical abilities, for example, surgical skills. . . . One of the most flagant abuses in this regard is the widespread practice of multiple recovery surgery. . . . What makes this practice abhorrent is the fact that recovery from surgery, as we all know, involves shock, pain, distress, and suffering.
>
> (Rollin 1981: 106)

The strongest argument in favour of survival surgery is not the mere acquisition of 'hands-on' expertise but the experience of postsurgical patient care, the observation of wound healing, and correction of possible complications. If the student does not recover the animal from anaesthesia, where will the experience of post-operative care come from? Alternative solutions to these problems, such as the study of wound healing and the use of surgical techniques on animals in need of them, have become more widespread and surveys by Nedim Buyukmihci (1986) and R. Playter (1985), for the American Association of Veterinary Clinicians, indicate that, since Rollin wrote, the practice is on the wane in North America. It is certainly a procedure where one could well argue that the potential for serious abuse is endemic and inherent rather than isolated and, with due care, preventable. The UK is surely better off without it.

Product testing and pharmaceuticals

Very different uses of animals are involved here. Some writers, like Michael Allen Fox, argue that testing for safety the thousands of new products that come on to market annually, from shoe-polishes to children's crayons, 'is often confused by the media with research, leading to a negative impression of the latter' (1986: 181). This is a fair point. Certainly most members of the general public will have heard of the Draize test for detecting the irritant potential of cosmetics, or perhaps the more widely used LD50, nor will they have been spared photographs of immobilised creatures in plaintive lines. (What is less widely known is that Draize testing need involve only minimal discomfort; the animals are under local anaesthetics and are humanely killed upon completion.) But Fox does not deny that research and testing are, without doubt, necessary. The problems arise in determining how both tasks are effectively and humanely carried out. It must be enough here to point to four main areas of debate, each of which has its political, economic, medical, and moral ramifications. They apply as much to the testing of new drugs by the pharmaceutical companies as to that of more mundane products.

1. How reliable are the present tests? On theoretical and practical grounds the experts differ. The British Home Office still takes the line affirmed in its committee report (1979) that live animals need to be used and the statement of the British Medical Research Council, included in it, that 'the LD50 test is the only reliable measure of acute toxicity and yields a result with the least possible expenditure of life'

(1979: 16). The official position in the USA is similar.[5] Yet the technical literature is littered with damning criticism of the LD50 (which signifies the single dose of the substance under scrutiny necessary to kill 50 per cent of a group of test animals within fourteen days). Robert Sharpe, for example, quotes from a major review by the toxicologists Zbinden and Flury-Roversi: 'For the recognition of the symptomatology of acute poisoning in man, and for the determination of the human lethal dose, the LD50 is of very little value' (1989: 104). Sharpe is equally critical of extrapolations from the Draize test as indicators of toxicity for humans (100–1). Rollin quotes F. Sperling, whose conclusion is even more abrupt: 'The LD50 is in fact only marginally informative, toxicologically inadequate, and misleading' (1981: 98). Rollin's own review (1981: 96–105) is also useful since it covers tests for carcinogens, mutogens, and for effects upon embryo development (teratogenicity).

2. The Home Office report (1979) indicated that 5 per cent of all experiments in the UK were in the nature of such routine testing. Need animals be used to this extent? The short answer is No. Product testing is a target area in the search for alternatives pioneered by organisations like FRAME. But a balanced reply must take account of less tangible issues like legislative simplicity and public confidence. The Draize test and the LD50, which has at least stayed the course since 1927, are both relatively straightforward and easy to regulate. They also serve as *international* standards. Any wholesale replacement of them will be a tortuous process on these grounds alone.

3. More impatient liberationists argue that since most of the products, typically cosmetics, are used voluntarily then animals should not be killed to protect the users from possible harmful consequences. (This is a variant of Regan's argument that the interests of farmers should not figure in the debate over vegetarianism since they are 'risk takers'.) However, even if the development of vital drugs like antibiotics was a permitted exception, the implementation of such a policy would have lunatic implications. Numerous forms of disease and injury are predictably related to voluntary activities. We might have to deny medical treatment to sufferers from AIDS and venereal diseases, alcoholics, those injured in sport or road accidents, on the grounds that more animals would be needed to test the new drugs and further the medical procedures necessary to treat the deluge of suffering resulting from the prohibition of testing with animals.

4. Since many of the products, and most of the drugs, emerge from

economies fueled by intense competition, is there not a danger of mere frivolous novelties or wasteful duplication, all of which will nonetheless require testing? The statutory requirements for the introduction of *any* new drug are particularly formidable. On average, four years of predominantly animal trials are conducted pre-clinically and may well continue after it has eventually been licensed. G.J.V. Nossal is particularly critical:

> One of the worst features of research in the drug industry is the work which needs to be done to make and test products which are only marginally different from existing ones. As soon as a real therapeutic advance occurs, there is a great temptation for a competitor to come along with a drug differing slightly in chemical composition which can then be marketed without patent infringement.
>
> (Nossal 1975: 46)

It is difficult not to agree with Nossal that such wastefulness is inherent in any system where consumer pressures predominate and is one of the less happy faces of market economics. Perhaps we should applaud the will to curb it whilst being sceptical of practical moves to bring it about. It is in this spirit that we can greet Rollin's attempt to resolve the 'entire question of toxicity', if we extend the field beyond drugs to insecticides, preservatives, children's toys, and the rest, by demonstrating that our own interests and those of experimental animals overlap: 'Basically, it is in both our interests to diminish the number of potentially toxic substances being introduced into the market and into the environment' (1981: 99). This may only be wishful thinking, but it is *worth* thinking.

'Pure' research

In the preceeding section it was accepted without question that if experiments were wasteful, presumably with or without animals, it would be best if they did not take place. Nossal also describes superfluous testing as, 'mentally stultifying and, with rare exceptions, of no benefit to mankind' (1975: 46). Colin Blakemore was pilloried in 1987 and 1988 not just because his work was considered (wrongly) to be excessively cruel but also because it was thought to be useless. Gill Langley, for example, was quoted in the *Sunday Mirror* as saying that Blakemore's research was 'cruel, barbaric and of no clinical value' (Askwith 1988: 19).

The assumption seems to be that research involving animals, particularly if they are to be harmed in any way, must at least be justified in advance by its probable benefits for human beings, or possibly other animals. But this is making demands which are wildly at variance with the methodology and history of the experimental sciences. It is illuminating that much of Askwith's article is devoted to Blakemore's apparent surrender to these demands having himself 'invited most of Britain's leading ophthalmologists' to bear witness to the clinical benefits of his work. (This was duly forthcoming.) Yet far less emphasis was given to Blakemore's denial, later in the article, that salubrious consequences affected the ethical justification of his experiments. 'Of course I'm very pleased', he was reported as saying,

> that my work has turned out to be medically relevant, but it might not have done, and that wouldn't have meant that it was useless or wasted. If I had had to justify my work in terms of clinical benefits before I started it, I would never have been given a licence. Like most researchers, I simply didn't know what I was going to discover.
>
> (Askwith 1988: 21)

There are two separable claims here. The psychologist Jeffrey Gray, who is also quoted by Askwith, more clearly distinguishes these, although perhaps unaware that he is doing so: 'How can you *know*, in advance, whether an experiment will be relevant? I would defend to the hilt the right of scientists to experiment on animals in the pursuit of pure knowledge' (21). The weaker claim is that although one cannot be *certain* that beneficial results will accrue, there are grounds for the probability that they will. The stronger, less compromising, position is that it is enough to have a problem, possibly due to lack of data or thrown up by another's findings, and plausible ways of solving it. It is a persistent misapprehension that the UK 1986 Act requires that a programme must be justified in terms of the weaker claim if it is to be approved by the Secretary of State. But this is not so. It is enough that a project satisfy the purpose of 'the advancement of knowledge in biological or behavioural sciences' (section 5.3(d)), although the applicant must then justify the necessity of using animals at all (5.5), and in specific terms if the use of larger mammals is proposed (5.6). What might be seen to be a hurdle is that the 'likely adverse effects on the animals concerned' will be weighed against 'the benefit likely to accrue as a result of the programme' (5.4). But a benefit can quite properly be judged in terms of the advancement of knowledge and not require a specific clinical spin-off. This is probably why Blakemore *would* have been given a licence had one been needed under previous legislation.

This is as it should be. It is quite wrong for such as Regan to claim that criteria such as these make a mockery of the statutory scrutiny of proposals. He quotes the psychologist C.R. Gallistel, whose position is close to Gray's: 'There is no way of discriminating in advance the waste-of-time experiments from the illuminating ones with anything approaching certainty.' But Regan wilfully distorts this into the implication that *we can never say in advance* that a given proposal has been drawn up by an incompetent researcher who doesn't know what he is looking for . . . Why not draw straws instead?' (1983: 383). But Gray and Gallistel are merely denying that there is any *certainty* in the selection. The assessors will be guided by probabilities, the reputation and track record of the project director, and so forth. Furthermore, Regan's incompetent researchers ought not to get to first base, at least under present UK regulations, for they would have been required to state objectives, if only of an 'advancement of knowledge', which the assessors would judge to be significant enough to outweigh any proposed harm (under 5.4) to the animals at risk. It is on these grounds that we could discount the 'rare exceptions' referred to by Nossal (1975: 46, above), since the superfluous testing which he condemns has a far greater probability of continuing to be of little benefit to mankind, even in the advancement of knowledge, than the work of Gray, Gallistel, or the early objectives of Blakemore.

The drawback of the argument in terms of the uncertainty of outcome, in support of the demand for pure research without beneficial strings, is that evidence in its support seems destined to be anecdotal. But Julius Comroe, sometime director of cardiovascular research at the University of California, has demonstrated that it need not be. Comroe's findings in his book *Retrospectroscope* (1977: 12), are here summarised and quoted by Fox:

> Comroe and Robert Dripps, with the assistance of consultants, studied 'the ten most important clinical advances in cardiovascular-pulmonary medicine and surgery' between 1945 and 1975. Out of 4,000 scientific publications they selected 529 'key articles' ('a key article was defined as one that had an important effect on the direction of subsequent research and development, which in turn proved to be important for one of the ten clinical advances'). Comroe notes, 'Our analysis showed

232

that 217 of the 529 key articles (41 per cent) reported work that, at the time it was done, had no relation whatever to the disease that it later helped to prevent, diagnose, treat, or alleviate'.

(Fox 1986: 140)

If this evidence is taken at face value it would seem spectacularly to support the uncertainty thesis.

Alternatives to animals

The field of 'research into research' is a highly active and fast moving one. The motivation behind the search for alternatives to animals need not necessarily be humane. D.H. Smyth (1978) in *Alternatives to Animal Experiments*, points out that several of its techniques, such as mass spectrometry, gas chromatography, and the use of isotopes in biomedical research, were developed much earlier in the century on the grounds of simple efficiency. Tissue culture, an ancillary method with a particularly high profile, 'was first used for vaccine production in 1949, a long time before the present demand for alternatives. The driving force was the need to find a better protection against poliomyelitis' (1978: 116).[6] Social minded reformers in the eighteenth and nineteenth centuries collated statistics which pointed to the influence of lack of sanitation and poor living conditions on a host of diseases such as diptheria, scurvy, smallpox, and TB, little aware that later generations would dignify their efforts as alternative medicine. It is ironic that even in the UK the National Anti-Vivisection Society (NAVS) urges us in its literature to look to our own self-interest. The species difference between animals and human beings can give rise to quite different reactions, as in the case of penicillin, digitalis, and aspirin, and with drugs which were thought to be safe after pre-clinical tests upon animals, such as thalidomide, clioquinol, osmosin, opren, and eraldin, the results were human death and tragedy. But obviously, although the NAVS encourages us towards alternatives such as homeopathy, a careful diet and relaxed lifestyle, and away from drugs, its main aim is to abolish the animal abuse implicit in testing them.

A concern for animals is also to the fore in the classic text of W.M.S. Russell and R.L. Burch (1959), *The Principles of Humane Experimental Technique*. Their 'three Rs' almost invariably provide the framework for classifying alternatives. In some cases methods will be employed to *reduce* the number of animals used in a programme.

Mathematical and computer-assisted models, for example, can enhance the data obtained from six subjects in an LD50 test which previously killed many times more than this. In other cases, techniques will be *refined* to reduce the suffering or stress of the animals as in the use of improved anaesthetics or postoperative drugs. Finally, there will be alternatives which *replace* animals entirely. The Ames test for detecting carcinogens or mutagens in hundreds of chemicals, where micro-organisms are used instead of vertebrates, is a paradigm case. FRAME (1985) make no secret of the fact that replacement is the final goal. I quote from its fact-sheet: 'The ultimate aim is to provide alternative methods for use in toxicity testing and in drug development, which will be so relevant and reliable that *no* animal testing will be necessary.'

But, it must be stressed, this is not a call for the *total* abolition of animals from the research laboratory. FRAME seems to be too well provided with practical, scientific expertise for such idealism. Rollin, in particular, is openly critical of utopian pressure: 'However well intentioned, an extremely heavy emphasis on replacement is misdirected. . . . The most currently viable hope for diminishing the total amount of suffering is by refinement of existing procedures' (1981: 104–5). Rollin is thus at variance with Regan who argues that *all* research involving harm to animals, and this includes killing them painlessly, must be stopped (1983: 397): 'If nonanimal alternatives are available, they should be used; if they are not available, they should be sought' (388). Whatever is supposed to happen in the meantime, or in the event that alternatives never become available, cowers the imagination. But the reason why Fox reports that 'there is virtually unanimous agreement among working scientists that animals will never be replaced entirely in the laboratory' (1986: 174), except perhaps in the fields of product and drug research and development, is that numerous research projects involve the study of fully functioning live animals (*in vivo*).[7] Smyth provides the clue:

> In general, the organ functions because of the coordinated activity of all the different kinds of cells. This has one very important result which has great significance in relation to alternatives. The organ will have properties which would not be apparent from studying the individual cells which compose it, or even the separate tissues . . .
>
> The various organs of the body do not function in isolation, but are mutually dependent on the activities of each other . . . This

234

kind of coordination can only be studied on whole animals, and
could never even be guessed at from . . . experiments on tissue
culture.

(Smyth 1978: 26–7)

But, in addition to the somewhat haphazard list of alternatives that
I have so far mentioned, there is a pre-eminent group which does
comprise whole animals, namely human beings. Man, as FRAME
(1985) puts it, 'is the ultimate experimental animal' since, individual
variability notwithstanding, interspecies difference (such as those
encountered with penicillin, digitalis, and thalidomide) cannot arise.
Human subjects have always figured in the history of medicine and
are now used widely in the testing of cosmetics and toiletries, and
treatments for common diseases like influenza, although there are
ethical limits to the severity of the ailments, or expected toxicity, to
which humans ought to be exposed. These limits have given rise to
thorny debate in at least two areas which serve as a reminder that it is
not only nonhuman animals which are put at risk:

1. Human subjects are volunteers; a fact which commends them to
those opposed to the use of animals incapable of choice. But should
there be limits? If the use of human subjects could promote dramatic
advances in research into hazardous surgery, such as liver transplantation, or the search for drugs to reverse Alzheimer's disease, angina,
or AIDS, but with possibly lethal side effects, why should we not offer
long-term criminals the choice of undergoing such tests in exchange
for a commutation of their sentence if they survive? If people are
honoured for risking their lives in the not obviously useful pursuit of
speed records and mountains to climb, why should they not be
encouraged to do so in more worthwhile causes?

2. In less dramatic contexts many of us already run such risks. The UK
Committee on the Safety of Medicines regularly provides General
Practitioners with questionnaires with which to inform it of any
irregularities encountered in the use of new, but *already licensed*,
drugs. It makes no secret of the fact that these drugs, despite having
passed their statutory pre-clinical tests upon animals, are now being
tested upon *us*. As a result of such returns, for example, the heart drug
Corwin (xamoterol fumarate) is presently in danger of withdrawal
from the UK market. Such procedures are quite routine. The Medical
Correspondent of the UK *Sunday Times* reported in May 1990 that
the anti-oestrogen drug, tamoxifen, used for several years to treat

women actually suffering from breast-cancer, is now to be tested on 30,000 human subjects over a period of five years to assess its potential as a preventative of the disease in *healthy* women. A 'small pilot experiment' has so far detected no side effects. Some might nonetheless think it justifiable to be fearful of the merely speculative dangers of a long-term reduction in the body's oestrogen levels. The problems associated with the common contraceptive pill, brought to light decades after its introduction, might seem to serve as an ominous precedent.[8]

ZOOS – FIELD SPORTS – FUR COATS – VIOLENCE

Introduction

These four phenomena form a continuum which is intellectually intriguing and for this reason they are treated in sequence. Zoo keeping would seem to be one of the least offensive of contemporary practices involving animals. Recent legislation exists in practically all western nations requiring that captive creatures be treated humanely, and where abuses occur, as undoubtedly they will, then legal remedies are available. Objections in principle will exist, such as those of the UK organisation Zoo Check, but these will be on the relatively anodyne grounds that animal nature is frustrated by captivity, rather than that healthy creatures are being deliberately harmed or killed. Zoos have the seemingly obvious virtue of preserving and exhibiting animals that human beings, who would not otherwise see them, may enjoy.

Yet zoos, often in countries with climates alien to their inmates, do not preserve the creatures' native habitats. It can be argued that it is the value of the traditional so-called 'bloodsports' of hunting, shooting, and fishing, that they ensure not only a continuing stock of the creatures that are pursued but that they conserve the natural surroundings in which they flourish. But the fury, resulting frequently in pitched battles between supporters and opponents of such sports, is aroused less by the truth or otherwise of these claims than by the violence of what goes on. Setting hounds upon a single fox arouses far more intense emotions than reports of lethal injections being given to fifty beagles by a PhD in a white coat. (And much the same goes for the clubbing of seal pups for their skins.) Yet it is ironic that two objectors to this violence, originally members of the Hunt Saboteurs Association, were founder members of the Animal Liberation Front

(ALF) in 1972 which specialises in even more robust methods, amounting in 1990 to the use of commercial high-explosives with sophisticated triggering devices, to register its displeasure at the activities of the PhD.

A brief background to zoos

Given our distant ancestors' varied needs for animals as food, labour, transport, companionship, and power symbols, it is hardly surprising that zoos have a long history. Certainly they existed 2,000 years ago in China, and the prolific needs of the later Roman games required that vast numbers be transported, mainly from North Africa, needing then to be caged and provided for. In the centuries that followed most European and Oriental rulers kept large collections of often exotic creatures, and those in cities such as Paris and Versailles, from which the Cartesians took specimens for dissection, served both as emblems of prestige and to entertain the public. The founding of the Zoological Society of London in 1826 was, however, a landmark, and the opening of the Zoological Gardens in Regent's Park a year later began the era of the modern zoo as we know it. (The diminutive 'zoo' was first used in the mid-1830s.)

The conditions in which the animals were kept in the typical European or American zoo of the nineteenth century were, to put it mildly, grim. Cramped and barred cages were the norm, little attention was given to the creatures' needs for exercise (apart from the tricks that those amenable were trained to perform to amuse the public), hygiene was non-existent, and only minimal research took place into the special problems generated by captivity. The impossibility of keeping chimpanzees alive for more than a few months was an instructive case in point. Being, for obvious reasons, an animal in great demand, numerous healthy samples were delivered from the tropics and then promptly died. It was not discovered until the 1930s that the apes were susceptible to our minor respiratory ailments which for them are lethal. (Capture and delivery, given the rigours of sea passage, was itself barbaric and incredibly wasteful. Normal procedure was, and still is, to shoot the powerful and ferocious adults and take the babies. Even in 1985 Dale Jamieson could write: 'The rule of thumb among trappers is that ten chimpanzees die for every one that is delivered alive to the United States or Europe' (1985: 117). Clearly such profligacy cannot be confined only to the capture of apes.)

Nor, in the nineteenth and early twentieth centuries, was much thought given to the actual purpose of zoos. Davy and Raffles, in London, had the provision of specimens for scientific research in mind but no sense of the need for conservation as the term now tends to be used. (Systematic captive breeding in something approaching a natural setting was not put into practical effect until the opening of the UK's Whipsnade Zoo in 1931, although the establishment by the US Congress in 1872 of the first National Park at Yellowstone was a significant omen.) There were nineteenth-century critics who were outspoken not only about the conditions in which the animals were kept but also the indignities and baiting to which they were subjected to please an unruly public (circuses were also a prime target in this respect), and the campaigns eventually led to the Cruelty to Wild Animals in Captivity Act of 1900. Even Darwin, it will be remembered, commented upon such goings-on:

> Several observers have stated that monkeys certainly dislike being laughed at. . . . In the Zoological Gardens I saw a baboon who always got into a furious rage when his keeper took out a letter or book and read it out aloud to him; and his rage was so violent that . . . he bit his own leg till the blood flowed.
>
> (Darwin 1909: 108)

The tasteless exhibitionism of certain zoological practices also aroused the anger of Charles Dickens. As Ryder nicely puts it, 'Dickens had criticized the public feeding of live creatures to zoo animals – once a favourite spectator sport at the Tower menagerie and a practice which continued surreptitiously in the Regent's Park zoo' (1989: 136).

Contemporary criticism: against zoos

Two books from the 1970s were influential in focussing enlightened opinion upon the issues to which the existence of zoos gives rise. Peter Batten's *Living Trophies* (1976) surveyed 200 American establishments in most of which the inmates experienced sub-standard conditions. He concluded that, 'The majority of American zoos are badly run, their direction incompetent, and animal husbandry inept and in some cases non-existent' (quoted by Jamieson 1975: 117). Bill Jordan and Stefan Ormrod's *The Last Great Wild Beast Show* (1978) revealed a similar state of affairs in many British zoos but also raised more basic questions about the reasons for having them in the first place. Both books were instrumental in influencing subsequent welfare legislation; Jordan and Ormrod's, in particular, helped to bring about the Zoo Licensing Act of 1981 under which all zoos must operate under the conditions of a local authority licence (Ryder 1989: 225).

Dale Jamieson (1985) clearly and concisely puts the case against the standard justifications.

1. The Victorian emphasis upon entertainment is a thing of the past. Most zoo administrators, he argues, regard highly publicised penguin feeding or chimps' tea parties as no more than necessary evils.

2. Zoos are frequently justified on the grounds that they play an important role in educating the public. Jamieson questions this claim on two counts. Firstly, many surveys have shown how ineffective zoos are in educating visitors who move quickly past cages tending to stop 'only to watch baby animals or those who are begging, feeding, or making sounds' (111). Zoo-goers have been shown to be far less knowledgeable about animals than country walkers, hunters and fishermen and they express predictable prejudices against such creatures as scorpions, rattlesnakes, alligators, and vultures and in favour of chimpanzees, koala bears, elephants, and lions. Secondly, to the degree that education *does* take place in zoos, it is not clear what its aims ought to be. Should it be facts about behaviour and physiology, for example, or attitudes favourable to endangered species? Nor is it obvious that wild creatures need to be kept in captivity to achieve these ends.

3. Despite Sir Humphrey Davy's ambition to assemble rare creatures 'as objects of scientific research – not of vulgar admiration', Jamieson points to the very severe constraints on the experiments that may be conducted on such creatures (112–13). Zoo animals, often partly tame and perforce living in artificial conditions, provide data which is controversial unless the project happens to relate to the effects of captivity. Even in the areas of anatomy and pathology, the most common types of zoo research, there are rarely the facilities for advanced manipulative and invasive studies that would compare with those in specialist experimental institutes. Zoos are perhaps unrivalled only in their ability to provide exotic specimens outside the repertoire of the standard laboratory supplier.

4. The enlightened policy which began with the founding of Whipsnade zoo now tends to be the dominant ethos, not only in the large civic menageries of western nations, but also in the more

specialist centres often run by dedicated private collectors (such as those of John Aspinall in East Kent). The talk is always of threatened or endangered species (adjectives with different legal implications) and the captive breeding programmes needed to preserve them. Now there have been some notable successes of this sort but as a justification for the conventional zoo it runs into difficulties. If we really are committed to preservation (the problems surrounding endangered species being an issue in its own right) then for biological reasons large numbers of creatures need to be involved and in relative seclusion. Many of the prestigious American zoos, such as those in New York City, Washington DC, and San Diego, locate their breeding programmes in remote, rural areas inaccessible to the general public. It was the view of Jordan and Ormrod (1978) that ventures such as these should provide the model for all zoos. Even with the will, there would be serious obstacles to the meeting of such criteria in islands as crowded as those of the UK and with its climate.

The 'moral presumption' against captivity

However strong we might think Jamieson's case to be, the suspicion will persist that he is setting too stringent standards for zoos to meet. What is wrong with their entertaining the public provided that the animals are humanely provided for; not subject to provocation nor indiscriminate feeding with chips and chocolate? Does it really matter if the zoo-goer is not transformed into a Konrad Lorenz and prefers giraffes to guano bats? Why not leave other than trivial experimentation to laboratories better equipped to undertake it, and captive breeding to remote facilities which can provide the zoos with specimens of the rare and threatened for exhibition? Additional implications lurk in the wings. The owning of *pets*, a practice of far more widespread interest than zoo-going, is at risk to arguments similar to Jamieson's. The owner of a pekinese or budgerigar will enjoy its company but typically have only the most rudimentary knowledge of the species; there is no question of either creature being in need of preservation nor, one hopes, will the possession of pets be justified upon the grounds of their experimental potential. Jamieson has a ready reply to my counter: 'Whatever benefits are obtained from any kind of zoo must confront the moral presumption against keeping wild animals in captivity' (116). This presumption is argued for on the grounds that zoos are detrimental to animals.

In the first place there is undeniable mistreatment which, most would agree, can be forms of cruelty. The wasteful killing employed in the taking of creatures from the wild is an obvious instance, and Jamieson uses the evidence of Batten's book which documents a whole series of abuses (overweight and diseased creatures, deformed by cramped quarters, unsuitably fed) all of which would by now be, and probably were even in 1978, illegal. It is this last point which defuses the relevance of such examples. The abuses are horrid and regrettable, of course, but they are not endemic to zoo practice; the law provides a remedy. But it is the second argument which is more interesting philosophically and upon which I shall concentrate. This is the claim that simply to 'deny animals liberty' by keeping them captive is also detrimental to them (116). It applies best to truly wild animals but a case is sometimes made that includes domestic ones as well. This is the breeder Phyllida Barstow, the self-styled sufferer from 'Noah's Ark Syndrome', quoted in my Introduction:

> Every activity the dog enjoys instinctively – from killing chickens . . . urinating on uprights and rolling in excrement to digging in newly-turned earth – offends the human sense of hygiene. . . . Complete brainwashing - euphemistically known as 'training' – is needed before humans and dogs can share living quarters. This often involves cruelty to the dog, and the trained animal is then obliged through fear of punishment to behave in an unnatural fashion for the rest of its life.
>
> (Barstow 1988: I)

Compare this with another animal trainer, Vicki Hearne: 'The fact that animals are so generous in answering us is what makes it not only okay to train them but a human duty' (1987: 265).

Undermining the presumption

Barstow's argument is so easily seen through that it hardly needs dwelling upon. The use of 'brainwashing' (a technical term, with precise implications, not applicable to animals) simply begs the question in her own favour since all but the most rudimentary animate forms adapt their instinctive reactions to changing demands *in the wild*. Even ferocity in wild animals like tigers tends not to show itself in habitats where it is not needed. Furthermore, her argument will apply to the training of young children. Is an infant that uses the pot rather than its pants, or puts the food in its mouth rather than depositing it on the floor, showing signs of being brainwashed? The use of 'unnatural' begs the same question and the depiction of the animal's fearful motivation is anthropomorphic in suggesting the plight of an adult human being in similar circumstances. But most serious, yet for our purposes most instructive, is the charge of cruelty; if it be taken to refer not to the means of training but the *result* of it. It needs to be substantiated. Most well-fed, well-cared-for, and well-trained dogs show no wish to leave the family home, are attached to their owners, and show every sign of well-being. If cruelty is the charge then it should be manifest either in aberrant behaviour, such as that described by Dawkins (1980), or expressions of pain. All that Barstow the breeder, rather than Barstow the amateur psychoanalyst, has to give us is the reasonable warning that the most obedient dog will sometimes disagreeably surprise us by rolling on a squashed hedgehog. (Hearne would, I think, agree with the spirit of my argument here.)

Zoos, however, are best known for housing *wild* animals. These exert an undoubted fascination upon most of us. To be within an arm's length of a feeding lioness who, as we like to imagine, would crush our skull with a blow of its paw, or to be a glass width from a tiny krait whose venom could kill us in seconds, is both captivating and repellent. Our admiration for such creatures, particularly the mammals whose resemblance to domestic pets (and to a lesser extent ourselves) encourages identification with them, can quite naturally give rise to reservations about the propriety of removing them from the wild, where they are able to pursue their often violent ways of life in freedom. This is the intuitive ground for Jamieson's 'presumption' that to keep animals in zoos is to deny them liberty, or, to put it in the more categorical language of James Rachels (1976), that they have a *right* to liberty; a claim echoed by most of the liberationists.

What is to be made of this? We may begin by questioning the tacit assumption that animals are truly free in the wild. Many ethologists in the twentieth century, such as Seton, Hindle, and Hediger, have stressed the limitations of such an existence. Hediger in particular, in his *Wild Animals in Captivity* (1964), describes in detail the diminishingly restricted habitats, niches, and territories, into which various wild creatures, including birds, are forced by pressures such as those of food supply, breeding, and biological and social rank. Furthermore they are struck down by natural predators and diseases which, quite reasonably, might be said to limit their freedom. The liberationist, however, can reply that similar restrictions apply to human beings yet we do not deny them the right to liberty. This counter is typical of a tactic, to which I have drawn attention on many occasions (and as early as in my Introduction in criticism of Lorenz and Hearne) that seeks a comparison with what we might say of human beings to give power and plausibility to a claim on behalf of animals. But the argument, if sustainable, that animals are incapable of language and are therefore, by comparison with ourselves, primitive beings, consistently undermines such tactics. Human liberty (to be brief and cut corners) is the right, with many provisos and within certain limits such as those of illegality, to make one's own choices or, as it is sometimes put, to live one's own life. To put a human being in a cage, against their will, restricts their liberty.

How goes the comparison with animals? They do not *choose* to live in the wild, for they are incapable of weighing alternatives; nor by the same token do they choose captivity. Nor can they *object* to it, as a human being incarcerated against his will would be expected to, because lacking self-consciousness they are unable to assess the merits of their new home against their old one. (This assumes that they were not bred in captivity which is to weaken the comparison still further.) The obsession with liberty, that lions have a right to live their own life, confuses the issue and often with tragic results, for we should not hesistate to extract animals from the wild when it is unequivocally in their interest or that of their species; although it might seem foolish to intervene merely to prevent a predator from killing its prey. Yet why then do we part fighting dogs, or rescue wild birds from cats? Because they are pets? As far as zoos and pets are concerned our primary guide can only be the creature's well-being; whether it is, as far as the veterinarians and other experts can judge, contented and healthy. (Even so, the predator-prey issue persists in zoo-management circles. If predation is approved of in the wild then why should it be so frowned upon in captivity, *if* certain species thrive upon a living diet which does not itself involve exotica?)

What constitutes an animal's well-being is not, as we have already seen, a straightforward matter. It is undoubtedly the case that although many domestic pets are mistreated, which is unfortunate, the vast majority are better off than if they were in the wild. But what is the virtue of attempting to compare the well-being of a domestic animal, born in captivity, with that of its feral equivalent? It is a largely idle exercise since domestic breeding rapidly changes an animal's nature; as the London pigeon-fanciers showed Darwin. The same problems of comparison face zoos for, in many cases, the majority of their charges will have been born in captivity. But what *can* be said is that in well run establishments the creatures live up to 20 per cent longer (not invariably, of course, – the opposite holds in the case of dolphins), and they have the benefit of regular feeding, veterinary care, and are saved an often violent and painful death. (Few birds die of old age in the wild. Robins, for example, last on average for only one-tenth of their potential lifespan.)

Yet the other side of this coin is not the possibility of blatant and painful abuse which even the untrained can spot, but the presence of *abnormal* behaviour patterns like pacing, weaving, or tail-biting, which are not infrequently observed in zoos and are treated as symptoms of an animal's *stress*. Marian Dawkins, whose *Animal Suffering* (1980) is authoritative on the medical details of this phenomenon, is cautious in her diagnosis of these criteria. Much so-called stress occurs in the wild, she points out, and is also beneficial to the animal, such as when hunting or otherwise searching for food; and she cites evidence that some African mammals seem to seek out stimulation for its own sake even when it puts them in extreme danger (1980: 59–62). She also argues against the assumption that because a captive animal fails to indulge in what we might expect of it in the wild, it is therefore suffering. (Again, this makes good sense. Listlessness, for example, is not itself a symptom of suffering since it is associated with all sorts of harmless conditions as well.)

The most that can be said in favour of Jamieson's presumptions against captivity is, I suggest, that society thinks it decent and civilised to avoid disturbing, alarming, or capturing other creatures without a good reason. Fishermen worthy of the name will, in this spirit, return excess or inedible catch to the water. We encourage our children to use their 'bugbottles' to entertain the odd insect for a few hours or so before returning it to the wild of the suburban garden. The existence of zoos, if they meet prevailing veterinary standards, is not at variance with such humane reflections. They are, in a sense, an extension of the pet principle, Barstow's 'Noah's Ark Syndrome' writ large, and despite their failure to meet all of Jamieson's too-exacting standards, they do enough to foster a familiarity with exotic creatures that the public would never otherwise see, to more than offset the over-dramatised ills of captivity.

Hunting, shooting, and fishing

My comments at the opening of this chapter gave a foretaste of the arguments to come. Field sports is one area of practical contention (the fur trade is marginally another) where the protestors so patently lose sight of what for them should be the main objective that they forfeit respect. This is not simply because the hunt saboteurs indulge in illegal acts of disruption; the hunting fraternity seems also to relish a fight and are not adverse to beating up protesters if given the opportunity (Ryder 1989: 185, 282). It is simply that the scale and shrillness of the campaigns over the years is so completely out of proportion to the number of animals that are allegedly abused as to suggest less worthy motives. If one excludes fishing and the shooting of small birds such as pigeons, which fail to raise hackles in any case, the animals killed are a fraction of those experimented upon, which is itself a comparative nothing in comparison with those eaten. What, of course, the objectors ought to be drawing our attention to, and indeed what should appall them, is the cruelty to animals (as they see it) to which field sports give rise. Yet much of the sound and fury seems to be generated more by a basic antipathy to the sorts of people who like to hunt and shoot and, in particular, by the fact that they do so for *pleasure*. But even if Oscar Wilde were right and so-called bloodsports are a question of 'the unspeakable in full pursuit of the uneatable', it cannot thereby be deduced that such pursuit is either cruel or unjustified. Even Lord Houghton, the respected chairman of the League Against Cruel Sports (LACS), flirts with this irrelevance in defending the Hunt Saboteurs Association: 'They are dedicated young people who risk insult and injury from brutal huntsmen because they are passionately opposed to hunting foxes with hounds for pleasure' (Ryder 1989: 186). The literature of the LACS reinforces this emphasis by comparing foxhunting with the illegal pastimes of cockfighting and bear-baiting. It almost invariably features arrogant or moronic-looking hunters crowding to view, or even triumphantly brandishing, a bloodied corpse. (The RSPCA and Scottish SPCA less sensationalistically, but probably more effectively, tend to stress the pain and torment resulting from dogfighting or the laying of snares.)

The obvious counter to my argument is that the pleasure *is* relevant because if people did not enjoy these pastimes then they would be discontinued, and with them the associated cruelty. But this legitimate point can be turned back against the abolitionist if field sports can be justified in other ways. The killing of animals for pleasure, it might thus be argued, is morally unacceptable (as even many people who are not otherwise liberationist contend) but only if it is not given respectability on *other* grounds. Such grounds are certainly forthcoming although the weight given to them, as is only to be expected, will vary enormously. One of the weaker defences is probably the argument that hunting is a form of pest control. Not only does this show every sign of being a recently concocted excuse for mink, badger, or foxhunting, where even in their case the less troublesome and perhaps more humane alternatives of shooting or poisoning are available; but it is of little comfort to the staghunters of the West Country and New Forest, or the elk, moose, or even salmon seekers of North America and Canada where the stocks are carefully conserved and the kills controlled, often by law. The same is true of grouse shooting (a regular target of UK abolitionist agitation when the season opens on the 'glorious twelfth' of August) where the heather moors are specially managed to encourage the breeding of young birds. The best defence of hunting lies precisely in these consider-ations of conservation which distance it from pest control – an important necessity in other contexts. It is, furthermore, on these grounds that attempts by the LACS to tar field sports with the same brush as bear-baiting or cockfighting miss the mark. Ryder spends some pages bemoaning the misplaced machismo, eroticism, and unemployment that he diagnoses as the cause of a recent eruption of inner-city baiting involving dogs, cats, rats, and horses, and he deliberately slips hunting into his psychiatric cocktail: 'the alienated young using non-humans as scapegoats for their anger, the emulation of the rich hunting set, the macho cult' (1989: 323). Clearly the justification for what these urban derelicts get up to can be *no more than* the pleasure to be derived from viewing creatures battling in torment. The traditional field sport is different, despite the sadistic nature of a few of its followers, because the further defence of its being conservationist is to hand.

Yet, amazingly, the argument against the largely illegal staging of animal combat is not conclusively won. The wholly respectable Vicki Hearne, trading upon both her wide experience of training dogs and her over-emphasis of their similarities with human beings, proffers a brave defence of dogfighting. It is, she contends, 'emblematic of glory, nobility, discipline in the old sense'; rather as one might justify gladitorial combat or Billy the Kid's gunfighting (1987: 221-2). Agreeing with the enthusiast, Richard Stratton, that pit bull terriers 'love fighting contact' she goes on:

When you read his tales of the great pit champions, you do begin to feel that, *with certain dogs*, not only is it not cruel to 'roll' them (give them real fighting, as opposed to mere scrapping, experience), it is cruel to prevent them from fighting, in the way it is cruel to put birds in cages, or at least in cages that are too small for them.

(Hearne 1987: 220)

It is at this point that Hearne's analysis betrays its idiosyncratic cash value.

The surveys that show that those who hunt, shoot, or fish are far more knowledgeable about animals than most zoo-goers will have surprised nobody. Much of the fraternity is strongly motivated towards, not only the conservation of the species they pursue, but the maintenance of the unspoiled countryside in which they have their natural habitats. In this respect their objectives are close to those who see the great National Parks, particularly in Africa and the USA (where controlled hunting is permitted), as having the edge over the conventional zoo. Caroline Yeates sums up the type in her obituary of the well-known sporting artist Michael Lyne, who, 'developed that strange paradox, incomprehensible to those who think field sports have no place in modern life, of delighting in the chase while at the same time having a deep commitment to all animals' (1989). The UK Nature Conservancy Council and the Royal Society for the Protection of Birds are typical in their criticism of the activities of the Hunt Saboteurs Association and the campaigns of the LACS. They contend that the heather moors of the grouse shooters provide a unique environment for numerous species of birds, including the merlin, and that its maintenance would be impossible without the income generated by the sport. Heather Mills reports Richard Porter, spokesman of the RSPB, as saying that, 'It is an economic truth that if there was no grouse shooting we would see the disappearance of these places' (1988: 2). Similar arguments can be fashioned from the need to preserve the lakes, rivers, countryside, and wilderness areas inhabited by other hunted creatures. Were it not for the interest in (and income from) field sports, they would lose much of the very special protection that influential political lobbies ensure for them.

Nonetheless, even if we disdain the use of snares and the squalid behaviour of the so-called 'terrier and spade brigade', which operates in the backwash of the traditional foxhunt, together with ratting and cockfighting, there is still the question of the alleged *cruelty* to the animals killed in the otherwise respectable pursuits, even if the numbers involved are relatively small. Three brief comments will suffice. Where hounds are involved even the LACS admits that the

247

death is 'relatively quick' and they put stress on the 'terror and trauma' of the chase. However, this must be judged in the light of all the qualifications that arise from my analysis of animals as primitive beings. The danger is to be over-impressed by the similarities of the pre-linguistic prototypes of such emotions to those that would be experienced by human beings in similar circumstances. The fox may be said to be in fear of its life but, unlike the beleaguered gladiator, it is not conscious of the fact. Secondly, as we have already discussed in the case of Dr Livingstone and some farm animals, account must be taken of the possible effects of thanatosis, shock, and such 'natural anaesthetics', which mitigate any suffering. Finally, it is worthwhile to compare even the most searing interpretation of such cruelty, and the fuss to which it gives rise, to the attitude of liberationists towards life in the wild where life expectancy is short and predation the norm. If the abolitionists are so quick to condemn the infliction of a certain amount of necessary pain in the otherwise justifiable cause of field sports why should they not regard life in the wild, with its attendant horrors, as a state to be remedied rather than one to be regarded with mixed feelings of resignation and approval? Clark, for one, is vehemently opposed to attempts to improve it: 'God save us from even well-meant benevolence' (1977: 167).

Hysteria and the fur trade

If field sports get a bad press, then it is nothing compared to the body blow dealt out to the fur trade in North America and the EEC during the 1980s. The achievement of the EEC ban on the importation of seal products in 1983 (and since renewed) was the culmination of fifteen years lobbying by the highly organised International Fund for Animal Welfare, founded by Brian Davies in 1969, and brought with it the virtual collapse of the Canadian seal industry in 1985. Highly successful publicity campaigns have since been waged by other organisations, like the 1989 fur 'amnesty' in Trafalgar Square organised by LYNX with the slogan 'Bring out your Dead'. The RSPCA, Greenpeace, and Compassion in World Farming, aided by effective posters, media coverage, and intense political lobbying, have all combined to turn fur traders into a threatened species. As Ryder puts it in his detailed account of the manoeuvring, 'In the mid-1980s the anti-fur campaign . . . had become the principal item on the animal rights agenda' (1989: 237).

But why the furore? It ought, as an issue, to be comparatively minor. The number of animals involved seems to be relatively small (although independent estimates are hard to come by) if comparisons are made with the other main areas of animal abuse, despite the neat Greenpeace slogan 'it takes up to 40 dumb animals to make a fur coat – but only one to wear it'. Even the notorious annual seal hunts off the coast of eastern Canada, which Davies highlighted with such success, resulted in estimates of no more than 100,000 deaths. Another anomaly is that animals are used to provide numerous other items of apparel, from leather shoes and jackets to belts and sheepskin coats, which occasions few protests. Certainly there can be some painful suffering involved, most notably for those creatures caught in steel leg-hold traps still, apparently, common in the USA and Canada. But this is typical of an avoidable abuse which, like many of those involved in other practices, it ought not to be beyond the wit of man to make illegal and eradicate.

Their mere existence, as we have already seen, is not enough to besmirch a whole practice. Furthermore, the majority of the animals used are specially farmed for the purpose, mink being the obvious example, and can be humanely killed; and even the clubbing of seals or other creatures by expert trappers is a very quick despatch. Nor, and finally, need it be a question of endangered species – the best of reasons for not killing animals. If the odd rare species is implicated then it ought *not* to be, and bodies like the UN-sponsored Convention on International Trade in Endangered Species (CITES) should intervene. But the majority of animals killed for their skin, the rabbit, mink, fox, and seal, are common ones.

The reasons for the priority of the fur issue are, in large part, similar to those aroused by the very term 'bloodsports', and are a reaction against the public image of the *violence* involved in the production of furs. Clever publicity, such as the famous photograph from 1968 of the Canadian sealer poised to club a seal pup,[9] or David Bailey's poster of a woman trailing a fur coat from which blood is streaming, intensifies and perpetuates this image. But it is largely a myth; which, to the extent that it *is* true, is avoidable. The wearing of furs also conjures up images of opulence and leisured superiority, not unlike those associated with foxhunting and grouse shooting, which, as grounds for disliking the members of either fraternity, can easily if confusedly transfer themselves into objections to everything they get up to. (It is possible to object to champagne on the same grounds.) Furthermore, the implications of the issue of fur production extend beyond the confines of Mayfair or Palm Beach. For many struggling people, in less fashionable places, animal skins are all they can afford to keep them warm.

A postscript on violence

The violence of human beings towards each other, apart from its uncomfortable reminder of life in the wild, might appear to have to do only with the *politics* of liberation (whether, for example, explosive tactics are justified to further the cause) rather than with animals as such. Ryder gives a detailed account of the campaign of alleged violence from the founding of the ALF in 1972 until 1989, but with the clear aim of rehabilitating the public image 'of the animal militant as a politically motivated left-wing terrorist perpetrating extreme violence against the invariably peace-loving and decent animal exploiter' (1989: 273-9, 289). His tactics are predictable.

1. He criticises the language used by judges and the media, in connection particularly with well-publicised trials of ALF members in 1986 and 1987, that the defendants were 'terrorists' and 'dangerous criminals'. He stresses, in mitigation, their professed desire to limit the damage they caused to property and their use of 'small non-explosive incendiary devices'. It seems incredible that Ryder, going on to mention the first use by the ALF of high explosive in an attack upon Bristol University in 1989 (227), should then conclude that, 'the use of the word "terrorism" in such a context is, surely, a deliberate slur and a debasement of the meaning of the word' (289), as if one could ignore the escalation. Events of 1990, featuring even more advanced devices used at Porton Down in Wiltshire and again in Bristol, when a baby boy in a pushchair was injured, underline the flimsy nature of this defence. What is terrorism if not a tactic to use force of arms to frighten someone into submission? If so, it would accurately describe the methods of the ALF, however small the incendiary device or high the explosive.

2. Ryder documents in great detail the apparently justified point that in terms of personal injury it is the animal sympathisers who have suffered (281-4). He includes several murders including those of the two members of the Greenpeace ship *Rainbow Warrior* in 1985, and that of the gorilla protector, Dian Fossey, and many less serious incidents involving hunt saboteurs. (Yet one can regret these happenings whilst wondering at their relevance. Have the huntsmen no rights of retaliation? Is it surprising that ALF fingers get burned?)

3. He blames governments: 'Violence is often the product of pro-longed frustration. By not recognising this fact, and acting upon it soon enough, irresponsible governments can become parties to its consequences.' And how, in Ryder's view, should governments have acted? His answer is, 'by meeting as many as possible of the actual demands for reform' (286).

The crux of the matter is here evident. The most that the ALF can be accused of, in Ryder's view, is poor tactics; of adopting violence without the certainty that it will be effective (287). Yet the view of many militants, as he admits, is that non-violence is equally uncertain: 'the non-violence of Gandhi and Martin Luther King was only effective because it appeared in the context of already violent movements' (285). At no point does Ryder, or the other liberationists, condemn the *abolitionist* aims of ALF militants as being misguided or even fanatical; nor, given his views, would we expect him to. Yet in so doing, or not doing, influential campaigners like Regan, Singer, and Ryder himself, bear the responsibility for providing *theoretical* justification for the conviction that what is occurring in the laborator-ies, slaughterhouses, or hunting fields of Britain and the USA, bears comparison with goings-on in Nazi Germany. If crazy people are then misguided enough to believe this to the letter it is small wonder that bombs are planted. Pious wringing of hands about violence is no good.

The militants must be shown to possess mistaken views about the nature of animals and the treatment properly due to them. Ryder and his friends are not the people for the task because they share the metaphysical confusions.

EPILOGUE

An idea that is not dangerous is unworthy of being called an idea at all.

(Oscar Wilde)

Many readers, painstaking enough to read to the end of my book, will be enraged by much of what I argue for. They will see my conclusions as both casting pagan doubt upon the theoretical sub-structure of the movement for animal rights patiently assembled by Singer, Clark, Rollin, Regan, and others, but also as giving aid and comfort to meat eaters, experimental researchers, hunters, and wearers of fur coats, whose behaviour they detest. I make no apology if this be so. My hope is that such readers will at least do themselves the favour of locating precisely where they think my errors lie, or they ought not to remain as secure in their convictions as hitherto.

I have tended to see my potentially more fruitful audience rather differently; as something of a beleaguered majority at variance with what they see as an almost irresistible bandwaggon of enthusiasm for animal rights which they are powerless to prevent. Why should they wish to prevent it? The answer I have in mind (apart, of course, from the violence) is that they entertain the nagging suspicion that the enthusiasm is misplaced yet are unable adequately to justify this. Michael Lyne, the sportsman-artist, would be just such a person; or the typical experimentalist, such as Blakemore or Gray, convinced that what they are doing is worthwhile, but with more pressing concerns than to pursue the argument. Yet pursued it needs to be; beyond ethics, beyond even our knowledge of ourselves, to an understanding of the true nature of conscious, appetitive beings, incapable of language. Without this theoretical foundation the readers for whom I have sympathy will be forever on the defensive; resentful perhaps at being forced into attitudes of apology, or even a guilty conscience, because they happen to work in a laboratory or enjoy a leg of lamb.

I personally neither enjoy hunting nor the wearing of fur coats, nor do I wield a scalpel. But that is not important. What matters is that for those who *do* feel strongly, or find themselves in situations of confrontation, reasonable justifications are possible which are strengthened by my philosophical conclusions. This is not, of course, to deny that disagreements will arise over the value of an argument or even its reasonableness. (I attempted, in Chapter 7, to show why this is a feature endemic to moral debate.) But the chance does exist of *sincerely* defending these activities with every chance of finding allies. What else is life all about?

The reply will be that life is also about the abuse and death of animals and that I am too ready to condone it. This is a matter of individual judgement. I am far from the position of the activist Celia Hammond, quoted with approval by Ryder, who puts the welfare of *individual* animals before all else: 'I would rather that there were no rabbits at all left in the world than that one of them should be subjected to unnecessary cruelty' (1989: 219). If this were held consistently there would be no animals at all, even in the wild, and if it were thought to apply also to children then there would be none of them either. We live in a world from which gratuitous cruelty and necessary pain can never entirely be eradicated and we should bend with these ill winds rather than capitulate. Individual animals, a lot of them, will continue to be harmed if we eat them, experiment upon them, hunt them, keep them captive, certainly if we attempt to preserve endangered species (for management involves the control of stock and the eradication of pests and predators). Even if we leave them alone in the wild they will not be immune to suffering. I condone these practices because it is in the *overall* interests of animals, being primitive beings rather than a competing race of human ones, that they are adapted to our ways. In the debate over 'conservation or welfare' I am firmly on the side of the former.

All of this is perfectly compatible with our treating other creatures humanely and with respect and it is a sign of a perverted human nature not to be instinctively inclined to do so. A humane researcher will painlessly kill some beagles whilst allowing others to undergo the minimum necessary discomfort, depending upon the experiment. Respectful pet-owners behave quite differently. But, as significantly, sensitive treatment will be dictated by our understanding of what we are dealing with. If we can allow that Michael Lyne could pursue foxes in a humane manner, it would nonetheless have been outrageous had he hunted children. But my differences with the liberationists surface at this point yet again. Their picture of animals mirrors human beings far more closely than my alternative allows. Theirs is the 'falsifying dream' that enthusiasts foist upon the hawk despite its own poetic protests. It is time they woke up.

253

NOTES

INTRODUCTION

1 Midgley (1983: 57–8) makes some rather casual criticisms of Wittgenstein. These I will discuss in Chapter 6. But the more notable exception is Vicki Hearne (1987), in her book *Adam's Task*, who mentions him approvingly on several occasions. She cannot however be described as an animal liberationist since she does not draw any practical conclusions. When she hints at one, as in her qualified defence of pit bull terrier fighting (1987: 220–1), to which I will return in my final chapter, she reveals herself as a highly individual voice.

2 'Noah's Ark Syndrome: an irrational compulsion to live surrounded by animals, generally in pairs. Commonly observed in childhood, with a slightly greater incidence in females. If carried into adulthood life may well become an obsession. Treatment: impossible. Cure: unknown' (Barstow 1988: I).

3 Hearne, a poet and sometime trainer of dogs and horses, is something of a latter-day Lorenz. *Adam's Task* is a source of fascinating animal anecdotes by an expert handler. She is also confessedly obsessive in just this sort of anthropomorphism (1987: 10). She talks of 'horses who are irredeemably dishonest' (14) and of her need, in training a dog, to 'be able to assume that he understands the moral significance of peeing on the couch or of biting certain objectionable visitors' (35–6). Unfortunately she enlists the aid of Wittgenstein in this endeavour. What she would make of his comments about the dog's inability to simulate pain we are not told since she cites hardly anything in support of her analysis. Readers will be able to judge for themselves, particularly in Chapter 5, the limited extent to which this squares with what Wittgenstein actually says.

1 THE UTILITARIAN BEGINNINGS

1 Singer has reservations about these types of example. The individuals concerned might not be at fault but, he rather quaintly argues, the state of a society which permits this *is*. 'So equality of opportunity is not an attractive ideal. It rewards the lucky, who inherit those abilities. ... It

penalizes the unlucky, whose genes make it very hard for them to achieve similar success' (1979: 35). Singer's social ideal is egalitarian rather than equalitarian; aiming to go beyond equality of opportunity to equality of *outcome*. But this step into the abyss does not, I think, reflect upon the arguments about animals to come.

2 Francisco Mendes Filho, a Brazilian ecologist and rural workers' leader, was murdered late in 1988 partly because he was instrumental in delaying an extension to the BR 364 Amazonian highway. (Report in the UK *Independent* 31 Dec. 1988.)

3 To be sentient is to have the power of sense-perception; to see, hear, smell, taste or touch. It is both unwarranted and misleading to extend it to include the capacity to feel pain as do all the liberationists who use the term, e.g. Clark (1977: 39) or Linzey (1976: 20, 1989: 36–7). It is used, one assumes, because feeling pain is associated with the tactile sense.

4 Originated by Cleve Backster (1968) and *The Secret Life of Plants* (1973) by Tomkins and Bird (see Frey 1980: 45fn. for a fuller citation).

2 R. G. FREY: THE CASE AGAINST ANIMALS

1 These five conditions owe much to Kenny's argument in *Action, Emotion and Will* (1963).

2 Reported in the UK *Independent*, 2 January 1989. Source: *Copeia, The Journal of the American Society of Icthyologists and Herpetologists*, 1988 (1): 92–101.

3 THREE CONTRIBUTIONS FROM TOM REGAN

1 Regan's attempt to reinstate simple desires appeared in the journal *Mind* (1982). But his other arguments against Frey are in the book (1983: 38–53).

2 It is illuminating to observe that Hearne falls into the same trap as Regan when she attempts to isolate a sense of a dog's knowledge *of* a familiar track which is independent of any knowledge *that* such-and-such is the case (1987: 101). The 'knowledge' in question, if it is to be so dignified, is grounded in no more than that the dog is in full command of its senses and uses them to stick to the track rather than stray from it.

3 Remarkably there are no extant 'primitive' languages. Careful field-work over many years by anthropological linguists has revealed 'only complex languages spoken by technologically primitive peoples'. Marshall goes on to say that although languages obviously change with time there is no evidence that the process is one of increasing complication 'in any general sense' (Marshall 1970: 230).

4 THE HISTORICAL PERSPECTIVE: ARISTOTLE TO DARWIN

1 All respectable editions of Aristotle's works carry marginal keys to the classic texts of Bekker. Quotations from *On the Soul* (*De Anima*: *DA*),

The 'Art' of Rhetoric (AR), *Nicomachean Ethics* (NE) and *The Politics* (P) will all be keyed to Bekker and should be easily locatable in whatever version. The *Summa Theologica* of St Thomas Aquinas will be abbreviated *ST* and is listed in the bibliography under its translator, Anton Pegis (1948).

2 In *De Anima*, Book 3, Aristotle does allow that one rational faculty is incorruptible. The so-called 'active intellect' is so depicted (430a) as to make it 'unreasonable that it be mixed with the body' (429a). These passages are much discussed.

3 Readers of science fiction will recall Philip K. Dick's novel *Bladerunner* where, in a future world denuded of animals due to war and pollution, cunning imitations are similar status symbols. Unfortunately the film excludes the electronic pets.

4 Richard Ryder (1989) is an exception. His factual account of the history of the controversy over Darwin's theories is worth investigating (1989: 99–123, 158–65).

5 LUDWIG WITTGENSTEIN: LANGUAGE-GAMES AND PRIMITIVE BEINGS

1 I will illustrate this chapter liberally with quotations from three of Wittgenstein's most celebrated, but posthumously published, works, in the hope that readers will be diverted to the primary sources: *The Blue and Brown Books* (1958), being material from Cambridge seminars in the 1930s, and the *Philosophical Investigations* (1953), and *Zettel* (1967), both put together mainly from later fragments up to 1949. These will be abbreviated to *BB* (citing page numbers) *PI* and *Z* (denoting numbered sections unless indicated otherwise). All italics will be Wittgenstein's own.

2 Section 27 illustrates a stylistic device which Wittgenstein frequently employs, not only in *PI*. He introduces, and often elaborates, an opinion to which he is *opposed* without always making it absolutely clear that this is what he is doing nor indicating precisely the point at which the criticism, or his own competing view, takes over. In *PI* 27 'whereas' marks the spot, although the repeated 'As if' intimates a lack of sympathy. The pitfalls awaiting the inattentive reader should be obvious.

3 This is the first reference to a *page* number in *PI*. Part I consists of the 693 numbered sections. Part II begins on p.174.

4 As Robert Hinde (1982) puts it: 'The basic supposition is that animals are adapted in such a manner that their biological inclusive fitness is maximised. Maximising inclusive fitness involves achieving many short term consequences. . . . The questions studied are thus of the form "Is the animal foraging as efficiently as it could?" or "Is it selecting that mate who will provide the greatest potential number of offspring?"' (1982: 112).

5 The status of *un*directed emotions is debatable. Anxiety and depression are given as examples (*Z* 489). But even when of clinical intensity these have their, frequently all-embracing, objects. In this respect animals could not qualify. But to the extent that these conditions resemble illnesses, with physical symptoms, then animals are certainly subject to them.

6 Midgley is critical of the remarks from *PI* p.174. Rightly so; given her

views. But the passages I quote, particularly if we add *PI* 25 ('they simply do not talk . . . they do not use language'), seem pre-eminently to underline how incredible it was for Hearne to select Wittgenstein as an ally for her aggressive anthropomorphism.

6   WHAT ANIMALS ARE: CONSCIOUSNESS, PERCEPTION, AUTONOMY, LANGUAGE

1 A philosopher who does make such assumptions is Thomas Nagel in his popular article 'What is it like to be a Bat?' (1979: 165–180). The confusions that result are well diagnosed by Churchill (1989: 315–6). A similar refutation of Nagel will be found in Patricia Hanna's article 'Must thinking bats be conscious?' (1990: 350–6).

2 Hearne gives no role to the pre-linguistic prototypes yet nevertheless seems to be forced into this confusion. It may well account for the obscure passage about Washoe which concludes: 'That doesn't mean she isn't talking' (1987: 41). Hearne has met Washoe and some of her Ameslan companions. Her sensitive description of the encounters is revealing background information (32–41).

3 Pheromones are odorous chemicals which act like hormones but from outside the body. In some cases, such as those of dogs, wolves, and foxes, they are in other secretions like the urine, but queen substance is specific for its variety of functions. Pheromones make possible individual recognition by smell and are important regulatory factors in a great range of animal behaviour, in particular sexual and foraging cycles (Burton and Burton 1977: 45). Protozoans are stimulated to reproduce by pheromones released into the water and some zoologists see this as a clue to the goal-seeking of the homing salmon, discussed in the preceding chapter.

7   AGAINST LIBERATION: THE ETHICAL DIMENSION

1 Bougeant's explanation is a brilliant counter to Descartes. The Jesuit argued, as Evans put it, that

> Even the strictest Cartesian would never think of petting his chronometer as he pets his poodle, or would expect the former to respond to his caresses as the latter does. Practically he subverts his own metaphysical system by the distinction which he makes between them, treating one as a machine and the other as a sentient being, endowed with mental powers and passions . . .
>
> (Evans 1987: 66–7)

Therefore they must have souls. But this would be contrary to Christian doctrine subverting, as it does, the pre-eminence of man over beasts. Bougeant threads this particular needle by invoking the alternative view that they are the incarnations of evil spirits.

2 Two useful sources are Bernard Williams *Morality* (1973), especially

Chapter10, and Samuel Scheffler (ed.) *Consequentialism and its Critics* (1988).

3 A useful and brief survey of some of these theories is to be found in A.G.N. Flew's *Evolutionary Ethics* (1968).

4 Detailed accounts of the history of this campaign will be found in E.S. Turner's *All Heaven in a Rage* (1964) and Ryder (1989).

5 Despite notorious and well documented abuses, slave-owning societies have tended to have strict laws regulating what is due such a valuable commodity. The background to Plato's *Euthyphro* is the trial of a respectable owner charged with such an offence. Aristotle, as we saw in Chapter 4, regarded slaves as the superiors of animals, even granting them the humanity that makes possible genuine friendships with free men. Plato was also exceedingly up to date in his views about women. In the *Republic* those that come up to the mark can attain the highest rank of philosopher-king. Although even his genius was unable to relieve women of the task of child bearing, he did stipulate that those fitted for high office would be free of the cares of bringing up their offspring; indeed would know nothing of them.

6 Hearne comes extremely close to attributing full moral agency in her succession of anecdotes in praise of police dogs and pit bull terriers. Readers can decide *how* close (Hearne 1987: esp. 206–12). See also Introduction fn.3.

7 The Parliamentary Reform Act of that year gave the vote to men of 21 and to women of 30. Not until the Equal Franchise Act of 1928 did women in Britain achieve full equal rights in terms of voting age.

8 Apart from the very useful article by Francis and Norman (1978: 507–27), which contains a wealth of obscure citations and deserves to be anthologised, other helpful sources are Michael Tooley's 'A defence of abortion and infanticide' (1973: 51–91) and Glover (1977: 156–8).

9 Michael Allen Fox (1986: 59–70) provides a more extended account of some of these arguments.

8 CHAPTERS OF DISCONTENT: EATING, EXPERIMENTING, ZOOS, BLOODSPORTS

1 I have benefited greatly from reading Williams but I intend no implication that he would support my conclusions. But it is fair to quote his comment on Clark (1977): 'I cannot see why, on any realistic view of our and other animals' "natural" relations to one another, it should be thought to exclude our eating them' (1985: 216 fn.).

2 Readers who would like to follow up the more intricate details of the political campaigns of the 1970s and 1980s to further reforms of alleged animal abuse on every front, can find them in Ryder's *Animal Revolution* (1989: 261–71). The book also provides a useful general history of the issues. Ryder writes as a vehement critic of contemporary practices. He is a political activist and a supporter of both Singer and Regan.

3 Aided and abetted in Europe by EEC regulations which financially encourage farmers to take surplus land out of use rather than to employ it in using less intensive methods.

4 Ryder recounts an example from 1983 when the Home Office minister, David Mellor, resisted acting upon an RSPCA report on painful experiments with the 'excuse' that 'there is and can be no definition of the term [pain]' (1989: 249–50). Ryder's alleged rebuttal of Mellor's point took the following form:

> Pain in animals is defined as abnormal behaviour which can be alleviated by analgesic procedures which relieve pain in humans. Severe pain in animals is defined as pain produced by procedures to which normal humans would not voluntarily submit without appropriate analgesia or anaesthesia.

We are not told whether the Home Office was taken in by this. The 'rebuttal' totally misses the point that pain is not behaviour but a *sensation* that is defined ostensively (see text below) in a behavioural context. One might as uselessly define a tickle as laughing and squirming resulting from touching certain parts of the body.

5 Judith Hampson gives a useful and detailed account of the varying legal requirements and regulating bodies in the EEC and USA. She is particularly critical of what she sees as a *laissez faire* attitude in favour of researchers in the USA, and of attempts to tighten up existing legislation (1989: 219–51).

6 Some animal and human tissues can be maintained alive *in vitro* (in glass, i.e. in the culture dish). Tissue culture, the preservation of tissues in a nutrient medium for 24 hours or longer, is one of a series of *in vitro* techniques. One donor animal can provide a great many cultures for experimental use. Their advantages, according to the FRAME fact-sheet (1985), include greater sensitivity, relatively low cost, greater speed, relative simplicity and absence of complicating factors. Their limitations 'stem from the absence of systemic mechanisms of absorption, distribution and excretion, and of nervous, hormonal and immunological controls.' Dallas Pratt's *Alternatives to Pain in Experiments on Animals* (1980) is also cited with approval in this connection.

7 A healthy chimpanzee, for example, is required for the testing of each batch of vaccine for hepatitis B since it is the only known animal, apart from man, susceptible to the virus. Furthermore, their anatomical similarity to human beings makes them, and other apes, essential in the development of experimental techniques in surgery, such as joint replacement and organ transplantation. In the words of the FRAME (1985) fact-sheet, 'the whole organism is more than the sum of its parts' (see note 6).

8 A related and ethically dark area, into which I shall not enter, is the area of *self*-experimentation by researchers. J.B.S. Haldane was a noted exponent of this in the 1940s and 1950s. It has been well documented in a recent book by Lawrence Altman, *Who Goes First?: The Story of Self-experimentation in Medicine* (1988).

9 This photograph re-emerged in July 1990 in furtherance of a campaign against seal culling in South Africa; the same month in which the UK Fur Education Council launched a counter-offensive (see the *Independent* 21 July).

BIBLIOGRAPHY

Altman, L.K. (1988) *Who Goes First? The Story of Self-experimentation in Medicine*, Wellingborough: Equation-Thorsons.

Aristotle (1948) *The Politics of Aristotle*, E. Barker (tr.), Oxford: Clarendon Press.

—— (1959) *The 'Art' of Rhetoric*, J. H. Freese (tr.), London: William Heinemann.

—— (1976) *The Nicomachean Ethics*, J. A. K. Thomson (tr.), Harmondsworth: Penguin Books.

—— (1986) *De Anima (On the Soul)*, H. Lawson-Tancred (tr.), Harmondsworth: Penguin Books.

Armstrong, D.M. (1973) *Belief, Truth and Knowledge*, Cambridge: Cambridge University Press.

Askwith, R. (1988) 'Experiments on animals: time to open our eyes', *Sunday Telegraph Magazine*, 10 July.

Augustine, St (1961) *Confessions*, R. S. Pine-Coffin (tr.), Harmondsworth: Penguin Books.

Austin, J.L. (1962) *How to do Things with Words*, Oxford: Clarendon Press.

Backster, C. (1968) 'Evidence of a primary perception in plant life', *International Journal of Parapsychology*, x.

Baker, G.P. and Hacker, P.M.S. (1980) *An Analytical Commentary on Wittgenstein's Philosophical Investigations*, Vol.1, Oxford: Basil Blackwell.

Barnes, D.J. (1985) 'A matter of change', in P. Singer (ed.) *In Defence of Animals*, Oxford: Basil Blackwell.

Barstow, P. (1988) 'Enjoying creature comforts', *The Daily Telegraph*, 28 May.

Batten, P. (1976) *Living Trophies*, New York: Crowell.

Bentham, J. (1960) *An Introduction to the Principles of Morals and Legislation*, Oxford: Basil Blackwell. (First pub. 1789.)

—— (1962) *The Works of Jeremy Bentham*, J. Bowring (ed.), 11 vols, New York: Russell and Russell.

Black, M. (1972) *The Labyrinth of Language*, Harmondsworth: Penguin Books.

Burton, M. and Burton, R. (1977) *Inside the Animal World*, Newton Abbot: Readers Union.

Buyukmihci, N.C. (1986) Report on the use of animals in surgical training of veterinary medical students (unpublished), listed in *Euroniche* (1989), 8.

Churchill, J. (1989) 'If a lion could talk', *Philosophical Investigations*, 12.4.

Clark, S.R.L. (1977) *The Moral Status of Animals*, Oxford: Clarendon Press.

—— (1978) 'Animal wrongs', *Analysis*, 38.3.

—— (1982) *The Nature of the Beast: Are Animals Moral?*, Oxford: Oxford University Press.

—— (1985) 'Good dogs and other animals', in P. Singer (ed.) *In Defence of Animals*, Oxford: Basil Blackwell.

Comroe, J.H. (1977) *Retrospectroscope: Insights into Medical Discovery*, Menlo Park, CA: Von Gehr Press.

Cook, J.W. (1969) 'Human beings', in P. Winch (ed.) *Studies in the Philosophy of Wittgenstein*, London: Routledge & Kegan Paul.

Cowley, G. (1988) 'The wisdom of animals', *Newsweek*, 23 May.

Darwin, C. (1909) *The Descent of Man*, London: John Murray. (First pub. 1871.)

Dawkins, M.S. (1980) *Animal Suffering: The Science of Animal Welfare*, London: Chapman and Hall.

—— (1985) 'The scientific basis for assessing suffering in animals', in P. Singer (ed.) *In Defence of Animals*, Oxford: Basil Blackwell.

Diamond, C. (1982) 'Anything but argument', *Philosophical Investigations*, 5.1.

Dworkin, R. (1977) *Taking Rights Seriously*, London: Duckworth.

Euroniche (1989), European Network of Individuals and Campaigns for Humane Education, Newsletter 2, September.

Evans, E.P. (1987) *The Criminal Prosecution and Capital Punishment of Animals*, London: Faber. (First pub. 1906.)

Feinberg, J. (1973) *Social Philosophy*, Englewood Cliffs, NJ: Prentice-Hall.

Flew, A.G.N. (1968) *Evolutionary Ethics*, London: Macmillan.

Fox, M.A. (1986) *The Case for Animal Experimentation*, London: University of California Press.

FRAME (1985) 'Alternatives to animal experiments', Nottingham.

FRAME News (1988) 'Animal welfare *versus* medical research', 18, Nottingham.

Francis, L.P. and Norman, R. (1978) 'Some animals are more equal than others', *Philosophy*, 53.

Frey, R.G. (1980) *Interests and Rights: The Case Against Animals*, Oxford: Clarendon Press.

—— (1983) *Rights, Killing, and Suffering*, Oxford: Basil Blackwell.

Garnett, D. (1932) *Lady into Fox and A Man in the Zoo*, London: Chatto & Windus.

Gendin, S. (1989) 'What should a Jew do?', *Between the Species*, Berkeley, CA, 5.1.

Gilby, T. (1951) (ed.) *St. Thomas Aquinas: Philosophical Texts*, London: Oxford University Press.

Glover, J. (1977) *Causing Death and Saving Lives*, Harmondsworth: Penguin Books.

Goodall, J. van Lawick (1971) *In the Shadow of Man*, London: Collins.

Griffin, D.R. (1976) *The Question of Animal Awareness*, New York: Rockerfeller University Press.

—— (1984) *Animal Thinking*, Cambridge, Mass: Harvard University Press.

Haldane, E.S. and Ross, G.R.T. (trs) (1970) *The Philosophical Works of Descartes*, 2 vols, Cambridge: Cambridge University Press.

Hampshire, S. (1959) *Thought and Action*, London: Chatto & Windus.

Hampson, J. (1989) 'Legislation and the changing consensus', in G. Langley (ed.) *Animal Experimentation*, Basingstoke: Macmillan Press.

Hanna, P. (1990) 'Must thinking bats be conscious?', *Philosophical Investigations*, 13.4.

Hare, R. (1978) 'Justice and equality', in J. Arthur and W. Shaw (eds) *Justice and Economic Distribution*, Englewood Cliffs NJ: Prentice-Hall.

Harrison, R. (1964) *Animal Machines*, London: Vincent Stuart.

Hearne, V. (1987) *Adam's Task: Calling Animals by Name*, London: Heinemann.

Hediger, H. (1964) *Wild Animals in Captivity*, New York: Dover Books.

Helm, S. (1989) 'Mad dogs and Europeans', *Independent Magazine*, 8 July.

Highfield, R. (1990) 'Animal tests lowest for 30 years', *Daily Telegraph*, 23 July.

Hinde, R.A. (1982) *Ethology*, London: Fontana.

Hollands, C. (1985) 'Animal rights in the political arena', in P. Singer (ed.) *In Defence of Animals*, Oxford: Basil Blackwell.

Home Office (1979) *Report on the LD50 Test*, London: Advisory Committee on the Administration of the Cruelty to Animals Act 1876.

Hume, D. (1902) *An Enquiry Concerning the Principles of Morals*, L.A. Selby-Bigge (ed.), Oxford: Clarendon Press. (First pub. 1751.)

—— (1911) *A Treatise of Human Nature*, 2 vols, London: J.M. Dent. (First pub. 1739–40.)

Jacob, F. (1989) *The Logic of Life*, Harmondsworth: Penguin Books. (First pub. 1970.)

Jamieson, D. (1985) 'Against zoos', in P. Singer (ed.) *In Defence of Animals*, Oxford: Basil Blackwell.

Jenkins, P. (1976) 'Teaching chimpanzees to communicate', in T. Regan and P. Singer (eds), *Animal Rights and Human Obligations*, Englewood Cliffs, NJ: Prentice-Hall.

Jordan, W. and Ormrod, S. (1978) *The Last Great Wild Beast Show*, London: Constable.

Kafka, F. (1961) *Metamorphosis and Other Stories*, Harmondsworth: Penguin Books. (First pub. 1916.)

Kalechofsky, R. (1989) 'What a Jew should do', *Between the Species*, Berkeley, CA. 5.3.

Kant, I. (1963) *Lectures on Ethics*, L. Infield (tr.), New York: Harper & Row.

Kenny, A.J.P. (1963) *Action, Emotion and Will*, London: Routledge & Kegan Paul.

—— (1970) *Descartes: Philosophical Letters*, Oxford: Clarendon Press.

—— (1975) *Will, Freedom and Power*, Oxford: Basil Blackwell.

Lambert, A. (1989) *1939: The Last Season of Peace*, London: Weidenfeld & Nicolson.

Langley, G. (1988) 'Defenders of vivisection mobilise', *Alternative News*, 29.

—— (ed.) (1989) *Animal Experimentation: The Consensus Changes*, Basingstoke: Macmillan Press.

Lewis, N. (1989) 'A harvest of souls', *Independent Magazine*, 1 April.

Linzey, A. (1976) *Animal Rights: A Christian Assessment*, London: SCM Press.

—— (1989) 'Reverence, responsibility and rights', in D. Paterson and M. Palmer (eds) *The Status of Animals*, Wallingford: CAB International.

Locke, J. (1965) *An Essay Concerning Human Understanding*, 2 vols, London: J.M. Dent. (First pub. 1690.)

Lorenz, K.Z. (1959) *Man Meets Dog*, London: Pan Books. (First pub. 1954.)

—— (1964) *King Solomon's Ring*, London: Methuen. (First pub. 1952.)

Lyons, J. (ed.) (1970) *New Horizons in Linguistics*, Harmondsworth: Penguin Books.

McClosky, H.J. (1975) 'The right to life', *Mind*, 335.

MacIver, A.M. (1948) 'Ethics and the beetle', *Analysis*, 8.

Malcolm, N. (1958) *Ludwig Wittgenstein: A Memoir*, London: Oxford University Press.

Marshall, J.C. (1970) 'The biology of communication in man and animals', in J. Lyons (ed.) *New Horizons in Linguistics*, Harmondsworth: Penguin Books.

Mason, J. (1985) 'Brave new farm?' in P. Singer (ed.) *In Defence of Animals*, Oxford: Basil Blackwell.

Midgley, M. (1983) *Animals and Why they Matter*, Harmondsworth: Penguin Books.

—— (1985) 'Persons and non-persons', in P. Singer (ed.) *In Defence of Animals*, Oxford: Basil Blackwell.

—— (1986) 'Discussion', *Between the Species*, Berkeley, CA, 2.4.

Miles, H.L. (1983) 'Apes and language', in J. de Luce and H.T. Wilder (eds) *Language in Primates*, New York: Springer.

Mill, J.S. (1910) *Utilitarianism*, London: J.M. Dent. (First pub. 1861.)

Mills, H. (1988) 'Saboteurs claim Glorious Twelfth as victory day', *The Independent*, 13 August.

Murdoch, A. (1990) 'Irish farms fatten on Islamic meat', *The Independent*, 20 January.

Nagel, T. (1979) 'What is it like to be a bat?', in *Mortal Questions*, Cambridge: Cambridge University Press.

Nossal, G.J.V. (1975) *Medical Science and Human Goals*, London: Edward Arnold.

Pacheco, A. and Francione, A. (1985) 'The Silver Spring monkeys', in P. Singer (ed.) *In Defence of Animals*, Oxford: Basil Blackwell.

Pegis, A.C. (ed. and tr.) (1948) *Introduction to Saint Thomas Aquinas*, New York: Random House.

Paterson, D. and Ryder, R. (eds) (1979) *Animals' Rights: A Symposium*, London: Centaur Press.

Playter, R. (1985) *Survival Surgery Survey*, unpublished report for the American Association of Veterinary Clinicians, listed in *Euroniche* (1989), 8.

Pratt, D. (1980) *Alternatives to Pain in Experiments on Animals*, New York: Argus Archives.

Rachels, J. (1976) 'Do animals have a right to liberty?', in T. Regan and P. Singer (eds), *Animal Rights and Human Obligations*, Englewood Cliffs, NJ: Prentice-Hall.

Rawls, J. (1972) *A Theory of Justice*, London: Oxford University Press.

Regan, T. (1982) 'Frey on why animals cannot have simple desires', *Mind*, 91.362.

—— (1983) *The Case for Animal Rights*, Berkeley: University of California Press.

—— (1985) 'The case for animal rights', in P. Singer (ed.) *In Defence of Animals*, Oxford: Basil Blackwell.

Regan, T. and Singer, P. (eds) (1976) *Animal Rights and Human Obligations*, Englewood Cliffs, NJ: Prentice-Hall.

Ritchie, D.G. (1976) 'Why animals do not have rights', in T. Regan and P. Singer (eds) *Animal Rights and Human Obligations*, Englewood Cliffs NJ: Prentice-Hall. (First pub. 1894.)

Rollin, B.E. (1981) *Animal Rights and Human Morality*, Buffalo, NY: Prometheus Books.

Rose, M. and Adams, D. (1989) 'Evidence for pain and suffering in other animals', in G. Langley (ed.) *Animal Experimentation*, Basingstoke; Macmillan Press.

Rowan, A. (1984) *Of Mice, Models and Men: A Critical Evaluation of Animal Research*, Albany: State University of New York Press.

—— (1989) 'Ethical dilemmas in experimentation', in D. Paterson and M. Palmer (eds) *The Status of Animals*, Wallingford: CAB International.

Russell, W.M.S. and Burch, R.L. (1959) *The Principles of Humane Experimental Technique*, Springfield, Ill.: Charles Thomas.

Ryder, R. (1976) 'Experiments on animals', in T. Regan and P. Singer (eds) *Animal Rights and Human Obligations*, Englewood Cliffs, NJ: Prentice-Hall.

—— (1989) *Animal Revolution: Changing Attitudes towards Speciesism*, Oxford: Basil Blackwell.

Ryle, G. (1949) *The Concept of Mind*, London: Hutchinson.

Salt, H. (1922) *Animals' Rights Considered in Relation to Social Progress*, 2nd edn, London: Bell. (First pub. 1892.)

Scheffler, S. (ed.) (1988) *Consequentialism and its Critics*, Oxford: Oxford University Press.

Schleifer, H. (1985) 'Images of death and life: food animal production and the vegetarian option', in P. Singer (ed.) *In Defence of Animals*, Oxford: Basil Blackwell.

Schopenhauer, A. (1965) *On the Basis of Morality*, E.F. Payne (tr.), New York: Harper & Row. (First pub. 1841.)

Sharpe, R. (1989) 'Animal experiments – a failed technology', in G. Langley (ed.) *Animal Experimentation*, Basingstoke: Macmillan Press.

Sidgwick, H. (1874) *The Methods of Ethics*, London: Macmillan.

Simonton, O.C., Mathews-Simonton, S., and Creighton, J.L. (1986) *Getting Well Again*, London: Bantam Books.

Singer, P. (1979) *Practical Ethics*, Cambridge: Cambridge University Press.

—— (1983) *Animal Liberation*, Wellingborough: Thorsons. (First pub. 1975.)

—— (ed.) (1985) *In Defence of Animals*, Oxford: Basil Blackwell.

Smyth, D.H. (1978) *Alternatives to Animal Experiments*, London: Scolar Press.

Spira, H. (1985) 'Fighting to win', in P. Singer (ed.) *In Defence of Animals*, Oxford: Basil Blackwell.

Sutherland, P. (1989) 'Farm Blight', *Independent Magazine*, 7 October.

Temerlin, M.K. (1976) *Lucy: Growing Up Human*, London: Souvenir Press.

Terrace, H.S. (1980) *Nim*, London: Eyre Methuen.

Tomkins, P. and Bird, C. (1973) *The Secret Life of Plants*, New York: Harper & Row.

Tooley, M. (1973) 'A defence of abortion and infanticide', in J. Feinberg (ed.) *The Problem of Abortion*, Belmont, CA: Wadsworth.

Turner, E.S. (1964) *All Heaven in a Rage*, London: Michael Joseph.

Voltaire (1971) *Philosophical Dictionary*, T. Besterman (ed.), Harmondsworth: Penguin Books. (First pub. 1764.)

Waismann, F. (1965) *The Principles of Linguistic Philosophy*, London: Macmillan.

Walker, S. (1983) *Animal Thought*, London: Routledge & Kegan Paul.

Warnock, G.J. (1955) 'Seeing', *Proceedings of the Aristotelian Society*, vol. 55.

Warren, M.A. (1986) 'Difficulties with the strong animal rights position', *Between the Species*, Berkeley, CA. 2.4.

Whitley, E. (1989) 'In a valley of vanishing penis gourds', *Independent Magazine*, 9 December.

Williams, B. (1973) *Morality: An Introduction to Ethics*, Harmondsworth: Penguin Books.

—— (1978) *Descartes: The Project of Pure Enquiry*, Harmondsworth: Penguin Books.

—— (1985) *Ethics and the Limits of Philosophy*, London: Fontana Press.

Wisdom, J. (1953) 'Gods', in *Philosophy and Psycho-Analysis*, Oxford: Basil Blackwell.

Wittgenstein, L. (1955) *Tractatus Logico-Philosophicus*, 6th imp., London: Routledge & Kegan Paul. (First pub. 1921.)

—— (1958a) *The Blue and Brown Books*, Oxford: Basil Blackwell.

—— (1958b) *Philosophical Investigations*, 3rd edn, New York: Macmillan. (First pub. 1953.)

—— (1967) *Zettel*, G.E.M. Anscombe and G.H. von Wright (eds), Oxford: Basil Blackwell.

—— (1969) *On Certainty*, G.E.M. Anscombe and G.H. von Wright (eds), Oxford: Basil Blackwell.

—— (1980a) *Culture and Value*, G.H. von Wright (ed.), Oxford: Basil Blackwell.

—— (1980b) *Remarks on the Philosophy of Psychology*, 2 vols, G.E.M Anscombe, G.H. von Wright and H. Nyman (eds), Oxford: Basil Blackwell.

World Society for the Protection of Animals, *International Alert: The Republic of Korea*, London: undated.

Yeates, C. (1989) 'Obituary: Michael Lyne', *The Independent*, 25 March.

INDEX

DATE DUE